Praise for *Chasing Wi*

'Elaine Pearson has a long histo
oppressed around the world whil
rights organisations, most notably Human Rights Watch.
Chasing Wrongs and Rights gives us an opportunity to explore
intersecting systems of oppression that operate in various
parts of the world. With a wealth of experience, the writer
opens our eyes to the intimate effects of such systems
as she interweaves her own personal narrative through
the text. Challenging and revealing, this book is an
important offering to young activists to come.'
Behrouz Boochani

'Few in Australia have the vast practical experience, courage
and unflappable purpose in championing human rights than
Elaine Pearson. In this book, her iron belief in the basic rights
of all, our shared humanity and a vision for a more equal
world is buttressed by real stories at the intersection between
not just rights or otherwise, but sometimes life or death.'
Craig Foster

'Many young people (even lawyers) dream of tackling some of
the local and global challenges described in this book. For Elaine
Pearson, every day brings new challenges which she meets with
endless reserves of energy, embodying the motto: "Never give up."'
The Hon. Michael Kirby AC CMG

'Elaine Pearson is hope and justice personified . . . fighting for
what is right in the darkest corners of the globe. She has spent
her lifetime listening to those denied their human rights, helping
them tell their own truths and fight their own fights. Her story
is a powerful read and reminds each and every one of us there is
always something we can do, and always more to be done.'
Fran Kelly

'This important and inspiring book provides an insider's account of the struggle for human rights, from interviewing victims in jungles to arguing over words in strip-lit UN conference rooms in Geneva. Essential reading for those who want to help, because it illuminates the courage, commitment and collegiality needed for working towards a better world.'
Geoffrey Robertson QC AO

'Refreshingly honest, captivating, funny, heartbreaking, illuminating and educational all at once. Everyone who values human rights should read this book. Everyone who dreams of, or cares about, faraway places should read this book. Everyone else should read this book too.'
Vicky Xu

'Elaine Pearson shows what it takes to become one of the world's leading human rights defenders. She displays a compassion for the downtrodden, a drive to come to their defense, and a willingness to travel wherever she is most needed. Her powerful memoir, filled with colourful characters and compelling vignettes, takes the reader to some of the most troubled spots in Asia and beyond – and includes her work on Australia's own human rights shortcomings. As she describes her research and advocacy to redress this abuse, she reveals the character of an activist determined to make a difference and talented enough to see her ambitions realised.'
Ken Roth

CHASING
WRONGS
AND RIGHTS

To Johnny,
With best wishes,
Elaine Pearson.

CHASING WRONGS AND RIGHTS

Elaine Pearson

SCRIBNER

SCRIBNER

First published in Australia in 2022 by Scribner,
an imprint of Simon & Schuster Australia
Suite 19A, Level 1, Building C, 450 Miller Street,
Cammeray, NSW 2062

Sydney New York London Toronto New Delhi
Visit our website at www.simonandschuster.com.au

SCRIBNER and design are registered trademarks of The Gale Group, Inc.,
used under licence by Simon & Schuster Inc.

10 9 8 7 6 5 4 3 2 1

A catalogue record for this
book is available from the
National Library of Australia

9781761104190 (paperback)
9781761104206 (ebook)

Cover design by Daniel New
Typeset in 12.5/17 pt Adobe Garamond Pro by Midland Typesetters, Australia
Printed and bound in Australia by Griffin Press

The paper this book is printed on is certified against the
Forest Stewardship Council® Standards. Griffin Press holds
chain of custody certification SGSHK-COC-005088. FSC®
promotes environmentally responsible, socially beneficial
and economically viable management of the world's forests

To all the human rights defenders
who are fighting for our rights

CONTENTS

PROLOGUE

Whenever I go home to Perth in Western Australia, I remember it's the big blue sky that I have missed. The earth there is so flat. The sky takes up all the space. It swallows you up and sucks up the energy. You can't help but look up into that deep shade of blue. Cloudless and intense with heat from the searing sun. I used to daydream a lot growing up, looking up at the sky, thinking about the world outside Perth, thinking about what people elsewhere were doing.

My family moved to Perth in 1981, when I was five years old. My mum and dad drove across the Nullarbor (no trees) Plain from Sydney for five days in our yellow Toyota station wagon packed full of all our belongings – I was wedged on some dusty pink pillows between the TV and the legs of our Formica dining table.

I was born in Blacktown, in the Western Suburbs of Sydney, to a white British father from South London and an ethnic Chinese mother from Singapore. It was Dad's second marriage; his first wife had died tragically, and he raised four young children alone – my half brothers and sisters.

My father worked for Qantas Airways, scheduling the flights in and out of Australia in an era before this was done by computers – he was made redundant in the 1990s. My mother was a nurse at the local public hospital. Nowadays, a lot of my friends' families are mixed race. But back then, in Blacktown and in Perth, our family looked different.

From an early age, I was always slightly self-conscious of not quite fitting in. Like most mixed-race kids, I had a crisis of confidence from my early years – am I white, am I Asian? Am I Australian? Am I British? I may have been born in Sydney, but my passport said I was British. I only got myself an Australian passport after I turned eighteen.

Dad emigrated to Australia as a 'Ten Pound Pom' with his young family around 1960, but he never lost his British accent. He had a photographic memory – he could remember bus and train routes from his travels twenty years earlier – and a brain made for crunching numbers. He never had the chance to attend university, but I always thought he would have enjoyed it.

My father talked a lot about his childhood – growing up in the Great Depression and World War II. He was one of over 800,000 children evacuated from London during the Blitz, and was relocated to Brighton.

He lost his own father to pneumonia when he was just four years old.

Dad would tell me, 'They kept all the windows open in the hospital, even in the middle of winter. No wonder he got pneumonia.'

Even on scorching days in the height of summer, Dad never opened the windows at home.

Dad had impeccable manners, which was a result of a boarding school education in South London for boys who had lost their fathers – mostly during the war. He would tell me horror stories of punishments inflicted by sadistic teachers, including sports teachers making the children exercise outside in the middle of winter in the nude, science teachers forcing them to breathe in over a jar of formaldehyde, the locking of children in cupboards, as well as regular hidings with the cane or sticks.

In typical stiff-upper-lip British fashion, Dad didn't bear any ill-will towards the school.

He thought it had taught them all good discipline.

Dad joined the Royal Air Force in 1950 after high school. He was stationed in Iraq and Aden (now Yemen) in the 1950s as a mechanic, when both were remnants of the British Empire.

He would tell me stories of this time in the Middle East, and about my grandfather whom I had never met – who had worked on the railroads in Cuba before returning to London, where he met my nan. I loved these stories of faraway places and my family. They made up for the absence of any family on his side; my father was an only child and my nan died when I was just a baby.

In contrast to my dad, my mother rarely spoke of her childhood in Singapore. But we made annual trips back there to visit grandparents, my great-grandmother, aunties, uncles, and cousins. No one spoke much of the past during those visits; we were too busy eating and shopping. I always thought this was a cultural thing in Asian families – the past was too painful, too shameful, and it was better for everyone to focus on the present.

My Singaporean grandparents did not speak any English. And I did not speak Teochew, a Chinese dialect they all spoke at home. My mother and her siblings had Western names, in addition to their Chinese names, which they had acquired at a British school during the colonial period in the 1950s.

3

'I didn't learn Mandarin,' Mum would say in exasperation when I tried to quiz her, 'I learned, "Jack and Jill went up the hill to fetch a pail of water".'

Mum left school at seventeen to study nursing, working in Singapore and the UK. My parents met in Singapore in 1971 and my father is a lot older than my mother.

When I was born, my mum gave me a Chinese name, but it never went on my birth certificate. According to my mother, there was no use in learning Teochew – 'Just dialect, lah', she would say, adding the distinctive Singaporean colloquialism. After a few years in Australia, she dropped the 'lah' altogether.

In Australia in the 1970s and 1980s, the migrant culture was all about assimilation and fitting in and shaking off the qualities that made you different. I felt like my Asian side was something to hide. I remember the kids at school relentlessly bullied one guy in my class from Vietnam because of his heavily accented English. It was awful. It made me not want to be Asian, not want to be different.

As a kid, I faced the usual low-level racism, sometimes in the school yard or on the street. Strangers calling out, 'go home, nip', 'Asian' or 'mongrel' for being mixed race. At school, when kids wanted to be hurtful, they'd say things like, 'Your mum is a mail order bride.'

I'd get more subtle and confusing questions from adults. 'Where are you really from?', or 'But you look exotic!' when I said I was Australian. I just felt awkward.

Because I was mixed race, I felt like I could blend in, but in Australia this meant pretending I wasn't Asian. I got so good at it that sometimes I forgot that I was Asian. I also had the whitest name ever.

My mother never complained about how hard it must have been for her as an Asian woman moving to Australia in the 1970s, to marry an older husband with four children from a previous marriage.

My mother is very pragmatic. She's always living in the present and planning for the future. Though – like my grandmother and my great-grandmother – Mum is also fiercely independent, and not one to shy away from an argument or sharing her views.

'Tell us what you really think, Mum!' I would tease her sometimes after another blunt outburst. I only realised later – with pride – that all the women in my family were strong and outspoken. When people cast stereotypes about Asian women being passive or docile, they've clearly never met the women in my family!

My older half-brothers and sisters all grew up in Blacktown, and they had it tough. In addition to his Qantas job, Dad was waiting tables at weddings to help make ends meet after his first wife died of a brain aneurism. His kids were aged two to ten when she passed away, in 1966 and he struggled for a while to keep them all together, living in a foreign country on the opposite side of the world. But he didn't want to go back to the UK.

By the time we moved to Perth my siblings were all in their late teens or early twenties and had already moved out of home or overseas.

I was a typical youngest child, spoilt and precocious. When you spend a lot of time alone or with adults who praise you frequently, it helps to build your confidence.

The one thing we all enjoyed as a family was travelling. One of the benefits of Dad working for Qantas Airways back then was ridiculously cheap flights at a time when flying was comparatively much more expensive than it is now. Most school holidays, from the age of ten or so, I'd be packed off to the eastern states of Australia to spend time with my brothers or my sister.

Because I travelled a lot, I was quite bold and self-assured, and had no qualms about navigating airports and travelling on planes alone. In fact, I rebelled after once travelling as an 'unaccompanied minor', and felt the flight attendant who chaperoned me treated me like a baby.

'Please, don't make me do that again!' I said to my dad angrily. I felt like I could take care of myself. He relented and let me go alone, but my brothers Nigel and Ian or my sister Chris would always be there to pick me up at the other end.

By the time I reached university, I became even more adventurous. At eighteen, I went to visit family in Singapore with my boyfriend, and then decided to just keep exploring. We got a bus to Malaysia, and then kept going up the peninsula to the beautiful tropical islands of Southern Thailand by bus, train, and ferry. At nineteen, we traipsed around South America. At twenty, I did a student exchange to Nottingham in the UK, made lasting friends at university, and went backpacking for six months around Europe.

I loved travelling. I felt like it was in my blood. Initially, I wanted a job where I could travel, explore, and write. I had read voraciously from a young age, and in my teens, I got into the Beat Generation and Jack Kerouac's *On The Road* and *The Dharma Bums* and dreamed of taking off on solo adventures across the world.

I was lucky to have an English literature teacher at my high school, All Saints College, who recommended interesting books for me to read outside our syllabus. Mr Gipson suggested John Pilger's *A Secret Country* about Australia's hidden past and untold stories. I read with horror about the massacres of First Nations people after white colonisation and the criminalisation of Aboriginal people that continues to this day. There is a line in the book that I can still remember, more than twenty years after I first read it: 'Every Aboriginal man, woman and child in the town of Roebourne, Western Australia, experiences arrest at the rate of three a year.'[1]

The book blew me away. I suddenly discovered a whole other perspective of history that we were never taught in school and that I had been ignorant of.

I'm no longer a Pilger fan, but the book had a lasting impression on me.

It ignited a passion for stories of injustice that were untold. But I wasn't just drawn to telling the stories, I became interested in how people could change and challenge systems that were discriminatory and unjust.

I suppose I also have One Nation politician and renowned racist Pauline Hanson to thank for starting me on my career as a human rights activist. It was her anti-Asian statements that led me to take part in my first protest.

In her maiden speech to Parliament in 1996, she said:

I believe we are in danger of being swamped by Asians. Between 1984 and 1995, forty per cent of all migrants coming into this country were of Asian origin. They have their own culture and religion, form ghettos and do not assimilate. Of course, I will be called racist but, if I can invite whom I want into my home, then I should have the right to have a say in who comes into my country.[2]

Something inside me snapped. As someone who was Asian and whose family had tried desperately hard to assimilate, too hard in retrospect, those words felt like a kick in the guts. I took it personally.

In May 1997, Hanson made a visit to Perth. She'd been booted out of the Liberal Party and had set up the One Nation party the month before and was on a national tour spouting her racist views. Back then, her targets were Asian immigrants and Aboriginal people, rather than Muslims.

When Hanson came to Perth, I wanted to make my voice heard. I joined the protests outside the venue where she was due to speak. We chanted loudly, 'Racists are not welcome here!' I got on the 6 o'clock evening news, angrily shouting and wearing my dad's green knitted jumper that was too big for me.

And I felt a wave of solidarity in the crowd of strangers. So many Australians were angered by Hanson's visit: Asians, First Nations people, and other Australians. It's a feeling I have often had when attending protests. It triggers a latent outpouring of emotion that has been buried, hidden deep down, and in that moment of raw unity with others – I fought back tears.

I remember afterwards the Australian Prime Minister John Howard criticised the protesters. He said:

> I think the demonstrations that have gone on around Australia over the last week or so have really been quite stupid and counterproductive and probably momentarily driven more people towards her rather than repel them. And I really think it is people who are interested in denying her oxygen, they shouldn't engage in those sorts of demonstrations.[3]

Howard's comments blaming the protesters and not Hanson's racism made me even more furious. Racism certainly played a role in my political awakening and throughout my career, I've seen racism as the silent factor that pervades so many other human rights abuses. Some people may not want to acknowledge it, but it is at the heart of why some people are treated differently and why unacceptable behaviour is tolerated or justified by governments.

I see it clearly in many of the abuses that I have documented over the years and abuses that feature in this book – whether they are ethnic Somalis in Ethiopia, First Nations people in Australia, refugees and migrants, or victims of trafficking everywhere.

I wrote this book because a lot of young people ask me questions about human rights work, what we do at Human Rights Watch, and how I got started. I have been with the organisation since 2007, working to investigate and expose human rights violations around the world. I wanted to give an insider's account of how we try to generate change. Sometimes we succeed, other times we fail, but the fight for lasting change requires persistence. Change also requires uncovering uncomfortable truths, exposing injustices that would otherwise be ignored or buried.

My colleagues at Human Rights Watch were supportive of me writing this book, and it is written with their blessing. I've tried hard to obtain approval from those individuals whose stories feature in this book, and I thank them for letting me share their stories. In a few cases I've had to change a name for security reasons, and occasionally I've merged a couple of characters to protect someone's privacy or because I've been unable to locate an individual to obtain their consent. These stories are told to the best of my recollection, with the caveat that some of the events happened a long time ago.

Beyond the reports, the press releases, the media interviews and advocacy meetings, there is a lot more going on behind the scenes to protect human rights. I wanted to give readers a picture of what it is like to be on my shoulder in various places, doing the job of being a human rights activist and 'chasing wrongs and rights'. This is the story of what I have learned on my journey.

PART I

HUMAN TRAFFICKING

CHAPTER 1

SEX, INTERNATIONAL LAW AND LOBBYING: GENEVA TO BANGKOK

In June 1999, as a twenty-three-year-old recent university graduate, I left Perth's big blue sky and flew to Geneva, a city on a lake surrounded by snow-capped mountains, to attend a meeting at the United Nations. It was a dream come true. I was beyond excited.

I was on my way to take up a volunteer role funded by the Australian government with the Global Alliance Against Traffic in Women, or GAATW – a small international non-governmental organisation based in Bangkok.

But I hadn't technically started yet.

Someone at GAATW had asked if I could get to Geneva in June, about six weeks before I was due in Bangkok. She said there was going to be a side meeting for activists from around the world which would be helpful for a project that I would be working on: developing a human rights handbook.

The catch was that GAATW didn't have any money to fly me there.

Was there any way I could pay my own way? Hell yes! I would find a way.

Back then, working abroad in the field of women's rights was exactly what I wanted to do. I'd graduated the past November from Murdoch University in Perth. I'd spent a semester studying and living in Nottingham in the UK, and then taken another six months off to travel, so it had taken me a bit longer than normal to finish my degree – most of my law school friends had graduated a year or two before and were working 'on the terrace', which meant toiling long hours on their clerkships and getting paid peanuts at corporate law firms in Perth's CBD. I'd never had any interest in doing that.

Instead, I was still living in a share house in the port city of Fremantle, going to nightclubs and all-night parties, and paying the bills by juggling the same part-time jobs I'd had as a student. These included shelving books at the university library, pouring beers at the university tavern (the Tav), and selling crystals and Buddhist trinkets at Crystal Palace, a stall at the Fremantle Markets. At the same time, I was editing a free newspaper focused on Perth's electronic music scene, a project that I had started with a group of friends in my final years of law school.

I liked all my jobs in different ways. The magazine wasn't just for fun: I wanted to develop some writing and publishing skills. The library was a calm, quiet place of work. The Tav was the opposite: busy, raucous and friends were always stopping by for a drink. And the market stall was where I could be a hippy for a few hours each week. But it was also where I was first inspired to consider volunteering abroad. One of my colleagues was a woman a few years older than me called Ros, who filled the quiet times with stories from her experiences working on development projects in the Pacific islands. It sounded exotic and challenging, especially to a restless and idealistic young law student who was keen to get out of Perth.

I began searching for volunteer opportunities overseas. I didn't mind where and my ambitions were vague: I knew I wanted to do something in social justice, ideally women's rights, maybe migration. But I didn't really know what exactly, or how to go about it.

It was Ros who told me about Australian Volunteers International (now known as the Australian Volunteers Program). And then I came across another program, funded by the government aid agency AusAID (now merged with the Department of Foreign Affairs and Trade) somewhat cringingly called Australian Youth Ambassadors for Development. They may as well have called it 'Little Lords of Southeast Asia', but the substance piqued my curiosity. AusAID sent young skilled Australians to live and work in the Asia-Pacific, on assignments between three and twelve months, covering the cost of travelling to Thailand, insurance, and a monthly stipend. My skills were basic – publishing and my law degree – but luckily for me, the Youth Ambassador program was brand-new, and I noticed that my university, Murdoch, was listed as a partner organisation. I made inquiries on campus and got the impression that AusAID was still figuring out how everything was going to work. Someone suggested I would have a better chance of getting chosen if I came up with my own project.

I asked one of my law lecturers for help: Fernand de Varennes, a French-Canadian, who got me interested in human rights when I had taken his course on human rights in the Asia-Pacific. Fernand is now the UN Special Rapporteur for Minority Issues, but I'll always be grateful that I had a lecturer who was willing to go out of his way to assist a student.

Fernand wrote to several non-governmental organisations working on women's rights in Asia, asking if they could use me, and GAATW replied saying yes. They got a fresh law graduate with some basic publishing skills for a year; in return, they would put me up in an apartment next door to the office, shared with another volunteer from Japan. I would get to build up some experience in my chosen field – and live in Bangkok. Perfect!

I'd backpacked through Bangkok as a university student a few times. The heaving, vibrant and chaotic 'city of angels' both awed and terrified me, a feeling that I loved. To my twenty-three-year-old self, Australia felt too small, too homogenous, too comfortable. Even before it began, I was hoping that this one-year experience would lead to a permanent future of working overseas – when I left home, I had no intention of returning.

Plus, migrating was in the blood. Both my parents had migrated to Australia from Singapore and the UK. While I've already mentioned the experiences on my dad's side in the Prologue, I also have a remarkable migrant history on my mother's side, though Mum never really spoke about it. Her mother – my grandmother or Amah as I called her – grew up in poverty in China. Amah was sold to a travelling opera troupe at age ten and taken to Singapore. At fifteen, the troupe owner sold her to another opera troupe, and they took her back to China. At nineteen, when the boss took a particular interest in her, she fled to Hong Kong on a boat, disguised as an old woman, and made her way back to Singapore, where she eventually met my grand-father in the early 1940s. As a young woman and a budding opera star, Amah toured all around Southeast Asia.

Amah didn't tell me all this directly – she couldn't because of our language barrier.

Regardless of the communication challenges, I had fond memories of Amah singing in Teochew, and dancing with me in their cramped Singaporean public housing apartment. My grandparents shared their apartment with my great-grandmother

(Laumah), my uncle, and his wife, Tina. (I never knew my uncle's name – my mum and all her siblings simply referred to him as 'Second Brother', because he was Amah's second-born son and their older half-brother from a previous relationship.) On the walls were pictures of a younger Amah in heavy theatre make up. As a kid, I remember thinking that she looked scary in the photos, intense. Amah often carried a mug with a pungent-smelling drink that I wasn't allowed to taste. Later, I discovered it was Benedictine, a herbal liqueur. She'd sneak cigarettes in the kitchen when my mother wasn't looking. I'd never really known my grandparents on my dad's side, so I thought that was what all grandmothers did – sing, and dance, and drink, and smoke all day. Amah was great fun.

My grandfather, Akong, was much quieter. His head was shaved, and he constantly wore white singlets, light blue pyjama pants and plastic slippers – the universal look for older Chinese men in Singapore. He would often be in the kitchen, chopping food, cooking something delicious, or just having a smoke. There would always be rice in the rice cooker, food under brightly coloured plastic food covers, and strong sweet black tea from a thermos.

Much later, while researching this book, on the internet I came across audio recordings of interviews with my grand-mother in the National Archives of Singapore. They were part of an oral history project in 1988 on vanishing arts, Teochew opera among them. It was a shock to hear her distinctive voice again, playing through my laptop so many years after she had gone. I still couldn't understand a word but family members in Singapore translated them for me. Amah spoke about experienc-ing the famine in China growing up in the 1920s. Her family was so poor, there was no food to eat. Amah and her sisters foraged the fields looking for food and hay to burn as fuel. If they were lucky, they ate potato porridge. Rice was a luxury. Four of her sisters starved.

I'd never known the details of how Amah was sold to the opera troupe. In the recording, she said that she had sold herself, willingly, because she was so hungry, and so that her mother could have money to buy back their land. Her story now feels chillingly familiar. Throughout my career, I've now heard hundreds like it. No one in our family ever described what Amah experienced as trafficking, and I only made that connection later myself, after I started working at GAATW. But that's what it was and although I wasn't totally aware of it as a young adult, Amah's life had a profound effect on the direction of mine.

By contrast, I had a very fortunate life growing up in Australia. I was the first child in our family to go to university, which was a source of pride for my parents. Given their own experiences, they both placed a lot of emphasis on my education, sending me to a private Anglican high school, All Saints College.

We were a typical suburban middle class migrant family – the ethos from both my parents was 'work hard, care for others, save money and keep your head down.' There was no history of activism in our household.

Since I was my dad's fifth child, he was pretty relaxed about my career choices. I think he was just pleased that I made it to university. My mother felt differently: I was her only child, and she was very much a 'tiger mum' as we Asians affection-ately call our mothers who are fierce, proud and always pushing their children to do better. Throughout my childhood, she would press me to get good grades, giving me cash for every 'A', and not hiding her disappointment when I slipped up.

This form of capitalism worked very well in the Pearson household. I got straight As in my final year of high school. I wanted to go on to university and study literature or journalism, as I loved books, but Mum tried her best to convince me that studying business would be more useful. Eventually we compromised – I would do a double major – Law and Arts (English and Comparative Literature).

And while the first few years of law school were tedious – property, contracts, constitutional law – I started to pay attention when I chose my own subjects like human rights in Asia, East Asian legal theory, feminist legal theory and jurisprudence. I became fascinated with the idea of social justice and how the law could be used as a tool to empower people – it reminded me of the injustices I'd read about as a teenager in John Pilger's book. But I didn't think I was cut out to be a lawyer. I was put off by the idea of doing anything remotely corporate. It would require even more years in Perth to get 'my articles' (the supervised clerkship required for new lawyers) and to get admitted as a solicitor before I had a hope of starting any more interesting work. I was impatient to go overseas and explore what was possible.

After getting through law school, Mum wasn't exactly thrilled with the idea of her only child giving it all away and galivanting off to volunteer in Thailand.

'All I want is for you to have a good job, get a house, earn good money,' she implored me as I was moving all my belongings out of the share house and back to the family home.

I'm sure a lot of first-generation migrant children have some variation on this conversation. I kept packing, keeping stubbornly silent, because all that I could hear was the disappointment in her voice, not her concern and deep love for her only child.

So, when the email came through asking me to attend the UN meeting in Geneva, I felt both elated and vindicated – 'See Mum, you will be proud of me – I'm even going to the UN.' Deep down inside, I still wanted to prove myself a worthy daughter.

But I still had the pressing question of how to find the money to fly there. I'd been saving up for the year in Thailand – the stipend from AusAID wouldn't be sufficient. A return flight from Perth to Geneva would put a big hole in that budget. In the end, I used an approach that I've always found worth a shot: I asked for assistance. The Murdoch law school was one of the Youth Ambassador program partners, and I inquired if they would be willing to sponsor the trip. The Dean agreed to pay most of the cost of the airfare so long as I wrote up a report about the UN meeting. I'd find some way to survive when I got there, even if that meant living off bars of Swiss chocolate. I was off to Geneva!

*

As a young woman from Perth, I didn't know too much about the UN. I knew from my law classes that the UN was where international agreements were made in the form of treaties, and that it monitored and reported on compliance with international law, though its powers of enforcement were limited. I knew that the global headquarters were in New York, but human rights concerns were dealt with in Geneva at the Human Rights Commission – the international body that held abusive governments to account for their human rights violations. (It's now the Human Rights Council.)

I imagined diplomats in suits from all over the world, drinking café lattes, eating croissants and Swiss chocolate next to Lake

Geneva, discussing the finer points of human rights treaties, far removed from the frontlines of human rights crises unfolding in the 1990s in Bosnia, Rwanda or Iraq. I arrived in June 1999, the start of European summer, and the city was indeed obscenely picturesque. The sun was shining, and the lake shimmered with the reflection of snow-capped mountains. Cute little trams serviced the city – I took one from the central station to our hotel, under strict instructions from Dad. In the days before Google Maps, my dad's recall of tram routes and numbers from his previous business trips was invaluable.

Some of my new GAATW colleagues were already at our small, drab hotel near the city centre. GAATW's founder was an immaculately dressed veteran women's rights activist from Thailand, Siriporn Skrobanek. She spoke softly, with a slight smile that inspired trust, and yet her comments were always razor-sharp and insightful, at times even cutting. I would sometimes wonder, did Siriporn *really* just say that?

A younger Thai woman Vachararutai (Jan) Boontinand was our energetic and whip-smart research director. Our thoughtful program director, Bandana Pattanaik, from India, welcomed me warmly: coincidentally, she'd only recently joined GAATW after a stint in publishing in Melbourne.

When our meeting started the next day, I was equally intimidated and inspired by the women around me – and I felt I'd found my calling. I met leading women's rights activists from Cambodia and Nepal – former Khmer Rouge survivor Kien Serey Phal and Meena Poudel (whom I would later go on to work for in Kathmandu). There was a representative of a domestic workers' union from Bolivia who wore her hair in long plaits under a Peruvian bowler hat. There were sex worker activists from India, Brazil, the UK and the US, human rights lawyers from the US and India, and academics from Canada and the Netherlands. Coming from Perth, it was the most diverse bunch of people I had ever met in my life.

GAATW was a global alliance of non-governmental organisations working on women's rights, especially trafficking, migration and sex work. Many of our members provided direct services to migrants and victims of trafficking. As a secretariat, our role was to provide research and advocacy support to the membership. On behalf of members and with their input, we advocated on common goals at international meetings. As part of these activities, we published reports, newsletters, and training manuals. I was quietly delighted that publishing a free music magazine was going to be just as relevant to my career as my law degree.

The reason we were in Geneva was the annual meeting of the UN Working Group on Contemporary Forms of Slavery. UN working groups are comprised of independent experts who publish reports and make recommendations to governments. In 1999, the Working Group was holding a two-day consultation with non-government organisations (NGOs) on trafficking and the global sex industry. Because GAATW wanted to make it possible for women activists from the Global South to participate in the UN meeting, they had organised a side-meeting and paid for several of its members to come to Geneva.

We spent our first two days in Geneva huddled in a conference room at the hotel The purpose of the GAATW meeting was to evaluate a series of human rights training workshops GAATW had organised in different regions of the world and to discuss a new document produced by several NGOs called 'the human rights standards for the treatment of trafficked persons'.[1] Activists pooled their collective experiences and views, including about the definition of trafficking and the responsibilities of governments to trafficked persons under international law. These standards were the basis for a new handbook on human rights that GAATW was in the process of drafting – the project I had been assigned to work on. I took copious notes trying frantically to absorb input coming from all directions.

I learned that after Geneva, some of our group would travel to Vienna to lobby a separate group of delegates who were negotiating the text for a UN Trafficking Protocol, attached to a Convention Against Transnational Organized Crime. While the Working Group could only make recommendations to governments, conventions and protocols imposed obligations on the governments that sign or ratify them. It was the first time in decades that governments were drafting a new treaty on trafficking – I didn't know it then, but this was a pivotal time in the anti-trafficking and human rights movement.

It was telling that the Trafficking Protocol was to be negotiated in Vienna, home to the UN Office on Drugs and Crime, rather than Geneva, the home of human rights treaties. It showed the real motivations behind this new international instrument on human trafficking – governments were worried about trafficking not because it was a violation of human rights, but as an issue of organised crime. Governments professed concern about criminal syndicates exploiting women and children through trafficking, but in reality, wanted to control the movement of people and to stop irregular movements, especially for 'undesirable' and often illegal occupations like sex work. Organised criminal groups were also generating huge illegal (and therefore untaxed) profits out of trafficking and the sex industry. In 1998, *The Economist* estimated that at least $US20 billion was spent in the global sex industry every year. [2]

23

Still, as far as GAATW was concerned, whatever the under-lying motives, a new international treaty outlawing trafficking was a chance to mandate specific human rights protections for victims, such as access to legal assistance, shelters and psycho-social support. Our task was to develop convincing strategies and arguments about why a protocol to a convention on organised crime needed to include protections for human rights.

This first experience of human rights work would prove to be reasonably representative of the rest of my career – while I've spent a lot of time in the field, interviewing victims of abuses, I've also had an unhealthy dose of days under neon lights in anonymous conference rooms. On my third day in Geneva, we caught the tram across town to the UN to attend the NGO consultation meeting with the UN Working Group on Contem-porary Forms of Slavery. It was a warm summer's day, and while I was excited to witness firsthand how activism could make a difference, I was also excited to simply get outside.

After the tram passed the stone façades of the city centre, I caught sight of a hideous giant sculpture of a wooden chair, with a broken leg. The tram stopped abruptly. This was where we got off. The sculpture, *Broken Chair*, marked the entrance to the UN buildings – the sweeping marble façade of the Palais des Nations (Palace of Nations). I wondered about the symbolism behind the sculpture which still sits at the entrance to the UN today: did it inadvertently betray the anxiety that the UN might be broken, and decorative rather than functional? Years later, I read that it was actually erected as a statement against landmines. Sadly, that was not obvious to me or any of my companions entering the UN, and it took some of the optimistic edge off our arrival.

The enormous complex of the Palais des Nations had been constructed in the 1930s to house the League of Nations, the intergovernmental organisation established in the wake of World War I, and (failed) predecessor to the UN. Its wings and annexes sprawled in all directions, snaking through beautiful alpine gardens. I glimpsed the deep blue and green plumage of peacocks roaming around the grounds. There was something so bizarre about these exotic Asian birds scratching around the gardens of a Swiss mountain town, yet no one gave them a second look. I guess peacocks and diplomats strutting around were a normal sight for those accustomed to UN life in Geneva.

We hustled through the warren of corridors to find our meeting room.

Until that trip to Geneva, I hadn't realised the definition of trafficking was hotly contested by NGOs – misguidedly, I'd thought that NGOs would largely agree on things, and the real job would be to convince the UN experts. But in fact, I had stumbled into one of the most epic battles between feminists working on trafficking and human rights in decades, largely due to differing views about sex work. GAATW was part of a coalition that included sex workers and argued for sex work to be recognised as labour, making a distinction between forced and voluntary sex work. We felt that while the first should be illegal, there was no point stigmatising and indeed criminalising women for the second, which may be their only option for income. Another group of NGOs excluded sex workers, arguing that *all* sex work was exploitative of women and that the sex industry should be abolished entirely. They were confusingly called the Coalition Against Trafficking in Women, or CATW. This was my introduction to NGO drama – acronyms and alphabet soup – duelling organisations with almost the same name but who hated being mistaken for the other.

I sat down at the back of a room filled with women from countries all over the world to observe what was about to unfold.

I can vividly remember the words of Janie Chuang, a young Asian American woman standing in for the UN Special Rapporteur on Violence Against Women that kicked off the discussions: 'We should not allow differences of emphasis to turn into divisions that prevent us from realising our common goal – to stand up for the rights of victims of trafficking wherever and whoever they are.' Yet it was the divisions and differences that would stand out for me over the next two days, and it became a familiar dynamic throughout my career working on trafficking.

There were three panels on the first day, one pro-sex work, one anti-sex work and then a panel of organisations somewhere in the middle. Early on, trafficking was very clearly defined by the straight-talking, middle-aged Dutch feminist Marjan Wijers. Along with Lin Chew (who would soon become one of my mentors), Marjan had literally written the book on *Trafficking in Women: Forced Labour and Slavery-Like Practices in Marriage, Domestic Labour and Prostitution* – which I read and re-read as my 'trafficking bible' in the years ahead.[3] As Marjan explained it, human trafficking involved three components:

1. movement from one place to another
2. acts of deception, coercion or debt bondage, and
3. for the purpose of putting someone in forced or bonded labor, servitude or slavery-like conditions.

There was a difference between adult and child trafficking – since children could not consent to things like sex work, the element of deception, coercion or debt bondage was not required to demonstrate that a child had been trafficked.

These three basic elements would become the mantra – a framework that I found myself repeating in a variety of situations – in much of my work on trafficking for the next seven years.

Marjan spoke of the importance of recognising adult sex work as labour. Women and children from developing countries often ended up being trafficked when they tried to migrate to avoid poverty or instability in their home countries, just as Amah had done. These days, restrictive immigration policies mean there are few options for legal migration. Domestic work, marriage or sex work become viable options for women who might have initially arrived as tourists or students. But the criminalisation of sex work made it harder for women in the sex industry to access their rights.

In 1999, the definition of trafficking was hotly contested. Historically, governments had focused on trafficking for prostitution, meaning that other forms of trafficking were seldom addressed. Their approach tended to concentrate on preventing women entering sex work, rather than improving the working conditions in sex work.

As Marjan explained it; 'The traditional concept of trafficking in women focuses predominantly on the protection of so-called innocent women from being lured or forced into prostitution.'[4] It didn't do anything for the rights of women working consensually in the sex industry.

In her definition, the core element of trafficking was coercion – '[t]he means by which a woman loses control over her own life, body and mind. It's not the nature of the work or services that's the problem but the conditions of deceit, violence, debt bondage or abuse.'[5]

Marjan's explanation made sense to me, and underpinned GAATW's approach: the emphasis needed to be on the abusive

27

and exploitative conditions – not judgements about the work trafficked women ended up doing. It did not matter what the industry was. It might not even be employment. Some people were trafficked into marriage, for example. If all three of Marjan's elements were present, trafficking had occurred.

Even more convincing was the testimony of sex worker representatives including Indian sex worker Mala Singh, and Americans Melissa Ditmore and Jo Doezema. Dressed in a bright blue traditional *salwar kameez* (a South Asian long tunic with pants), Mala spoke passionately in Bengali, gesticulating with her hands and becoming more animated the longer she spoke. My GAATW colleague Bandana translated for her into English.

Mala was a founding member of the Durbar Mahila Samanwaya Committee (the Durbar Women's Collaborative Committee, commonly known as DMSC), a sex workers' union in Sonagachi, the red-light district of Kolkata (then known as Calcutta).

'I am speaking on behalf of 40,000 sex workers,' Mala began. 'I'm not doing anything criminal. I pay my rent. I work hard. I don't beg and I don't steal. I see myself as a worker and an artist.'[6]

I realised I had never seen a sex worker speak up in public about their job in any forum before, let alone at the United Nations. Mala wanted the word 'prostitution' eliminated, speaking of the discrimination that she and others faced on a regular basis because of their status as sex workers. 'If people know that I'm a sex worker, I can't buy land. I can't send my kids to school.' Like people everywhere, women in the sex industry were trying to do their best by their kids. It reminded me of my own mother's strong emphasis on education and good grades.

Mala made it clear that no one was forcing her to work.

'It's a transaction. I make people happy, and that makes me happy. I see my work as someone who cures people. I am rather like a doctor. Meanwhile, the people who make cigarettes make people sick – and no one asks them to stop working.' Mala said it with a defiant smile.

Years later, I found out that Mala herself had been forced into sex work as a child, at only nine years of age. Back then, during a brothel raid she was taken to a shelter because the brothel madam didn't have enough money to pay police a bribe to get her out. One night a drunken police officer came to the shelter and collected her. He took her to the police station and raped her. 'Where are we supposed to go for safety?' Mala asked. 'My safe space is with other sex workers. It's not with the police.'

The fear of police and lack of police protection would also be a recurring theme in many of my conversations with sex workers and victims of trafficking around the world.

Mala described how her organisation sought to protect children from the sex industry, explaining how they established their own regulatory board to prevent child prostitution and protect the welfare of anyone below the age of eighteen.

'It's the people *in* sex work who are the best people to combat trafficking,' she said simply.

Melissa and Jo were two eloquent and persuasive sex worker activists from the US, both completing PhDs on trafficking. Melissa represented the Global Network on Sex Work Projects (NSWP). Like Mala, she talked about why using the term 'sex work' rather than 'prostitution' was important: it emphasised the labour aspects of the sex industry, without moral judgement. Making similar arguments, Jo Doezema had co-written a seminal report in 1997, with Jo Bindman, *Redefining Prostitution as Sex Work on the International Agenda*.[7] With her peroxide blonde hair in a pixie cut, fashionable clothes and loud American accent, she turned heads wherever she went. I found her captivating and intimidating, and she held the full attention of the room when explaining how migrants forced to work in the sex industry are unlikely to seek help if they fear deportation and arrest.

Melissa and I came to be good friends. On my first ever trip to New York, the following year, Melissa arranged for me to go up to Harlem and spend a few hours with a sex workers' mobile health clinic. She also took me to a burlesque show in the Lower East Side with the iconic Jo 'Boobs' Weldon – the queen of New York burlesque. Melissa would go on to publish the *Encyclopedia on Prostitution and Sex Work*.[8]

After hearing these three remarkable women speak, I felt sad and frustrated that governments ineptly applied such simplistic policies, further harming rather than protecting the rights of vulnerable people. I also felt proud that these were my new colleagues.

The CATW panellists, by contrast, considered all forms of prostitution – whether coerced or not – to be trafficking in women. They argued that prostitution is unlike any other work and is inherently harmful to women, normalising misogyny and violence against women. For CATW, prostitution itself was a violation of human rights: women in prostitution did not have agency and therefore no woman could consent to it. Regulating the sex industry enabled the commodification of women and gave 'legal cover' to prostitution, which emboldened traffickers to continue their practices. Trafficking laws should criminalise both 'forced' and 'free choice' prostitution, helping to abolish prostitution period.

Listening to the CATW arguments, I did not agree. I thought there was a clear difference between women who are forced into prostitution, and those who chose to do so due their personal or economic circumstances. I knew the line was blurry sometimes, especially when people are poor and have limited options, but that didn't mean there wasn't an important distinction. Even in my suburban upbringing in Perth, I had met women who worked as 'escorts', including one of the waitresses at a café where I had worked. She wasn't trafficked, it was her choice. She left sex work of her own accord and she didn't need to be rescued.

As I listened to the anti-prostitution panellists, it struck me that they were largely ignoring the voices of sex workers, rather than responding to them. The CATW panellists not only refused to accept the views of people like Mala, Jo and Melissa, they thought they were brainwashed, or even paid representatives of the sex industry. It seemed patronising to me, it infantilised women working in the sex industry, literally treating them like children by denying that they were able to grant – or withhold – consent.

Even as a very recent newcomer to human rights activism, I knew that the participation and empowerment of affected communities was a key principle of human rights work. Our job as activists involved some judgement about whether an act was a violation of international law or not, but after that, our role as I saw it was to support the people who had lived these experiences to voice those experiences, assert their own rights and represent themselves wherever possible.

The third panel attempted to find middle ground. I didn't envy their task. But if anyone could do it, it would be Mike Dottridge, the Director of Anti-Slavery International. A sharp, thoughtful Englishman and an experienced human rights activist, Mike was somehow both diplomatic and direct – something I later tried to emulate.

Above all, Mike was pragmatic. Pointing to the failure of previous UN Conventions to stem trafficking into the global sex industry, he suggested that focusing on the worst aspects of exploitation would be a good starting point. A similar approach had been taken to tackle child labour: instead of attempting to find a universal definition that could eradicate it entirely, more headway could be made by focusing on the most egregious abuses and targeting those areas first. He also tried to find common ground on the question of whether sex work should be recognised as work by including unequal global economic development into the equation. Globalisation meant women from poor countries were often the ones providing sexual services to men from industrialised countries – in much the same way that women in domestic work were overwhelmingly from poorer countries serving employers in richer countries. This inequity created a class of 'low status women' in the Global North who tended to have less rights than locals. Poverty sometimes drove women with limited choices to choose to do sex work, but if they ended up in slavery-like conditions and were trafficked, their initial consent to do sex work was irrelevant.

I thought Anti-Slavery's analysis made sense. It balanced acknowledging the reality of sex work and giving priority to ending forced prostitution, while recognising there can be inherent inequality in people's circumstances and the racist discriminatory treatment that women from poorer countries face. And that fact itself facilitates trafficking.

Debate in these sessions was intense, and it was even fiercer in the smaller groups afterwards, when we gathered to negotiate a series of written recommendations for the UN Working Group. I sat back taking everything in – and watching the fireworks. This wasn't the elegant lake-side discussion between diplomats I'd imagined: it was a bunch of intelligent and passionate, but polemically opposed, groups of women activists arguing non-stop about language. This introduced me to something that

I would become very familiar with: how fixated advocates at the UN become on words. Coming to Geneva, I naively thought we'd be battling with governments about human rights protections. Instead, we were fighting with other feminists. The faces of activists like Jo, Melissa, and Marjan got redder and angrier as their frustrations compounded. Some activists, like Siriporn, simply bowed out altogether.

By the end of the day, I felt like my head was about to explode, not only with all the new trafficking concepts that I had learned, but with the ferocity of the heated discussions.

I needed to get my thoughts straight. On the second and final day at the Palais, there was some time allocated for other organisations and individuals to give speeches, known as interventions. Back then, I found public speaking both liberating and terrifying in equal measure but I offered to speak, eager to synthesise what I had learned over the past days. It was a challenge to myself to try and put into words what I had seen and understood. The great thing about working for small and scrappy NGOs (like GAATW) is that my bosses were often amenable to my bold suggestions. Also, we never had enough staff to do all the work.

And so, I made my first ever speech at the United Nations.

I was shaking like a leaf, but my voice was steady.

It seemed clear to me that we needed a definition of trafficking that wasn't limited to prostitution. People were trafficked to farms and factories, but no one was talking about shutting these down, I argued. So why should we treat sex work differently? Women everywhere do jobs they don't want to do to make ends meet and earn money for themselves and their family. What gives some women the right to judge what others choose to do?

It was all very earnest. But given everyone else was so burnt out by the last few days of fierce feminist battles, no one objected to the baby-faced Aussie Eurasian law graduate making this final impassioned plea. In fact, it was what got me noticed by the older female activists. Until then, I was just the quiet one at the back of the room, who had been soaking everything in.

In the end, the group was able to find some agreement on a narrow set of recommendations to ensure basic human rights protections for all victims of trafficking, including those trafficked into prostitution. Beyond these *very* basic principles, the CATW and GAATW positions were like two parallel lines that would never converge.

It was a painful, bruising week, especially for the sex worker activists. But I realised how fortunate I was to be invited to that Geneva meeting. I learned a huge amount about human rights advocacy. Having the two sides stake out their positions so clearly and forcefully helped me to clarify and understand trafficking immediately, in a way that otherwise could have taken a long time to grasp. I understood how underdeveloped international law on the subject was. And finally – and perhaps most enduringly – I understood that putting the voices of affected groups of people front and centre of our human rights advocacy is critical. They're insights I've never forgotten.

*

I moved from Perth to Bangkok in July 1999. It is still one of my favourite places in the world. I love the anonymity of big cities, and I found the Thai capital intoxicating. I loved the mix of old and new, the street food vendors, the hot humid nights, the spontaneity, and the quiet narrow lanes (or *sois*) that crept off the main thoroughfares.

While most visitors to Bangkok spend their time on the eastern bank of the Chao Phraya River where most of the tourist attractions are, our office was in a *soi* on the Thonburi side, west of the river, in older Bangkok. It was down a muddling maze of left and right turns, past suburban houses and industrious street vendors.

A large white condominium block housed both the apartment that served as our office, and the homes of several staff, including me. I loved taking motorbike taxis down the *soi*, sitting side-saddle like the Thai women did, and getting my takeaway noodles and warm soy milk, served in plastic bags tied with rubber bands at the market.

In my first year there, I tried hard to crack the language. In addition to learning to speak Thai, I spent hours studying the complicated Thai script – if you've ever wondered why you see different variations of English spelling of Thai words, consider that the Thai language has forty-four consonants and twenty-eight vowels. The twenty-six characters of the English language are a poor substitute. While I was never completely fluent in Thai, my language skills became good enough to get around, and I could read a menu and street signs.

In addition to my colleagues at GAATW, and the other Australian volunteers, I made friends with young expats working at the UN, and with Thai sex workers at EMPOWER, the sex workers' union located in Patpong, the heart of the seedy tourist red light district.

I met the EMPOWER women at a regional HIV/AIDS conference in Kuala Lumpur in October 1999. They found it cute that I was a *farang* (foreigner) living in Bangkok, earnestly attempting to speak Thai.

I enjoyed hanging out with the EMPOWER women because they were astute, feisty, and fun. We sat around their office above clubs with names like Superpussy eating *gai yang* (grilled chicken) and fiery *som tam* (papaya salad). I learned more about their lives and their relationships. We even did a trip together to the famous temple and UNESCO heritage site, Angkor Wat in Cambodia, after a meeting in Siem Reap with the Cambodian Prostitute Union.

The EMPOWER acronym stands for Education Means Protection Of Women Engaged in Recreation. These women were a powerful example of what Mala had been talking about in Geneva. They smashed the stereotypical trope of Thai women in the sex industry as demure, passive women interested in sex. 'We don't want to be rescued; we don't want the police to raid our workplaces,' one of the sex workers Pom (pseudonym) told me. 'What we want is a safe, clean place to work and respect.'

I felt like a sponge soaking up all the information and experiences from everyone around me. I learned how to listen to people, and not to judge others too quickly. I learned how to connect with people from very different backgrounds to mine. I didn't think much of it at the time, but in retrospect, my own background as a mixed-race child of two migrants helped: I was used to being different and trying to find ways to blend in or build connections with people.

I hustled to prove to my new employers that I could do the work, and be useful to them. I started out drafting the newsletter, and then policy documents and providing research assistance on GAATW's human rights handbook.

The handbook was a guide for NGOs and governments on what a 'human rights approach' to trafficking actually involved. In a stroke of luck, the consultant employed to draft the handbook decided to quit after a few months, and – boldly – I asked if I could take over the project. My boss Jan agreed and, fortunately, there were two mentors to counsel me and oversee the project – Ann Jordan, a human rights lawyer in Washington, DC, and Lin Chew.

During my year in Bangkok, I travelled back to Vienna with Jan to participate in the UN Trafficking Protocol negotiations – the negotiations that might actually result in binding international law, at least for the countries who adopted the Convention. Several activists from Geneva were also there, like Melissa and Jo, and under the leadership of Ann Jordan we lobbied delegates from numerous governments to include human rights protections in the draft UN Trafficking Protocol.

We divided up these diplomats by region and collared them as they were coming in and out of the conference rooms. Jan and I got the Asia delegates. We would request a moment for a coffee and a chat, and then argue our case for why the definition of trafficking should be broader than just sex and why human rights protections for victims should be included in the text. If governments wanted to combat trafficking, then protecting the human rights of victims had to be part of the equation to be effective. We used the GAATW document we had discussed in Geneva – the human rights standards for the treatment of trafficked persons. But I was also developing my own style of lobbying, which was to lead with real cases of trafficked women to hammer home the point about why human rights protections were necessary. One was the story of a nineteen-year-old from Cambodia, Dinah (pseudonym).[9]

Dinah was living in poverty in Cambodia when a recruiter told her that she could earn money for her family by working in a factory in Bangkok and offered to help make the arrangements.

When she arrived, the owner of the factory forced her to work long hours every day, locking her and other workers in a guarded compound. The employer never paid Dinah but claimed her salary was paying off the debt that she owed to the agent who brought her to Thailand. After several months, police 'rescued' Dinah in a raid.

Dinah's initial relief at being rescued soon turned to dismay. She was never identified as a victim of trafficking, but an undocumented migrant worker and held in a large cell with dozens of other women awaiting deportation and sleeping on the floor. Dinah spoke hardly any Thai and there was no translator when investigators spoke to her.

Dinah's employer was fined for underpayment and hiring illegal workers, but not for illegally confining Dinah and the other women.

Dinah was also fined, for working unlawfully. Because she didn't have any money, she was transferred to jail for three months, and then back to an immigration detention facility, pending deportation back to Cambodia.

I used Dinah's story because it showed how the problems don't end when a victim is removed from a trafficking situation. We urged delegates to include practical measures in the Trafficking Protocol like requiring governments to provide legal and social assistance to those who were trafficked, to afford them due process, and to ensure that, first and foremost, they were being treated as victims, not as lawbreakers.

I included cases like Dinah's in the handbook that I was drafting: GAATW's approach centred on the lived experiences of individuals. And later, when I joined Human Rights Watch, similarly our emphasis was on including the testimony of victims of human rights violations in our reports.

Negotiations for the UN Trafficking Protocol concluded the next year, in December 2000. Eighty governments signed immediately, and twenty years later the Protocol has been signed by nearly every government in the world. For the first time in international law, we had an agreed definition of trafficking that was broader than just sex work. The Protocol defined trafficking as the transfer of a person though means of the threats, coercion, abduction, deception, abuse of power – and 'abuse of a position of vulnerability' (a slightly more nebulous term, that worried some of us in GAATW) into conditions of exploitation.

But so much of international rights work is one step forward and at least half a step backwards. Exploitation was defined to include 'exploitation of prostitution of others or other forms of sexual exploitation, forced labour or services, slavery or practices similar to slavery.'[10] The meaning of 'exploitation of prostitution' was deliberately not defined – the UN Protocol left it up to individual governments to determine their approach towards sex work. To those in the sex workers' movement, it left the door open for the old problem of governments criminalising sex work under the guise of preventing trafficking. It felt like a big failure.

Moreover, while the Protocol included a list of basic protections for victims of trafficking, the wording was quite weak. While the criminal aspects of the Protocol imposed hard obligations – 'states shall' do this or that – the protection aspects, such as provision of shelter, and access to legal and support services, were worded saying things like 'states shall endeavour to . . .'. The discretionary language and the vagueness of definition meant we would need to advocate intensely with individual governments to secure human rights protections under national law.

Still, some progress is better than none. At the time, we got so caught up in these failures that we did not take the time to reflect or celebrate the areas where we had won. Looking back on it now, we did achieve some success by setting the groundwork for governments to introduce legislation on trafficking and shift their focus beyond the sex industry. But it certainly felt like the battle was just beginning.

Around the same time that the Protocol was finalised, I finished *Human Rights and Trafficking in Persons: A handbook* for GAATW.[11] Jan (who by then had taken over from Siriporn) told me it would be translated into six languages. We released it at an event at the Foreign Correspondents' Club of Thailand in Bangkok. I was proud of the final result, and grateful for the input from my mentors and colleagues. But it was only years later – when I was working in places such as Nigeria, Cambodia, Thailand, Nepal, and the UK – that I saw firsthand why GAATW's handbook on a human rights approach was so necessary.

I would come face to face with government officials and staff of anti-trafficking NGOs who were often well-meaning, but paternalistic, and damaging the very victims they sought to protect.

CHAPTER 2

SLAVERY, TRAFFICKING AND THE COPS: FROM AMSTERDAM TO LAGOS

'Have you ever been in a window before?' the brothel owner asked me.

'No, I haven't.'

'Stay here for a bit then, feel what it is like.'

He stepped back out of view, leaving me alone in the window of a brothel in the red light district of Amsterdam.

These days, a lot of sexual services are arranged online. But back in the early 2000s, prostitution windows were a common feature of several European cities, and especially famous in Amsterdam.

I sat in the window on the stool provided. The window was effectively a little cubicle with a door that could open to the street if you wanted to invite your client inside. The thick velvet curtains were pulled back and a red neon light bathed everything in a pinkish glow. I knew sex workers closed the curtains when they had customers. Then there was a small room behind a partition for having sex.

In my job, I do my best to remain calm, not to react strongly when people tell you things that *should* make you feel shocked.

I try to listen and accept. So I found myself applying that emotional steadiness to my current situation. I tried hard to be Zen.

I sat there and looked out onto the street.

I'd been on the other side looking into the windows as a tourist many times, exploring the bars and coffee shops, ambling around the streets in the red light district. Amsterdam's red light district is a tightly packed group of streets in the old medieval part of the city centre, with crowded cobblestoned laneways and small bridges over canals. In addition to the windows, there are bars, clubs and the famous Amsterdam coffee shops. At night, it comes alive with groups of drunk and stoned tourists, these days popular with hen's nights and stag parties.

It was around midday now, so the street was much quieter. The sky was grey and gloomy, drizzling with rain, that moist air that lingers.

A middle-aged guy walked past and casually glanced up at the window. That was enough for me: I called out to the brothel owner, 'I'm done now, thanks!' and jumped off the stool, slipping behind the partition.

Looking back at it now, the man passing by was probably just surprised to see someone fully clothed in the window. But I panicked, suddenly feeling vulnerable.

The room behind the partition was small – it had a single bed, a sink and an attached bathroom. Marieke, a Dutch woman who worked for Mr A. de Graaf Stichting (at the Dutch Institute for Prostitution Issues) – an organisation that facilitated health services to migrant sex workers – was chatting with the middle-aged male brothel owner. Marieke had brought me there for a site visit. The owner pointed to the panic button on the wall above the bed.

'See, it's safe here,' he said. 'You press the button if you have problems.'

He seemed happy to be showing me around his business – the institute developed relationships of trust with the women working in the windows and the brothel owners, and it appeared that trust extended to me.

'To work here, it is for the legal sex workers. But if you don't have EU papers, then you can't work here. You'll get deported.'

'So where do they go?' I asked.

'Who?' he responded.

'The ones without EU papers?'

Marieke replied. 'Ah, they work on the street, the Tippelzone. You want to go there?'

Tippelen is a Dutch word meaning to walk by taking small steps, but it is most often used to mean street-based sex work – walking to attract clients.

'Of course!'

I was in Amsterdam on that drizzly day back in 2001 because I was working for Anti-Slavery International in London. After nearly two years of living in Bangkok, working for the Global Alliance Against Traffic in Women, I had accepted a role at the world's oldest international human rights organisation. Anti-Slavery International was founded as the Anti-Slavery Society in 1839 to combat the transatlantic slave trade. In late 2000, they were hiring a Trafficking Program Officer to carry out research in several countries, comparing witness protection schemes for victims of trafficking. It seemed a logical next step to move to a slightly bigger organisation with a broader focus, and the job was a good match of the skills I had learned on the job at GAATW and my legal background. I prepped hard for the interview, treating it like an exam, and after a conversation

43

on a crackly landline from Bangkok, I was thrilled to be offered the job.

Mike Dottridge was the director. He was a revered expert in slavery and human rights, but I remembered him as the calm and intelligent man with exceptional manners, during that bitterly divided feud of feminists in Geneva. I respected Anti-Slavery's position on trafficking and sex work and I thought I could learn a lot from Mike. I was also beyond excited at the prospect of moving to London. I'd always wanted to live there – I'd spent six months in Nottingham as a university exchange student, and I had a deep affection for the UK. London was my dad's hometown, and I'm half-British after all.

With the UN Trafficking Protocol now complete, governments were starting to adopt laws to criminalise trafficking. But even with national and international laws in place, stopping human trafficking requires successful prosecution of the traffickers. That relies on the laborious collection of evidence and usually the co-operation of victims, which is not always as easy to obtain as you might think. They tend to come from countries with deep suspicion of authority, and are terrified about reprisals against themselves and their families.

In the countries where trafficked victims end up (known as destination countries), they often lack legal status and work permits. They are understandably anxious about how their families back home will survive. So how governments treat victims and potential witnesses is vital to a successful prosecution. And that's what I was in Amsterdam to explore.

Over the next three years at Anti-Slavery, I got to see the problem of trafficking at both ends – why victims take risks to leave their home countries, and how they are treated by authorities at home in places such as Nigeria, and in destinations such as Europe.

I knew from my work with GAATW in Thailand that trafficked women were very scared to give evidence against the people that abused them. Often, they simply refused to cooperate with law enforcement and so were just deported to their home countries. In some cases, the women were re-trafficked.

The Netherlands had a different approach. Rather than rushing into prosecutions, the government provided suspected victims of trafficking with a 'reflection delay' of three months. This was basically a bridging visa that did not require victims to cooperate with law enforcement immediately: when someone is initially rescued or removed from their trafficking situation, they need time and space to recover from their ordeal, rather than immediate pressure from police to make a criminal statement. As victims have time to build up their resilience and recover, they are more likely to want justice.

Victims of trafficking were terrified of retaliation from their abusers, especially if they had to return to their home countries in Asia, Africa or Eastern Europe – they would usually return to the same place and circumstances that had led to their being trafficked in the first place, and where police were ill-equipped or unwilling to protect them. In some cases, corrupt police were in cahoots with the traffickers. Some victims still 'owed' huge debts to their traffickers or those who had arranged their travel. Sometimes they or their families were threatened and harassed for repayment.

For these reasons, many victims wanted to safely stay in the country where they ended up, usually a wealthier country in which they also had a better chance of earning an income than the home they'd left.

In the Netherlands, after three months, further residency was contingent on cooperation with law enforcement. Belgium had a similar reflection period, but it was only forty-five days. In contrast, the Italian government offered a six-month residency permit, that could be extended by twelve months at a time. It was not contingent on cooperating with law enforcement, but it was tied to successful social integration and recovery – such as enrolling in school or getting a job. The US was also exploring new visas to encourage victims to cooperate with police.

The UK had no such residency permit. Victims who were not willing to cooperate were deported, usually within forty-eight hours, whereas those who agreed to testify could be granted exceptional leave in the UK for four years if the information they provided was useful and if they were judged to be at risk if they were to return home.

My new job was examining the effectiveness of how these different programs worked in practice. I was also to look at what happens in countries of origin when victims were sent home. The study was funded by the European Union, and the outcomes would be used by Anti-Slavery International to lobby governments to better protect the rights of victims of trafficking.

We selected ten countries for the research. On the destination side, it was Belgium, the Netherlands, Italy, the UK, and the US – all chosen for their different approaches to residency permits for victim witnesses. For countries of origin, we chose Colombia, Nigeria, Poland, Thailand and Ukraine. We picked these based on where victims in Europe came from, where we had local NGO partners, and where our partners thought the research would help to change government policies on the ground.

In some countries, our NGO partners helped us to understand the local situation and who to talk to, but I conducted the interviews myself (often with the assistance of translators). In other countries, we effectively 'contracted out' the research to local NGOs as a way of deepening our collaboration with other organisations and helping to build their research and advocacy capacity. We interviewed police, judges, prosecutors, lawyers, health care workers, organisations assisting trafficked persons and migrants, as well as victims themselves.

Although Mike gave me a lot of autonomy and trusted me to do the research as I saw fit, he would regularly ask probing questions, offering useful advice throughout the research process. One of the most valuable things I learned was how to conduct interviews with victims of trafficking in an ethical manner. Always ask for their consent, making sure they understand how the information will be used. Ask open-ended questions, do not lead them – some victims may simply agree with you, or say what they think you want to hear. Be aware that it's painful for victims to talk about some of their experiences, so don't push people to share intimidate details that make them uncomfortable. Be ready to offer referrals to support services. End interviews on a positive note. Don't rush, try and build rapport.

I started in the Netherlands because I wanted to see how having a legal sex industry impacted human trafficking and the abilities of police to investigate the crime and protect victim witnesses. My interviews with Dutch authorities and NGOs suggested a logical answer: authorities could concentrate their efforts on the illegal areas – aspects of the sex industry that were under the radar, where people were being forced or coerced to work, and where children were being sexually exploited. But to understand the Dutch approach (and to get a sense of whether it would work elsewhere), I wanted to see a fuller picture of how sex work was being regulated. That's how I ended up in the window.

Around 10 pm, Marieke drove me to the Tippelzone, which was in an industrial part of Amsterdam, a short drive from the city centre. The zone was open seven days a week from 9 pm to 3 am. It was the only place where sex workers could legally offer their services on the street.

We pulled off the main road into what looked like a suburban car park. It was a chilly, wet November evening. There were a couple of bus shelters to protect working women from the elements. We sat in our warm car watching women in high heels and short skirts attempting to attract clients. Even though we were there for our research, I felt a bit uncomfortable.

Marieke said the Tippelzone had opened in the mid-1990s in an attempt to reduce sexual services from being conducted on the streets of Amsterdam and to provide a safer environment for street-based sex workers.

Vehicles drove along a 'pick up' loop, where the drivers could negotiate with and pick up a sex worker. We drove round the loop, passing about thirty or so women. They looked at our car, and noticing that we were female, looked away. We weren't worth their efforts.

Several of the women were African, most likely from Nigeria. Marieke also pointed out the young, white women, probably from former Soviet Bloc countries.

'A lot come from Moldova these days,' she noted.

Away from the 'pick up' area was a separate area of parking bays with wooden privacy partitions between each car space – the 'service area'.

'This is where you have sex,' Marieke pointed out helpfully.

'In the car?' I asked, confused.

'Yes. It's safer for the women. It is all taking place in the zone. There's less risk of violence, rape or not getting paid. It is part of the rules. The drivers can't take women outside.'

It all felt a bit like a McDonalds drive-through. Sterile, but safer.

Sex work was legal in early 2000s Australia – there are working brothels within several hundred metres of where I now live in Sydney – but everything is discreet, largely off the street and out of sight. I realised it was the visibility of sexual services that I found confronting.

On the second drive around the zone, Marieke pointed out that we weren't the only ones observing.

'A lot of these men in the cars aren't customers, they are pimps. It's how they keep tabs on their women. That's how they control them, make sure they are working. The pimps aren't allowed to get out of the car.'

I noticed a police car parked near the entrance to the Tippel-zone.

'The police come and go – they monitor the zone throughout the evening. It's for safety and to discourage the pimps. But the police aren't allowed to ask the women for their papers,' Marieke explained.

The police largely left the women alone, unless they approached them with a problem. There was a two-storey building between the 'pick up' and 'service' areas, and once we parked the car, Marieke showed me inside through a back door, the staff entrance. Inside a health care worker was on duty. We chatted to her briefly. As well as helping with health concerns on site, she could also refer women in trouble to services like shelters and informed women of their rights, including their right to the three-month period of stay if they were victims of trafficking. The building contained restrooms, a shower, and a living room area where the women could come inside to get warm, take a break, get a coffee or a snack from the vending machines. There were free condoms. I noticed stickers advertising a hotline for women to report violence.

Marieke explained that trafficking was still happening in the Netherlands, but 'it's more hidden. It's now in the phone hotlines, the escort services. Not in the windows. And here in the Tippelzone, there's still a little trafficking and problems with abusive pimps, but it's easier for the women to connect with each other and know what their rights are. They can get information about services and how to get out. So it does provide a layer of protection.'

I had read academic studies that showed sexual assaults and drug-related crime fell after Tippelzones were introduced in Amsterdam and other Dutch cities.[1] I wondered whether women forced into sex work in the Netherlands went to the police for help – certainly the authorities and NGOs seemed to think so. The system wasn't perfect, but the women seemed safer, and more aware of the resources there to help them. I soon learned this was a rarity even in European countries.

*

A few months later, I travelled to Italy with a colleague from Anti-Slavery International who spoke Italian. Driving on the outskirts of Turin and Milan in the north, I soon witnessed how the absence of regulation could facilitate trafficking and violence against sex workers. Scantily clad African women stood on the side of the highways, in the rain, trying to wave down truck drivers or motorists. They positioned themselves near the exits and rest stops but getting in a client's vehicle was risky – they were vulnerable to violence or non-payment. Some of these women were likely victims of trafficking.

At the time, Nigerian women and girls were increasingly being trafficked to Western Europe for prostitution. We had heard that traffickers forced them to undergo ritual ceremonies before they left Nigeria, known as 'juju', where they swore blood oaths to repay the travel costs and be loyal to their 'sponsor' in exchange for a safe journey. People laughed it off as voodoo, but these spells cast a powerful hold over a lot of women and girls. I knew of one Nigerian in London who adamantly refused to give a statement against her trafficker because she had taken such an oath. Eventually, a social worker persuaded her to file a police report naming her abuser. Soon afterwards, the girl got hurt in an accident. She blamed it on breaking the oath she had sworn.

In Turin, while visiting a shelter run by a Catholic religious organisation, I met Mary (pseudonym) a young Nigerian woman who had been trafficked. The shelter was a large apartment on an upper floor of a low-rise building. There were no signs advertising its presence, its location was a secret except to the staff and the women staying there, usually four or five women from Eastern Europe or Africa.

It was early evening and there was the smell of coffee and cigarettes. An Italian espresso pot sat on the stove in the kitchen.

I introduced myself to Mary and tried to converse with her – initially in my terrible high-school-level Italian, though we didn't get very far, so we switched to English. She told me she'd recently moved into an apartment across town. She returned to the shelter to meet us and do the interview. It felt like a second home to her, she said. She'd spent nearly a year there.

Mary was around twenty-five years old, with long hair in braids. She was dressed simply in jeans and a pale pink jacket. The three of us sat around the kitchen table drinking coffee, Mary chain-smoking cigarettes. As a former smoker, the smell made me crave a cigarette myself.

I began the interview explaining what Anti-Slavery International was, what my role was, and why we were doing this research – we wanted to hear the voices of women who were trafficked so that we could make recommendations to governments based on their experiences.

Mary listened, expressionless. Maybe she was bored, maybe she didn't think much of our ambitions. I asked for her consent to conduct the interview and told her she could refuse to answer any question that she didn't like, or just didn't want to answer. I explained we might use her testimony in a public report which would be available on the internet, but we would not use her name or personal identifying information. Mary nodded her agreement.

I focused particularly on Mary's 'post-trafficking' experiences and her treatment at the hands of the Italian government, the main subject of our research. Also, I didn't want to retraumatise her by asking her too much about the abuses she had suffered. We already knew that she had been trafficked into sex work, that was enough.

She politely answered my questions about the police, prosecutors, court process and support services, but in fairly abrupt short sentences. The process to get a residency permit allowing her to remain in Italy had been long and difficult, she said, but other than that, it was hard to get a sense of what her experience had been like.

'Did you have any interactions with the police when you were working on the street? Did you ever go to the police for help?' I asked.

Mary smirked.

'No. Why would I trust the police? They would just send me back to Nigeria. In Nigeria, the police are in it – they are involved in the trafficking,' she said, exhaling deeply in a big puff of smoke.

'How so?' I asked.

Mary paused and stared intensely at the bottom of her coffee cup. She didn't answer. I let the question linger for a while. We sat in silence.

It is difficult doing interviews when you have not had sufficient time to build up a rapport with someone. Perhaps Mary didn't want to talk to us after all. I thought I should offer to wrap it up.

I asked her the final vague question that I asked all interviewees: 'Is there anything else you want to tell us?'

Often people say no, and that's it – end of interview. But sometimes they want to talk and clearly Mary did. Now the words came tumbling out, delivered in a low monotone, at times switching from English to Italian, telling her entire story. Mary didn't make eye contact with either myself or my colleague.

'I'm from Nigeria, from Benin [City], in Edo state. I went to Italy because I heard there were jobs here and I needed to earn some money. I didn't finish high school.' Mary described how a friend from her village helped arrange the travel and loaned her money, telling her she could repay it once she got to Italy. 'Before I left Nigeria, I had to swear an oath with a juju priest to pay back the money and be loyal to my sponsor. It was scary, they killed a chicken in front of us. But they said it was for my safety.'

Mary said she thought she would be working as a nanny, but she was instead forced into sex work on the street. They told her she had to pay back 30,000 US dollars.

'I had to go with a lot of men. I had to work even when I was sick, even when I had my period. The Madam had my passport, which was fake anyway. She said I would get it back when I paid off the money. I didn't know what to do.'

At this point Mary started to cry, and I grabbed her some tissues. We took a break for a while, and I made a fresh pot of coffee. After some time had passed, I gently asked her some more questions, to see if she wanted to continue.

She explained that after a year, a 'friend' – a former client – helped her to escape and move to another Italian city, putting her in touch with this shelter.

'When did you go to the police?'

Again, Mary avoided talking about the police. She lit another cigarette and continued telling us her story.

'At first, I didn't want to report the Madam. I was so scared. I was scared of the juju. I was living in a flat that he [the former client] was paying for. But then, the traffickers back home, they started going to my family and asking them for money, saying that I ran away. I was too ashamed to tell my mum what happened. And then some men, they found out where I was living, they came to the flat, they beat me up. They said I still owed the Madam.

'I moved in [here]. I didn't want to go home, I was afraid. Anna [from the Catholic organisation running the shelter] said I needed to report it to the police. So I went to the police. I told them what happened. They arrested the Madam. But I still feel scared. Those men found me after I escaped. And I'm worried about my family.

'My mum said [Nigerian] police came to the house to get a statement, but they asked for money. This is the police in Nigeria. They are crooked.'

Later, the shelter manager told us the Madam who forced Mary into sex work was charged and convicted of 'exploitation of prostitution'. The police did not charge her with slavery or trafficking, saying they didn't have enough evidence. The Madam was fined and imprisoned for twenty-two months.

The Catholic organisation had contacted the Nigerian embassy in Rome to report the threats to Mary's family back in Edo state. Local police went to her family home, but as Mary had recalled, they demanded money to investigate.

It took ten months from when Mary filed the police report to when she got a residency permit that allowed her to work. But for now, at least, she was safe.

I always tried to end interviews on a positive subject, especially after discussing traumatic events. We spoke about Mary's current life – she was working as a sales assistant in a retail store – and she planned to study. She wanted to be a beautician. Mary smiled and I had no doubt that with her steely resilience and street smarts, she would make a good life for herself in Italy.

A few months later, I was to have a much richer understanding of Mary's experience, when our research project took me to Nigeria. It was my second visit to the country – my first had been a fleeting visit to the capital, Abuja, for a conference in 2001. Mike, who had lived and worked in the country, briefed me in advance about Nigeria's political and economic context: despite Nigeria's abundant natural resources, especially oil, most Nigerians faced dire economic circumstances due to endemic corruption, government mismanagement and widespread inequality.

I was excited to be going back to Africa's most populous country, but also a little nervous about its notorious reputation for corruption and fraud. Nigeria gets a bad rap in the Western press, but I found it a warm and dynamic, albeit chaotic place. I loved the energy of Nigerians, their hustle, their candour and irreverence. Still, the chasm of inequality between rich and poor was galling, and visible everywhere. It underscored many of my interactions while travelling in the country.

My travel partner for the trip was Bruno Moens, executive director of a Belgian NGO, Payoke, that we were partnering with for the project. We were going to visit three cities – the sprawling mega-city of Lagos; Benin City (not to be confused with the country Benin to the west of Nigeria), the historic capital of Edo state, which was the recognised point of origin for many of the trafficking rings operating in Europe; and Abuja, the capital, for meeting with government officials and diplomats.

I arrived alone after an overnight flight from London; it was early morning and the Lagos airport terminal was already bustling with people, mainly West Africans. As I went through customs, uniformed officials scanned my bags, and took an unusually long time examining my passport.

'Present?' one of them eventually asked smiling. 'You have a present for us?' I knew this was a polite way of asking for a bribe. Even though I had been warned by Nigerian friends in London that something like this might happen, I was still shocked at the brazenness of it occurring in the international airport.

'No,' I said bluntly. 'No present.'

My lack of enthusiasm to pay bribes meant I had to wait longer for my bags to be checked and re-checked. Eventually my passport was returned to me, without the big smile. I was free to go. I exited into the arrivals terminal and tried my best to casually glance around for my name on a sign – to do this too obviously was to invite energetic offers of cheaper rides from the pushy touts crowding the hall. Unfortunately, the driver who was meant to collect me was nowhere to be found, and soon I was swamped by offers of a ride. I declined them all, found a pay phone, and called Bisi Olateru-Olagbegi, the vivacious lawyer and director of the Women's Consortium of Nigeria (WOCON), who was helping us organise our trip. She had insisted a driver was safer than taking taxis.

Bisi welcomed me warmly over the phone, but then I heard her voice drop.

'Oh, the driver. Sunday . . . Eh! He forgot! So sorry.'

I wasn't sure who had forgotten but I could hear her in the background simultaneously carrying on another conversation, presumably in Yoruba, the language of Nigeria's south. It sounded intense – like she was berating someone.

I had no idea what was going on, but it sounded like Bisi had bigger issues at home to deal with than a foreigner stuck at the airport. I hung up the phone and accepted a ride from an older driver who had the most appealing negotiation tactic in my eyes: he didn't talk too much or hustle too hard. The ride to the hotel was eye-opening.

Lagos is a port city of fifteen to twenty-two million people, spread over 'the Island' (actually a collection of islands) and 'the mainland'. The streets are wide, but buildings, bridges and roads were in an advanced state of decay. I was accustomed to grid-locked traffic and vendors plying their wares in the streets of cities like Bangkok, Jakarta, and Manila. But Lagos street vendors took it to another level in the crowded traffic jams. They weren't just offering cool drinks – you could buy electric kettles, slippers – even puppies.

I kept the doors locked and windows up, as Bisi had advised, but it was hot and stuffy, and the AC didn't seem to work. I wound the window down barely an inch. Drowsy from my overnight flight, I soon dozed off. I awoke to someone trying to stick their fingers through the window to grab my glasses off my face. After that, I always kept the windows wound all the way up, no matter how hot the car was.

At the hotel, I met Bruno who was both a colleague and a friend. Payoke provided support to victims of trafficking and he was interviewing trafficked women staying in their shelter in Antwerp, Belgium. He was an ideal travel partner – funny, curious and nothing much fazed him. Bruno and I had first met at a trafficking conference in Brussels and we bonded over a love of travel, especially to difficult and unusual countries. Bruno told me wild stories of his solo travels through Yemen and Lebanon, where he had been taken hostage briefly by Hezbollah. In return, I told him about how I accidentally (but successfully) crossed the Gaza Strip as a naive backpacker looking for the most direct route from Cairo to Jerusalem. We subsequently travelled together through Vietnam and Myanmar.

When I said I was going to Nigeria, Bruno was one of the few people in my circles who was genuinely enthusiastic about it, and I was pleased to have his company for the trip. An increasing number of trafficking victims coming to Payoke's shelter in Antwerp were from Nigeria. Bruno wanted to see things firsthand and get a sense of what happened when people returned home.

We finally met up with Bisi who introduced us to our driver, Mr Sunday, who arrived in a battered but reliable silver Toyota sedan. I had met Bisi in person twice before in Nairobi and Abuja and she greeted us warmly. In her endearing but disorganised fashion, Bisi flitted between the topics of which officials and NGOs we should meet, where we should go, looking over our agenda of planned meetings and passing on phone numbers, meanwhile making suggestions of Lagos's best nightlife and offering up her adult children to escort us to nightclubs when we were done with our interviews.

Mr Sunday was a huge hulk of a man, who was a devout Christian and mainly spoke Yoruba with only a little English – or at least, little that he was inclined to reveal to us. For several days, he drove us around Lagos and then on the five-hour journey to Benin City – and gradually, we managed to break down his stoic demeanour and even got him to laugh a few times. Moreover, if Mr Sunday's spoken English was rudimentary, his skills in police management were advanced.

As anyone who has been to Nigeria can attest, police checkpoints are frequent, and they are often a pretext to shake down motorists for money. In 2010, Human Rights Watch published a report about how armed police officers regularly extort money from taxi drivers, market traders, and motorists.[2] If they refuse to pay, they risk arrest and detention, physical and sexual assault, torture, and even execution. Negotiating police bribes at roadblocks is therefore a delicate art, and one at which Mr Sunday excelled. He seemed to have wads of naira [Nigerian currency] in small denominations stuffed all over the car. Money was hidden in his pockets, by his feet under the floor mat, and tucked into the car's sun visor.

As we approached a checkpoint, he'd speak loudly and assertively to the police in Yoruba, always with a smiling face. I had no idea what he was saying. He'd almost throw the money at them (in a technique known as money spraying), trying his best just to slow the car down to a crawl rather than bringing it to a complete stop. I guessed that he was telling them that the annoying foreigners in the back were in a hurry.

These 'tips' weren't just for police at checkpoints, but part of a whole ecosystem of petty payments by motorists. Tips were given to boys on the street who provided unsolicited guidance to Mr Sunday on where to park the car; to the boys who watched over our car while we went into a building or a restaurant; or to the parking attendants working their patch of the street.

We mostly avoided travelling at night because both the number of police checkpoints and the risks of carjackings was much higher.

We soon set off on from Lagos to Benin City and the road was potholed and in bad shape. Although it had been sealed, it had obviously not been maintained. We seemed to go through at least a dozen checkpoints manned by police and uniformed civilians – all with demands for payment – during the five-hour drive. Ironically, the presence of police was meant to keep motorists safe from bandits on the road.

At one point, as we bounced down the muddy road, I looked out the window and saw several handmade signs advertising tyre repairs. *How weird,* I thought. *Who would get their tyres fixed here, in the middle of nowhere?* I wondered if it was because of all the logs on the road to make people slow down for the checkpoints – they functioned as makeshift speedbumps. But suddenly the car lurched to a complete stop as Mr Sunday slammed on the brakes and cursed in Yoruba – or at least it sounded like that. Immediately ahead on the road was a group of menacing young men wielding large planks of wood studded with nails. One was thrown down onto the road in front of the car. They seemed to be dressed in a uniform – I didn't know if they were a disaffected road crew or just robbers in matching coloured outfits. Mr Sunday had the window open and was yelling angrily at them. This particular shake-down seemed to anger him – perhaps because it threatened his vehicle, not just the passengers. With his head out of the car, it looked like he was about to launch through the window. But they didn't budge.

Begrudgingly, he flicked them some naira. They removed their makeshift spikes from the road, and we motored on. We had gone less than a kilometre when we saw a car jacked up and a tyre being changed by a similar road crew. I laughed – that slightly hysterical laugh that happens when you are tense. I tried to focus instead on the lush greenery of the landscape as a welcome distraction from the highway.

With a population of about 1.5 million, Benin City is much smaller than Lagos. It was the capital of the ancient empire of Benin, a kingdom which had flourished from the thirteenth to the nineteenth centuries. It had been ransacked and looted by the British in 1897 and burned to the ground. The city still had a king – the *Oba* of Benin, a traditional and ceremonial ruler. His palace was in the centre of the old town. But the city around it has fallen on hard times. Benin City had only a few paved roads and endured frequent power cuts. The city centre and its ring road was hectic, rowdy with crowds of people, cars, and minivans, and a gigantic moat. Vibrant colourful street markets were full of vendors yelling to attract your attention and hawking their wares in wheelbarrows. Beggars with disabilities crawled around the cars asking for money. Half-built buildings were everywhere, paralysed in a state of decay. Earth seeped up the white walls of buildings, staining them brown. It was a city that once had such a rich history, destroyed by foreign conquest and then neglect.

Benin City was now more famous for trafficking of women to Europe than its ancient kingdom. Edo state isn't the poorest state in Nigeria, but since the 1980s it has had well-established migration links to Italy for trade and business. As more Nigerian merchants travelled to Italy, some of them started to use those same routes to lure women into sex work and debt bondage. Nigerian Madams got wealthy by running trafficking networks in Italy and built opulent homes back in Edo state. 'Sponsors' lured young women to Europe with vague promises of work, offering to arrange their travel and documents. When they arrived, the Madams told them how big their debt was, and that they must repay it by engaging in sex work. And initially, officials did very little about it.

In Lagos we had interviewed various NGOs and international organisations working on trafficking. In Edo state, we met with several more NGOs and local officials who lamented that human trafficking was rising due to rising crime, poverty and high unemployment in the region. They complained about a lack of resources from the federal government to fight trafficking. Back then, the Edo state government did not assist trafficked women returning home – there was no counselling, no medical care, no legal support or financial assistance.

In the absence of government, civil society organisations were emerging to support women and girls. To help prevent trafficking, they ran awareness-raising campaigns and skills-training in subjects like sewing, catering, and computer studies to help them find work. We visited young women learning to make scotch eggs in a cooking class, an improbable sight that reminded me of my own ill-fated high school home economics classes.

Providing effective support to trafficked women returning from Europe was harder. An order of Catholic nuns working closely with the International Organization for Migration (IOM) said they had helped nine women in the past year, a tiny number. They, too, spent much of their time trying to prevent trafficking in the first place. And while the program was well-meaning, it felt paternalistic: I could see why the strong, resilient women escaping sex work on the streets of Europe wouldn't find the nuns' focus on religion and rules a good fit. Survivors of trafficking wanted to assert control over their lives, not have someone new tell them what to do. And most Nigerian women were deported back to the country as undocumented migrants instead of returning through IOM's reintegration program.

The nuns told us that many of the deportees were probably re-trafficked, especially if their debts were not paid off. This matched with what we'd been told in Europe by several victims who had been re-trafficked. Bonded to their traffickers by the juju ritual oaths, they felt they had no choice – Bruno and I had interviewed a number of them, and for them the power of the magic was very real.

One day, when we were wandering among the tightly packed streets near the *Oba*'s palace and state government buildings, we stumbled across a juju priest at his shrine. I noticed a small sign in English about warding off the presence of evil spirits. Curious, we stepped through the front gate. The priest was dressed neatly in white robes. He wouldn't let us into the shrine, but we spoke to him sitting on plastic chairs in an overgrown garden with exotic plants and life-size macabre carved human statues. Bruno immediately started peppering him with questions about rituals for the trafficking of women to Europe. The priest explained the ritual process as something that women and girls want to do to keep them safe for their journey. They offer a bit of hair, fingernails, clothing, blood, and usually a chicken or a goat was sacrificed. They drank some concoction, incantations were made, and a spell was set.

Traditional religious beliefs in the supernatural were strong in Benin City. Many people seemed highly superstitious. Pacifyingly, the juju priest claimed that he didn't offer rituals to girls travelling to Europe anymore. I didn't believe him. The whole place sent a shiver down my spine.

But change did eventually occur. As well as being the king, Benin's *Oba* is the sacred spiritual leader with authority over all juju priests. In 2018, sixteen years after our visit, the *Oba* responded to concerns about trafficking and banned juju priests from making ritual oaths for Nigerian women travelling to Europe. Moreover, he annulled all oaths previously sworn, effectively setting women free from the curses. Writing in the *New York Times*, Nigerian author Adaobi Tricia Nwaubani claimed, 'What the Oba has done is likely to be more effective than anything the international anti-trafficking community has managed to do after millions of dollars and many years.'[3]

After meeting the juju priest, Bruno and I took separate motorbike taxis, or *okadas*, to get back to our guesthouse as the sun was setting. On my way home, I experienced yet another random police shakedown for a 'tip'. The next day I told Mr Sunday what happened and he responded like my dad would have, clicking his tongue, shaking his head, and chastising me for not calling him to pick us up. Observing the blatant police corruption everywhere, I thought of what Mary had told me in Italy: to her, the police weren't the protectors, they were the predators, to be feared. Ordinary Nigerians avoided them at all costs. Instead, people relied on their own streets smarts, like Mr Sunday, or sought the protection of those stronger than themselves. I'd only been in the country a short time, but I could already understand why.

Back in Lagos, Bisi suggested we pay a visit to Alagbon Close – a police station next to an immigration office – she had heard that a group of women who had recently been deported from Italy were there. It could be an opportunity to interview them about their experiences.

'Do we need to make an appointment?' I asked Bisi.

'No, you just turn up. African way,' she told me.

The immigration office was a noisy hub of activity, with several uniformed police coming in and out, a caged off area which was a mass holding cell and plenty of bystanders milling around. Later, I realised many of the bystanders were relatives of the women and girls who had been deported, eager to see their loved ones.

The police let us in to interview the officers, though they refused our requests to speak with the women. We learned that a charter flight of 160 Nigerian women deported from Italy had arrived several days before. The women were taken directly from the airport to the police station and held in the cell for several days without charge, the victims along with the Madams and anyone else who had been deported for criminal activity.

As we spoke to the police, we could see the women's faces behind the fence. They were yelling at the police officers, clearly distressed about their situation – it was chaotic. According to the officers, some had escaped the previous night by breaking down a gate, although they'd since been rounded up and brought back.

I glimpsed one reunion between a woman who appeared to be in her late teens and a relative, perhaps her sister. She was crying and saying in English, 'I have nothing. They [the Italian authorities] let me take nothing, I'm sorry, I wasn't able to bring anything back . . . not even my clothes, nothing.'

I tried to imagine Mary, back in Turin, being locked up in this holding cell with these women. It would be re-traumatising for anyone who had been trafficked.

According to the police, the women were detained for the purpose of collecting their details, they were screened against a criminal suspects database and tested for HIV. It was unclear what was done with the test results. Police said that the women's details were collected to share with government officials to block them from obtaining passports as a means of preventing trafficking – all these women, including trafficking victims, were now supposedly barred from international travel. This seemed particularly perverse, forcing women who needed to migrate to take even greater risks – and rack up higher debts – by obtaining fake documents or attempting illegal border crossings. And according to several of the waiting families, the length of time for screening and health checks was just another opportunity for police to extort money from their relatives. 'If we can pay, they come out, but we just don't have any money,' one family told us.

We asked the police what happened to the women once the screening was complete. Officers replied that the women were handed over to relevant state officials and that 'ninety-five per cent of deported women came from Edo state.' Several NGO sources later told us that sometimes the Edo state officials refused to accept the deported women, so they were just left in Lagos, vulnerable to re-trafficking.

The only way for women to avoid this messy process was to identify as a victim of trafficking and accept 'voluntary return' through the International Organization for Migration. This meant going through programs like the order of nuns that we had met in Benin City. There just didn't seem to be any good options available to them.

The final stop on our visit was Nigeria's capital, Abuja, some 700 km northwest of Lagos. We were going to meet government officials, diplomats, and visit an NGO shelter established by the Vice President of Nigeria's wife, Titi Atiku Abubakar. Maybe they would be able to tell us why more couldn't be done to help the deportees.

Abuja was full of surprises. Our first meeting scheduled with the ministry of women's affairs turned out to be an impromptu press conference for Nigerian media – for which I was completely unprepared, but as circumstances demanded, I just rolled with it. Our second meeting was at the trafficking shelter, where it quickly became clear that the young women there were far more interested in braiding hair than discussing trafficking and they talked me into getting my hair braided too. The moment we'd finished, NGO staff unexpectedly summoned me to meet the Vice President's wife and founder of the NGO. In my casual dress, my hair in corn row braids, I looked like a Spice Girl. I could have died.

Thankfully, Titi Abubakar didn't seem to notice, and even gave me some Nigerian clothes to wear. She was keen to plug her organisation's plans for expanding shelters across the country, wrongly assuming that Anti-Slavery was a donor. In a way, it summed up my trip to Nigeria perfectly, the spontaneous unexpected swirl of chaos and the inexorable energy and charm of Nigerians who do not take no for an answer.

I haven't been back to Nigeria since that trip in 2002, but my memories of it remain strong. Saying goodbye to Mr Sunday at the airport, I thanked him sincerely for keeping us safe. I still marvel at his negotiation tactics, and I have – on occasion – tried to imitate them. My greatest lessons, however, were about the value of having colleagues and partners whose judgement you trust, people like Bruno and Bisi.

I spent the next few months in London writing up our report.[4] One of the main arguments was that trafficked persons were being 're-victimised' when they acted as witnesses – practical measures were needed to protect them and their families from reprisals. Many victims weren't even recognised as such by authorities, such as the deported women I encountered in Lagos. We urged destination countries to issue a three-month 'reflection delay' residency permit, like the Netherlands, to allow people time to recover from their situation and consider their options. Residency after that should not be limited to those who cooperate with law enforcement, like the Italian model.

At the same time, a ground-breaking court judgement in Italy found that even situations that allowed some limited freedom of movement could be slavery. Trafficking was not merely about locking someone up in a brothel – traffickers could enslave and control women in other ways, such as through the ritual oaths sworn to juju priests, confiscating ID papers or passports, or controlling their movements by use of mobile phones. This was a huge step forward for victims like Mary.

The report did lead to lasting change. Even before the report was complete, we started advocating for better victim protection based on the preliminary findings. Myself, Bruno, Bisi and our other research partners attended conferences all over the world sharing what we had learned with governments, the media, and international organisations. We drafted submissions and journal articles. And working with other civil society organisations, we succeeded in making governments take victim protection seriously and start discussing reflection periods. We educated police and prosecutors across Europe about our findings. Anti-Slavery International was invited to join an EU Experts Group on Trafficking. And three years after our report, in 2005, the Council of Europe – an international organisation representing forty-seven European countries – mandated states to allow suspected victims of trafficking a reflection delay, of a minimum period of thirty days. While it fell short of the three months we advocated for, it was at least a partial success.

And things improved in Nigeria too. In 2003, the Nigerian government established a National Agency for the Prohibition of Trafficking in Persons (NAPTIP) and the government adopted a trafficking law that complied with international standards. The law mandated the establishment of a network of shelters across the countries, and that victims should not be criminalised. These measures have helped to improve the investigation and prosecution of trafficking cases.[5]

I've returned to Amsterdam many times over the years. Whenever I am in the red light district I look up into the windows, wondering who is really sitting behind that glass. Whether it is an independent entrepreneur, a mother saving money for her children, a victim of trafficking paying off a debt or a young researcher trying to understand the experience. I think about how much the scene has changed in twenty years. The efforts to improve legal and health protections, new conventions and protocols, policing and law enforcement, and the efforts to establish and protect women's human rights.

I also think about how my perspectives and experiences have changed since it was my own face being illuminated by that famous pink-red glow.

CHAPTER 3

TRAFFICKING, HUMAN SHIELDS, AND ARRESTED IN KATHMANDU

I've always had an itch to travel, which is why I left Perth in the first place. After three years at Anti-Slavery International, I felt like I'd achieved what I could in that role. I needed a break and was keen to explore more of the world. So, in 2003 I quit my job and spent several dusty but delightful months backpacking through East Africa with a boyfriend. Along the way, to support myself, I picked up consultancies for a German aid agency – human trafficking by now was a priority of many governments and so consultants with expertise in trafficking were in demand. It also made my travels through Africa more interesting, with a purpose.

I started on the spice island of Zanzibar in Tanzania, summited Kilimanjaro, got robbed in Uganda's capital of Kampala before volunteering for an organisation working with child soldiers in Gulu, Northern Uganda. It was there that I came across a dog-eared report by Human Rights Watch which with devastating clarity described the horrors inflicted upon children forcibly recruited into the Lord's Resistance Army (LRA). Every night in

Gulu, I saw kids walk in from their villages kilometres away at sunset to sleep on the pavements and shopfronts around town. It was safer to sleep on the streets of government-controlled Gulu than in their villages where they risked night raids and abduction by the LRA. In the morning, they'd walk back to their homes and their schools.

One night, watching the BBC program *Hard Talk* in my hotel room, I saw an interview with the Executive Director of Human Rights Watch, Kenneth Roth. He powerfully and persuasively made the case to protect civilians and safeguard human rights on a whole range of crisis situations. Between the report and the interview, I thought to myself, Human Rights Watch is an impressive organisation and one day I would like to work there.

From Uganda, I hitchhiked and bounced around on the back of cattle trucks from Kenya to Ethiopia on a road notorious for bandits, not realising that later in my career I would gain a much deeper understanding of Ethiopian and Somali politics.

After Ethiopia, I bought a one-way ticket to Delhi: I had no idea what my next career move would be, or what life would bring. I spent three months zigzagging around India by train, staying in a monastery in Bodh Gaya – the town where Buddha attained enlightenment under a bodhi tree – to doing a job interview with a UN agency by phone from an internet café in the holy city of Varanasi on the banks of the Ganges (I didn't get the job).

In January 2004, I went to the World Social Forum in Mumbai, partly for fun but also to network and see what was out there professionally. The World Social Forum was a heady jamboree of social justice activism, full of people from all over the world concerned about the inequalities caused by capitalism and globalisation, and protesting for peace, human rights, and the environment. It was far removed from the stuffy UN conferences in Europe where officials obsessed over procedure, and NGOs felt like interlopers. Here, activists and community organisers of all ages from diverse backgrounds ran the show, jostling to bring attention to their causes. There were workshops, talks, performances. In my late twenties and still not jaded yet, I loved every minute of it.

At one point during the Forum, I was sitting on a bench and noticed these remarkable Indigenous men and women in elaborate, brightly coloured clothing and head-dresses. They were from India's far northeast – Nagaland. I couldn't help but stare. I was trying to pluck up the courage to ask them if I could take their photo, when one of the men plonked down right next to me, put a camera in my face and snapped my photo. This happened in India quite a lot back then with foreigners, especially young women. At times, I felt irritated at the invasion of my personal space, but this time, I burst out laughing. I guess I was just as exotic to them as they were to me. We looked at one another and smiled. I pulled out my camera, and we each got the shots we wanted. To me, that exchange summed up the World Social Forum – solidarity and friendship overcoming language and difference.

At one of the many on-site demonstrations, I ran into Brad Adams, the Asia director of Human Rights Watch, whom I knew from my time in London. A few years later, Brad would become my boss. I also reconnected with Bandana Pattanaik, my former colleague from GAATW, whom I had worked with in Bangkok. Bandana was now the Executive Director. We had stayed in touch while I had been at Anti-Slavery International as our work lives crossed over a lot. Bandana mentioned that the humanitarian group, Oxfam, was looking for a consultant to do some research on anti-trafficking efforts in Nepal. I had no plans and had never visited Nepal before. Of course, I knew of its breathtaking mountains and the sleepy capital of Kathmandu sounded intriguing. I also knew the country was in the midst of a civil war, but it didn't seem too dangerous, at least not for foreigners. I'd met Oxfam's representative in Nepal, Meena Poudel, in Geneva back in June 1999; she remembered me, and after sending her my resume and some samples of my work, we spoke by phone, and she offered me the position on the spot. I was off to Nepal!

I flew from the busy, chaotic streets of Mumbai to the much smaller but still hectic Himalayan city of Kathmandu. Squeezed between the world's two most populous countries, China and India, the mountain kingdom of Nepal is one of the world's poorest. Kathmandu is in a valley, and the air hanging between the mountains was heavily polluted from motor vehicles and open fires. It was noisy from honking cars, buses, and trucks. And it was smelly from the fumes of exhausts and rotting garbage which littered the streets, where random cows roamed.

Yet there was something intoxicating about Kathmandu's vibrant street life, the tiny dusty lanes that suddenly opened and revealed these historic, spiritual squares with ornate wooden temples that hadn't changed in centuries. In contrast to India, Nepal's slower pace of life felt more relaxed. On a good, smoke-free day, the stunning snow-covered mountains of the Himalayas beckoned. Here, the mountains touched the sky.

In 2004, Nepal was still a constitutional monarchy and in the midst of a brutal civil war between the government and the Maoist faction of the Communist Party of Nepal. I was pretty clueless about Nepal's politics before I went there. All I knew was that the Maoists were communists, and wanted to overthrow the monarchy and form a people's republic.

Nepal's monarchy had achieved worldwide notoriety in 2001, after the Crown Prince Dipendra went on a murderous rampage, killing his father, the king, his mother, the queen, and seven other members of the royal family before shooting himself in the head. Briefly declared King while in a coma, Dipendra died a few days later and his uncle, Gyanendra, assumed the throne. It was no secret this new king was not popular in Nepal.

The Maoists began their 'People's War' in 1996. Much of the fighting occurred in rural areas, so the 'insurgency', as people called it then, wasn't always immediately obvious in Kathmandu. Daily life carried on in the city. The most visible manifestation was the frequent *bandhs* (or strikes) called by the Maoists, that forced the closure of businesses, schools, and modes of transport.

By 2004, trafficking in women and girls was a serious problem in South Asia. As the wealthier, more-developed neighbour, India attracted Nepalese women and girls across the open border, desperate to provide for themselves and their families. Many lacked skills and education, with little experience of life beyond their village. Traffickers exploited the insurgency and poverty in Nepal to lure women and girls to India on the pretence of work. Instead, some were trafficked and forced into sex work in brothels, into private homes as domestic workers, and into factories making clothing, carpets, or bricks.

The Nepalese government lacked capacity and resources to address the issue, and was preoccupied with the insurgency. But unlike Nigeria, at the time Nepal did have a plethora of NGOs devoted to preventing trafficking and assisting in the recovery and reintegration of victims. Most were funded by foreign governments or international organisations, like Oxfam. Some were successful, others less so.

In Nigeria, I'd witnessed how the authorities violated the rights of deported women. In Nepal as I would learn, over-zealous NGOs can also violate the rights of people under the guise of 'protecting' them, by restricting people's rights to free movement or detaining them in shelters. Oxfam wanted me to write a report recommending what a rights-respecting approach to trafficking would look like. In my research, I would come to learn a lot about the complexities of working in a country experiencing armed conflict, and experience firsthand what it feels like to be detained – albeit briefly – for exercising basic rights.

Meena Poudel headed the Oxfam office. She was a no-nonsense feminist: she spoke quickly and liked to get stuff done. The twenty or so staff were all Nepali. We hired a small team for my project including Naresh (pseudonym), a dynamic young anthropologist who had recently completed his masters and was teaching part-time at a university in Kathmandu. Naresh was my research assistant and translator. Stocky with a broad smile, he dressed in casual Western clothes and nearly always wore a baseball cap. He was immediately welcoming and introduced me to his circle of friends; we bonded from day one. His perfect English was a product of attending a Jesuit high school.

'Are you Catholic?' I asked, surprised.

'God, no – Hindu,' he replied. 'But it had the best English-language education, so my parents sent me there.'

Naresh spoke passionately and proudly about his country and the many beautiful places he had visited. An avid hiker, his enthusiasm was infectious, and soon I was planning my own hiking adventures in the Himalayas for once my contract ended.

Also on my team was Priti (pseudonym), who worked with an organisation formed by trafficking survivors called Shakti Samuha (Women of Power). Priti had long dark hair, glasses and usually wore a sari or *salwar kameez*. Softly spoken, it took time for Priti to lose her shyness, but we bonded as we spent more time together. Later, Priti and I discovered we were both at the UN consultation meeting in Geneva in 1999: she spoke in Nepali (through an interpreter) on the panel with Mike from Anti-Slavery International.

It was because of the experiences of Priti and other women in India that Oxfam had commissioned this report. Priti did not like to talk about it, but she had been trafficked to a brothel in India as a teenager. She had spent five years in brothels in Mumbai and then, after paying back a large debt, she worked for herself. Priti's case illustrated the blurred lines for trafficking victims – she was initially trafficked, but later, with few other options, she had accepted the work and had managed to earn an income and send money to her family.

Priti was one among hundreds of women and girls from Nepal, Bangladesh, and India rounded up in police raids on the red-light district in Mumbai in 1996. They were treated appallingly by both the Indian and Nepali authorities. The Indian government initially detained the women and girls in government-run homes for child offenders – effectively swapping one form of captivity to another. As Priti put it, 'Actually during the raid, it was more exploitation on us. It was a very painful time, even more than when I was in the brothels.'

On the other side, Nepali authorities refused to help repatriate them. Eventually, several NGOs stepped in with support, counselling and vocational training and tried to mediate with their communities and families they had left behind.

But even back in Nepal, the experiences of survivors were mixed. Some NGOs detained the women in their shelters, keeping them from their families. Some sent the women and girls for HIV tests without their consent, just as the Nigerian police had done. HIV/AIDS was immensely stigmatised for anyone who had worked in the sex industry, forced or not. Priti had spoken of this in Geneva:

> When I went back to my country, I wanted to go back to my home, but it wasn't possible because of social rejection. After a while, after counselling, my family was ready to accept me, but society was not, and if my family accepted me, society would reject them. So I decided to go back to the organisation [Shakti Samuha] and I have been there two years. But I am lucky, because many women do not have organisations, and no one will accept them.

Out of all these horrible experiences for trafficking survivors, Shakti Samuha was formed. It was a unique organisation because it was actually led by trafficking survivors, rather than career NGO staff. Oxfam supported Shakti Samuha financially as well as helping to build their capacity, the aim being that Priti would learn skills in conducting human rights research and interviews from myself and Naresh. It would also be a chance for Priti to learn some English, as I sadly spoke no Nepali. In turn, I would learn from her how to incorporate the perspectives of trafficked women in Nepal into my report.

Naresh, Priti and I were a great team, despite or perhaps because of our different backgrounds. We were all around the same age (late twenties) and we shared a sense of humour. Priti and I stayed firm friends, and years later, those English skills came in handy: by chance we would both end up living in the same city on the opposite side of the world at the same time – in New York.

During the next few months in Nepal, we interviewed trafficking survivors, family members, government officials, police officers, and staff from civil society organisations. We visited shelters and group homes for survivors. We collected experiences, good and bad, as we travelled around the country, security permitting. We would go to a town or village and meet with individuals or groups of women who would tell us about the initiatives they had taken to combat trafficking, some which were funded by Oxfam.

Shiny white 4WDs are the stereotypical vehicle of the Western aid worker. Oxfam had two of them and two drivers. In Nepal, the 4WDs were not just a status symbol, they made it much easier to navigate bumpy, windy mountainous roads and to cross rivers when bridges were washed away. So, we'd either get a ride in the Oxfam car or take taxis or buses to get around.

In 2004, the Maoists controlled swathes of territory in rural areas and civilians were increasingly caught in the crossfire. There were serious human rights abuses by both sides – the conflict had racked up thousands of deaths. Both the military and the Maoists engaged in killings, torture, arbitrary arrests, and abductions of civilians and captured combatants.[1] Security forces raped and 'disappeared' people suspected to be rebels or Maoist sympathisers. Meanwhile the Maoists forcibly extorted money from civilians in the form of 'taxes' and recruited children into their ranks as cooks and porters.

One day Naresh arrived at the office looking grave. He was usually so cheerful and chatty, but this day he was silent, and his face was dark.

'What's up?' I asked.

'The military visited us in the middle of the night. Soldiers asking lots of questions. It happens,' he said quietly.

I wondered why the military would be visiting his family.

I did not know it then, but at the time, Nepal had the highest number of enforced disappearances in the world, according to the UN.[2] Enforced disappearances are when people – usually young men, sometimes young women – are taken by security forces on suspicion of supporting opposition groups but the authorities deny responsibility or knowledge of their where-abouts. Most of those who 'disappear' are never heard from again: they are missing, presumed dead. Chillingly, Nepalese government officials had recently said that anyone working for human rights organisations, even the UN, were considered 'Maoist sympathisers' and therefore aiding and abetting terror-ism.[3] But all of this I discovered later, and I would become very familiar with disappearances when I started working for Human Rights Watch.

Some of the villages that Naresh, Priti and I went to were in Maoist-held areas. Of course there were no signs telling you that you'd entered Maoist territory, but I could always tell from the hushed silence that would come over my Nepali colleagues sitting in the car, or the furtive glances of families that we interviewed. Sometimes, when the white 4WD attracted too much attention, our driver dropped us off and we continued our journey using public transport or walking from village to village.

When I travelled outside of Kathmandu, I tried to blend in. I wore the *salwar kameez* and with my southeast Asian features and olive skin, I could almost pass for a light-skinned Nepali. I have often found that an appropriate change in clothes is helpful to avoid unwanted attention from authorities in places across the Asian continent. When we went through military checkpoints in the car, I'd usually pretend to sleep so that soldiers wouldn't get curious. And I always sat in the back with Priti.

In some small towns, it was safer for us to sleep on the floor in the NGO offices we were visiting rather than stay in hotels. These areas had curfews; it was dangerous to be out after sunset because of the fighting and movements of rebels and soldiers. One night, I remembered hearing the pitter patter of gunfire: my first thought was of fireworks, because apart from a brief stint in Northern Uganda, I had never been in a war zone before.

One day on a field visit in Maoist territory, having slept the previous night on the floor, I was feeling a bit cranky from lack of sleep and lack of food. Breakfast was sweet chai tea and boiled eggs – I'd taken the tea but passed on the eggs. We stood by the side of the road for what felt like hours but was probably thirty minutes, waiting for a bus to take us to a neighbouring village. It was humid, and I felt sweaty even though we were in the mountains. I wanted to put my hat and sunnies on, but I thought it would look a bit odd with my Nepali clothes. Finally, the bus came, already crowded, and we squeezed on with everyone else.

'Don't talk in English,' Naresh whispered forcefully in my ear as we stood in the aisle.

It was then I noticed the bus was full of young men with guns . . . machine guns. And although they had plainclothes on the top – Western-style t-shirts and jackets – some had combat army fatigue pants on. Someone turned over a bucket for me to sit on in the aisle, and from that vantage point I could see that the bus was also loaded with cases of ammunition.

I felt my stomach drop. I suddenly felt very uncomfortable surrounded by all these men with weapons. Both Naresh and Priti looked tense. I wondered why the Maoists would take the public bus. I noticed a couple of the guys staring at me, and I figured I should just do my sleeping trick before anyone started talking to me and realised I wasn't Nepali. I rested my eyes and tried to breathe and not think about it too much, although my mind was racing.

About forty-five minutes later, the bus stopped and all the young men with guns got off, taking their ammunition with them. We carried on, lighter physically and mentally in the half-full bus winding through the mountains.

'What the hell was that? Were they Maoists?' I asked Naresh.

I kept my voice low, as I knew in these areas it could be dangerous even to say the word aloud.

'No,' he replied whispering. 'They are army. Nepal army.'

'But don't the army have their own trucks?' I asked, confused. I'd seen heaps of army vehicles driving around Kathmandu.

'They do, but this is a Maoist area, so they don't want to be seen. Safer for them, but not for us,' Naresh said, his voice low and tense.

At that moment, the penny dropped, and I realised we had just been used as human shields.

I felt sick and angry. I'd read stories in the newspapers about public buses being blown up because of the presence of soldiers. I thought it was outrageous that people, mainly poor villagers, who had no other means of transport between towns, would be used as human shields for the Nepali military. What bloody cowards, I thought.

A few years later, I would study a short course on international humanitarian law at Harvard University. We learned about the laws of war and when it was acceptable to kill combatants or not. And I thought about that exact situation, and whether a bus full of enemy soldiers in plainclothes with a handful of civilians would be considered a legitimate military target for the Maoists.

Using people as human shields is in fact a war crime – military forces are never allowed to deliberately use civilians to protect their forces from attack. At Human Rights Watch, I would advocate on this topic – the practice, although banned under international law, was unfortunately still in use in conflicts around the world, for instance in Sri Lanka and Syria. That experience in Nepal was always in the back of my mind.

Meanwhile, the war was also one of the main drivers for trafficking in women. Young people were caught in the middle – regarded with suspicion by government forces, and vulnerable to recruitment or indoctrination by the Maoists. People were displaced from their homes due to the violence and the lack of jobs.

NGOs in Nepal had embarked on anti-trafficking programs with mixed consequences. The same split I'd seen in Geneva was evident in Nepal – organisations that were vehemently anti-prostitution and considered all prostitution to be trafficking, opposed to those that were more like GAATW, that made a distinction between consensual sex work and the force, coercion or deception in trafficking. In Nepal, there wasn't much discussion about legalising sex work, but the organisations that recognised sex work tended to be more pragmatic in their prevention campaigns, recognising many trafficked women and girls came from very poor rural areas with few work opportunities. Migration therefore was almost inevitable.

These NGOs prevented trafficking by advising women on their options, including how to migrate safely, to understand the risks, and know their legal rights if they got into trouble. They set up migration information booths, radio talk shows and hotlines.

The organisations that adopted a moral position that all sex work was trafficking were most problematic on human rights. Their interventions were often well-meaning, but at times did more harm than good. These tended to be the shelters that detained women and girls behind walls and locked gates, thinking it was the best way of protecting them, without realising they were mimicking the harmful behaviour of traffickers. Some organisations stopped women from travelling to India at all, thinking that would prevent trafficking. Several of these NGOs reinforced unhelpful gender stereotypes through their vocational training programs or touted marriage as the solution for survivors facing the stigma of sex work. In fact, encouraging vulnerable women and girls to marry could easily end in more violence of the domestic kind.

Naresh, Priti and I visited the busy Sonauli border crossing between Nepal and India as part of our research. There, we witnessed this 'moral saviour' approach playing out in real life. Nepal and India have an open border meaning no documents are required for local people to cross. At the border, an NGO had trained former trafficking survivors to monitor female movements across the border and interrogate those leaving Nepal who appeared 'suspicious'. They then wielded the power to turn back any women and girls they felt were vulnerable to trafficking and stop them from travelling. I understood the reasoning behind this approach, but I found it deeply troubling. These border monitors were not police, nor government officials.

In Kathmandu, we had interviewed a leading women's rights activist, Dr Renu Rajbhandari, who founded the Women's Rehabilitation Center (WOREC) in Kathmandu. She was Nepal's first ever Special Rapporteur on Trafficking, a government-appointed position established as part of Nepal's Human Rights Commission. Renu was small, slightly built with short hair and glasses but she spoke with fierce authority in telling us about a case involving more than thirty women intercepted at the border and taken to a shelter.

'In my capacity as National Rapporteur, I interviewed these thirty-two women. It wasn't clear to me that they were being trafficked. They wanted to go abroad for work, for opportunity. Yet this NGO prevented them from leaving. Who is going to pay for these women's expenses, now they are out of pocket because they missed a plane or a train?'

Soon after we arrived at Sonauli, we met two young women working for the NGO stationed at the border and I asked them to explain their work.

'We see if a boy and girl are crossing the border together, we try to find evidence of their relationship. If they are together and look suspicious, then we separate them and ask them questions. If the stories don't match and we are not convinced that they are related, then the boy is taken to the police. And the girl is transferred to a transit home [run by the organisation],' one of the border monitors told me, via Naresh of course who was translating. The other woman wiggled her head side to side in fierce agreement with her colleague.

'How do you know who to stop and question?' I asked.

'Because we've been here a while, we know the local community. But if there is any girl we have not seen before, then we question her. Girls who are not from here, they look different,' she responded.

They told me that in the past week, their border monitors had interrogated twenty to thirty girls and of that they prevented sixty per cent from travelling to India, taking them to their 'transit centre' instead. The border monitors acknowledged that not all the girls they 'rescued' were in danger of trafficking; some of them were runaways. On their website, they have a running tally of intercepted girls and women – more than 42,000 the last time I checked. It might sound impressive to Western donor agencies, but based on my conversation with these two women, I doubted all these women and girls were at risk of trafficking. The next answer confirmed my scepticism.

I asked the border monitors if mistakes happen and if people who weren't at risk of trafficking are prevented from travelling.

'Often,' the young woman replied. 'It's the nature of the work.'

But there was zero accountability for the process and no compensation for mistakes. Renu had also flagged that. Missing a bus or a train for someone in poverty was not just an inconvenience, buying a new ticket cost them dearly. Then, there was the impact of sending someone mistakenly and by force to a shelter home. In human rights language, it was discriminatory and violated freedom of movement; some might even call it arbitrary detention.

The border area was a constant flow of people back and forth on foot, in rickshaws, on motorbikes, and in cars. It was hot and dusty. Very few girls were travelling to India the day we were there, but the border monitors intercepted a young man and his wife. We stood within earshot and Naresh quietly translated for me.

The man said he worked for the Indian army. He showed his paperwork and their train tickets to Assam. The border monitors asked for their marriage certificate. They didn't have it. His wife was eighteen years old.

The border monitors then questioned the couple separately. Most aspects of their story matched, but the name she called her husband differed from his documents. This immediately raised the alarm bells for the border monitors – the couple cannot cross and must return home to get their marriage certificate. The man is exasperated and says he must report to work and cannot miss the train. He asks to go ahead alone, but they tell him he can't leave his wife.

To me, this was bizarre. If the young woman was at risk of trafficking, then why insist the two of them stay together? Later, when the border monitors were distracted, we spoke to the man ourselves. Naresh asked him why the names didn't match.

He hesitated for a while and then sheepishly blurted out,

'To work for the Indian army, you need to have finished your Year 5 schooling, but I only finished Year 3. So, I used my friend's ID to get the job, and that's the ID I showed to the checkpoint ladies,' he told us.

I believed him. The couple's ordeal illustrated all the complexities of Nepalis crossing the border, especially those who are poor and lacking education. He had shown his ID card and train tickets voluntarily. The young couple seemed genuine. But in the end, they dutifully obeyed the border monitors and turned back. I saw the power dynamic at play in which the poor, young and uneducated did not question instructions coming from two women appearing to be in positions of authority. I wondered if these two cases would be chalked up as another successful border interception statistic.

Later that day, we interviewed a female police officer in the nearby town of Bhairahawa. The police officer was part of a women's unit that received specialised training in combating violence against women. She seemed exasperated when we asked about the role of NGO border monitors:

The NGO checkpoint workers are not very well-trained. They don't know how to interrogate girls, they speak in a very direct way, they don't know how to extract information. They are too strong in stopping women. Sometimes they don't seek permission from police before taking girls to the transit home. In one case, they kept a girl in the transit centre for one month before they let her go – when they found out she was not going to be trafficked.

We saw several other well-meaning but misguided and harmful anti-trafficking interventions. Back in Kathmandu, we visited an NGO shelter – in stark contrast to most of Nepal's ramshackle buildings that easily topple over in the frequent earthquakes, this was a slick compound of new brick buildings funded by foreign donors. The imposing structure was encircled by a wall topped with barbed wire and had guards at the gate. It felt like a prison but was home for up to 600 women and girls, some of whom were trafficked or victims of sexual violence. Others were 'at risk' of trafficking – that risk determined by the moral values of the organisation who detained them.

I'd been warned that Nepali visitors would not be welcomed at the NGO headquarters. Naresh usually arranged all our meetings, but this time he said I should call them myself. I made the appointment and we turned up, the three of us. Initially, the staff refused entry to Naresh and Priti.

'Why?' I asked. No reason was given, just smiles and a nod of the head which in Nepal, confusingly for foreigners, means no.

'It's because you're a foreigner,' Naresh said, under his breath. 'They want to show off to you, but see how they treat us – Nepalis are not welcome, no transparency.'

I was outraged. It reminded me a little of the special treatment we got in Nigeria, where Bruno and I had received a warm welcome from some organisations under the mistaken impression that we were potential donors with capacity to fund their programs. Now, here in Kathmandu, it was even worse because they were blocking access to our local staff.

'We are a team,' I insisted. 'And we have visited many homes together all over Nepal. I'm not going in without them.'

Eventually, after some discussion amongst themselves, the staff relented and the three of us entered the compound. Priti rolled her eyes at me. Naresh grinned.

The staff gave us a tour of the facility – heavily sanitised. It was a tour meant for Western donors and international humanitarian groups. The physical condition of the facilities was impressive. Rooms were freshly painted in white with fans and electricity in impeccably clean dormitories and classrooms. There was also a medical clinic. But the heavy institutional feel of the property reminded me of a prison inside as well as out. When we asked to talk to any of the women staying at the shelter, the staff unequivocally refused.

The scale and institutional-feel of the shelter was in stark contrast to the smaller family-style atmosphere of the group home run by Priti's group. Shakti Samuha's shelter was a ramshackle house in a low-key suburban neighbourhood of Kathmandu that welcomed us warmly when we dropped in. Of course, it made things easier that Priti was a trusted staff member. We sat on the floor, interviewing trafficking survivors who told us about their experiences in other NGO shelters – how some shelters had detained them, preventing them from reuniting with their families, and how if they failed to follow the rules, they were punished, sometimes physically.

At Shakti Samuha, women could choose to stay or leave. They could also choose their vocational training. Several were learning new skills like driving or hair dressing – there was an effort to try and move away from gender-defined roles and let women themselves choose their path. It felt like a home to me, a more nurturing environment for women and girls who had faced some of the most horrendous abuses and had all their choices taken away from them.

These visits helped form my views on providing assistance to victims of trafficking, and I shared what I had already learned in other parts of Asia, Africa, and Europe. The best interventions were the ones that put the rights of trafficking survivors at the centre and gave survivors agency – let them make choices in aspects of their daily life rather than forcing people into institutional regimented routine. A few rights-respecting organisations were trying to move away from shelters entirely and looking for alternative safe living arrangements for women – like shared housing. Shakti Samuha's self-organising structure reinforced its focus on building resilience and empowerment rather than simply treating the women and girls as passive victims. This seemed to be effective in fostering their recovery, in contrast to other shelter homes that created a new dependency on the organisations that 'rescued' them – or 'captured' them, depending on how you viewed it.

My final weeks of work in Nepal were in April 2004, with almost daily large-scale protests in Kathmandu, mostly pro-democracy and anti-monarchy demonstrations organised by students, workers, and political parties. People were agitating for a return to democracy and against the parliament hand-picked by the King. During these weeks, Naresh, Priti and I would travel across the city for meetings and end up in gridlocked traffic for hours because protesters had shut down the city centre. *Bandhs* (strikes) were called more often now by the Maoists. Power cuts were also becoming more frequent.

On 8 April, to quell the growing demonstrations, the government banned gatherings of more than five people, claiming that Maoists could infiltrate the protests. The ban had little impact on the protesters.

Later in the month, as I was leaving work one afternoon, Meena called me into her office and asked me if I wanted to attend a women's rights protest happening the next day. I didn't hesitate, from the streets of Perth to London, I had always loved a good protest. And I was curious about these demonstrations which, so far, I hadn't seen up close. In retrospect, I was also naive in thinking that the protest was simply about women's rights.

The next morning, Meena collected me from the hotel, and we took a rickshaw to the grounds of a small temple on a nondescript side street to meet other women activists. Priti was there and a few other staff I recognised from Oxfam, Shakti Samuha, and other women's rights organisations.

In all, less than a hundred Nepali women gathered wearing traditional saris or *salwar kameez* and just a few men (Naresh had decided not to come). I was the only foreigner, and that morning I'd deliberately decided to wear my 'western clothes' – jeans and a colourful top. I had a feeling that I might be better off playing the hapless tourist if anything went wrong.

As we gathered by the temple, one woman was handing out pieces of black cloth to wear as armbands; many of the women were wearing them and I took one too. Journalists were there reporting on the growing crowd, with photographers capturing the moment. Someone suggested I put the black strip of cloth around my head for a photo, which I did, somewhat foolishly – that photo has lived on forever in internet searches.

We hadn't been there long, maybe thirty minutes, when suddenly a bunch of police in full riot gear appeared at the temple. Police trucks blocked the road. The riot police reminded me of stormtroopers dressed head to toe in blue combat fatigues, helmets, and some of them wore body armour. Instead of guns, they carried long wooden sticks. Many of them were female, so clearly, they knew in advance this was a women's march.

The mood quickly shifted from one of jubilation to defiance. The Oxfam staff scattered but a group of the women protesters remained, refusing to be intimidated. I stuck close to Meena. Female police officers quickly encircled our group blocking the exit. Some of the women started chanting slogans. And just like that, police moved in.

Two of the women police officers grabbed me, forcefully but not violently, and frog-marched me to a waiting police truck. They pushed me into the back of the vehicle. They said nothing and I didn't try to resist. Meena was right behind me, and Priti was already in the truck. Some of the protesters kicked, some yelled, but all got dragged into the police trucks. No one was handcuffed. In the back of the truck, we smiled and linked arms, because at least we were together – and it felt like an important moment of solidarity.

I had the same feeling that I first experienced at the protest against the racist Australian politician Pauline Hanson – overcome with emotion of being with other women, of solidarity even if we didn't share a common language. Some of the women started singing songs in Nepali. We stood in the back of the truck, and they sang all the way to the police station. It felt strangely festive. I wondered what had happened to our other colleagues.

After several minutes, we arrived at police headquarters, a large, gated compound of buildings and open space surrounded by a wall and razor wire. I'd been in plenty of police lock-ups as a visitor, but this was the first time I was entering one as a detainee. When the truck stopped, we were ushered out of the truck and filed one by one into the nearest building. I tried to go with them, but police officers wouldn't let me.

'No, you stay,' a male riot police officer said, also clad in the blue combat fatigues.

'Why? I don't want to stay. I want to go with my friends,' I replied.

Meena yelled something at them in Nepali: it sounded like she was giving them a lecture. But they weren't having any of it.

'No, you stay here with us, please,' the officer repeated in English.

Reluctantly, I obeyed and stood with police officers in the large courtyard between several buildings. I could see the holding cell on the other side of a wall where my friends were being detained. I was worried about what would happen to them, but at least they were all together. It was only then, in that moment surrounded by police officers, and separated from everyone I knew, that the seriousness of my predicament sunk in.

I had never been arrested before. I had been in stressful situations with police officers in other countries, in Nigeria, Australia and Thailand. But I had always managed to get out or talk my way out of difficult situations. Now, here I was stuck in police detention. I later learned that police arrested more than thirty women's rights activists at the temple that day. Three of the women, unknown to me, were former members of parliament.

A policeman brought over a plastic stool for me and I sat under cover outside the cell block, staring gloomily and silently ahead. I looked out at the sky, my solace and calming reference point, now brooding and oppressive with clouds. I had a good view of the car park and main gate where police trucks pulled in. It was humid, I was sweating – it must have been even hotter in the cell.

'Are you hungry? Thirsty?' The male police officers – still in their blue combat fatigues – kindly offered me tea and biscuits.

'No, thank you,' I said.

'Do you want to call your embassy?' an officer asked me.

'No, thank you,' I said. 'If you won't let me inside, I just want to leave – can't you let me go?' I tried to put on my best smile.

'Cannot' they said, smiling back. 'You need to wait to see the superintendent.'

As the hours dragged on at the police station, it was clear the police didn't really know what to do with me. No one seemed to want to take responsibility for putting me in a cell, which is why they sat me in the outdoor corridor area together with the police officers. At one point, I even tried to slip inside when some of the women were going back and forth to the bathrooms. I made it in for a few fleeting moments. Priti and Meena both cheered when they saw me.

'I just want to be with my friends,' I said to the police officer who wearily came in to fetch me back.

'No, you can't. You have to sit here. Outside,' he replied, firm, but polite.

Nepalis are generally friendly hospitable people, and the police were no exception. Some of those who spoke English had been to East Timor as UN peacekeepers. They had spent their R&R in Darwin, and they were keen to reminisce about their time in Australia. It was surreal, talking to them about Australia and some of them practising the Aussie slang they remembered. 'G'day mate,' they would say chuckling.

But as the afternoon wore on, after infinite offers of cups of chai, the situation was changing outside. Ours was not the only protest happening that day. In fact, ours was a small demonstration by comparison. As I learned later, tens of thousands of people at different pro-democracy rallies had converged on the streets of Kathmandu, not far from the royal palace and close to the police headquarters where I was detained.

Dozens of protesters had begun gathering in the streets outside the police compound. They lit fires – I could first smell the burning rubber and then see the smoke. Some threw stones into the police compound, even several large rocks that would cause serious harm if they struck anyone. Helmeted riot police officers started throwing the rocks back over the fence at the protesters. It was kicking off.

More vans of arrested protesters arrived and started filing into the holding cells. One of the vans was full of protesting lawyers, mainly men, arrested at a nearby legal demonstration. The lawyers were neatly dressed in their black suits and white shirts, and arguing passionately with the police officers. Some of them flat-out refused to go into the cell. The police by this stage seemed weary and more concerned about the deteriorating security situation outside the station. Some of the lawyers sat with me for a while outdoors.

'Who are you? What are you doing here? What is your name? Where are you from?' The lawyers peppered me with questions and then sent a flurry of text messages.

'Don't worry,' one of them said, 'we have reported your case to Amnesty International.'

Meanwhile, the situation outside was descending into anarchy, with more fires, rocks and other projectiles being thrown in and more police rushing out to deal with the protesters.

'Do you want to speak to your embassy? We can call them for you?' one of the lawyers offered.

'No, that's okay,' I said.

I felt a bit embarrassed about my predicament.

At that stage, if I am completely honest, my biggest worry was my Nepal visa – I needed to get a visa extension at the immigration office the following week. It sounds very superficial, given everything that was going on in the country at the time, but all I could think about was the fact that my parents were just about to fly from Australia to Nepal to visit me. I hadn't seen them in more than a year – in fact I had seen them rarely over the past five years. I was worried the authorities might deport me before they arrived. I wasn't too worried about the police charging me. I knew from Meena, the police tended to release the protesters without charge, the main aim being to disrupt the protests. But still, I was a foreigner in their country. Maybe they didn't want me here anymore.

After about six hours, I was finally summoned to meet with the police superintendent. We went to his office for tea. Meena was allowed to accompany me to help translate. The police superintendent calmly asked me some questions about politics. I answered truthfully that I wasn't involved in politics or in anything against the monarchy. It was a women's rights march, and that's why I participated. They asked me to write and sign a brief statement stating that I was not involved, and would not be involved, in any politics in Nepal. Then, I was free to go. It was around 4 pm.

I asked them to release Meena, but the superintendent refused. Police ordered her to go back to the cell while an officer escorted me to a rickshaw.

'Don't worry,' she said. 'We'll be fine, I'll see you at work tomorrow,' she waved me off.

Getting released was such a blur, I can't even remember how I got home. It was chaos near the police headquarters, with smoke from the burning tyres and crowds of people, mainly young men, and police officers on the streets. I remember paying close attention to the protests on the TV news that night. Soon after I left, the police let off tear gas; I learned later that Meena, Priti and the others were choking on it in the cell. Eventually about 8 pm, they let them all go home.

The next day, I turned up at work as normal. Meena and Priti were fine. My other colleagues had sheepish smiles and admitted they ran away as soon as the police arrived.

'But you were so brave!' they said. 'We put the word out about you, we got them to announce on the radio that an Australian woman was arrested. That's probably why they released you.'

The idea of media coverage made me nervous about my visa again, but I thanked my colleagues for their support. About 500 protesters had been arrested across Kathmandu, and few of them would have had the backing I got.

Shortly after I got to my desk, the office phone rang and someone put it through to me: it was an Australian diplomat calling concerned about my welfare. I wondered how the embassy got my number, before I realised they must have heard about my arrest in the local news. Ten minutes later, reception put through another phone call. This time it was a male journalist from the Australian Broadcasting Corporation calling from Delhi to interview me about the protests. I answered his questions factually over the phone. He told me that it was for ABC's radio news.

'When will this air?' I asked.

'The next news bulletin probably in about thirty minutes,' the journalist replied.

'Oh god!' I said, 'I better call my parents.'

I hadn't called them the night before because I didn't want them to worry. But now, I couldn't dial fast enough – I could just imagine them home in Perth, driving down the freeway, and my dad having a virtual heart attack when he heard my voice on the radio about getting arrested in Kathmandu. I was also anxious they would get cold feet and want to cancel their trip to Nepal.

There was no answer – my parents didn't have mobile phones back then – so I left a message on their answering machine: 'Mum, Dad – in case you hear anything on the radio, I am totally fine, please don't worry. Everything is all good, and I am so excited to see you here in Kathmandu next week.'

After that, I told Oxfam's front desk to screen my calls. I didn't want to speak to any more journalists. I didn't feel comfortable being the centre of the story: the protests were not about me, they were about Nepal's future, and if anyone should be talking to journalists it was the brave Nepali lawyers and women's rights activists whom I met in detention.

Thankfully for me and my worried parents, my visa did get extended at the immigration office the following week. My parents visited, and we went trekking in the Himalayas near Pokhara; it was just as beautiful as Naresh had promised. My dad later admitted he was concerned the entire time that someone would suddenly appear and arrest me. But he hid it well.

In May 2004, I filed my report with Oxfam and my time in Nepal came to an end. I headed off to Hong Kong and then to Bangkok, and a stint working as a consultant to the United Nations. As for my Nepali colleagues, Naresh went back to his work at the university and got married. Priti returned to Shakti Samuha, but within a few years moved to the US where she became a housekeeper. When I lived in New York, we occasionally met in Jackson Heights in Queens for authentic meals of *dahl bhat* (dahl and rice), *momos* (Tibetan dumplings) and other Nepali delicacies. Priti worked hard in the US and regularly sent money back home. On one occasion when work took me to

Kathmandu I visited her family who lived on the outskirts of the city. Her younger brothers proudly showed me the brick house that Priti had built for them, with the money she had earned in the US.

It was a good reminder of the lessons we had learned during our time researching anti-trafficking interventions in Nepal. Women who have endured trafficking, don't necessarily want to go back to their home villages and back to the lives they had before they were trafficked. They might still want to migrate for work. They might still want to take risks, have adventures in foreign countries. And why should we stop them? Ultimately, people want to be able to provide for their families in their own way.

As for Meena, she left Oxfam soon after we completed our project and took up a PhD on the social stigma affecting trafficking survivors returning to Nepal at Newcastle University in the UK.

Nepal's civil war ended in 2006. That August, the government and the Maoist rebels agreed to accept the United Nations to monitor the peace process. By November, the government, political parties known as the Seven Party Alliance, and the Maoists signed the Comprehensive Peace Accord, which formally ended the civil war. The monarchy was dissolved and Nepal became a republic. Maoist leader Pushpa Kamal Dahal, known widely by his nom de guerre Prachanda, became Nepal's prime minister in August 2008 after elections in which the Communist Party of Nepal (Maoists) won the most votes. It's rare these days for rebel forces to win, but the Maoists effectively won their war. Sadly, Nepal is still racked by political instability, poverty and trafficking remains a problem.

By the time I left Kathmandu, it had been almost twelve months since leaving London on my backpacking adventure.

I had seen and learned a lot in the course of the year. Getting arrested and witnessing the impact of the conflict on ordinary Nepalis made me realise that addressing the underlying social and political issues was critical. Protecting women's rights and combating the trafficking of women could not be done in isolation. They were driven by complex root causes, including in Nepal's case a civil war in one of the world's most impoverished nations. And so those few months in Kathmandu also awakened in me a desire to broaden my work in human rights. While I knew I had much more to learn, I had no idea that my work would have me sifting through the evidence of war crimes in an even bloodier civil war, this time in Sri Lanka.

PART II

ASIA

CHAPTER 4

FATE OF THE DISAPPEARED
IN SRI LANKA

After years of focusing on trafficking, migrant workers and women's rights, I found myself increasingly interested in the bigger picture of human rights. People wound up trafficked or exploited because they were trying to escape poverty, conflict, violence or discrimination: I wanted to help tackle the root causes of these abuses. I'd worked for several smaller, scrappier NGOs, and then consulted for donor agencies and the United Nations: I was thirty-two years old and felt inspired to join one of the world's leading human rights organisations. So in October 2007, I moved from Bangkok to New York for my dream job – Asia Deputy Director at Human Rights Watch.

Human Rights Watch was founded in 1978 with the creation of Helsinki Watch, largely to monitor government compliance with the 1975 Helsinki Accords across Central and Eastern Europe. When I joined in 2007, we had just over 200 staff and worked on more than 70 countries. As of 2022, that has grown to more than 550 people working on more than 100 countries worldwide. The objectives of the organisation are to investigate human rights abuses through our reporting, expose those abuses through publicity and 'naming and shaming' and try to change the situation through policy reform, and advocacy for justice and holding perpetrators of abuses to account.

I had always been impressed by the professionalism of Human Rights Watch staff. All the researchers and advocates I had met in Bangkok and London knew their stuff, and they weren't afraid to speak the truth. When I walked into their New York headquarters that first day of work, it felt like a movie. I couldn't believe that I had my own office in the Empire State Building.

But I didn't have much time to indulge my dreams about the bright lights of the big city. It felt like Asia was on fire. Thousands of saffron-robed monks were taking to the streets of Yangon protesting against military rule in Myanmar. Lawyers were demonstrating against emergency rule in Pakistan. In Sri Lanka, full-blown fighting had returned, as government forces pushed into the east of the country controlled by the successionist Tamil Tigers.

For the first year, I felt inadequate and out of my depth as I struggled to get to grips with these emergencies and adapt to my new role. I was used to excelling at my job and being respected in my specialist field. But suddenly I was responsible for a range of countries, staff, and a kaleidoscope of issues. I felt like I was surrounded by people who were smarter and more articulate than me, who spoke effortlessly in full paragraphs. I acted like I knew what I was doing, but on the inside, I worried that I couldn't possibly have anything to offer Human Rights Watch. Now I know there is a term for what I experienced – imposter syndrome.

All of a sudden my brain felt like it was exploding with the sheer amount of information I had to absorb. Every day, I read an improbable number of emails and articles, and I prepped hard for every interview and advocacy meeting. I had managed teams before, but it was a challenge to supervise staff on the other side of the world, some of whom had been with the organisation for a long time. Our Asia researchers, bless them, were mostly very patient with me, helping to get me up to speed on their countries and answering my naive questions.

Fortunately, the person who had previously held the role of Deputy Asia Director, Sophie Richardson, had moved to Washington, DC as our Asia Advocacy Director. Sophie welcomed me warmly. She is still the only person I know who can pull off a shaved head, heels, and a set of pearls. Sophie was both funny and fierce with an acerbic wit, but she was also personable and kind in helping me to navigate this strange new organisation of terrifyingly capable people.

I also had a boss who believed in me, Brad Adams. This made a big difference. He was based in London, but in those first few months we spoke every day, and he guided me patiently through the job and what I needed to do. Brad was strategic, had good political instincts but above all, cared about the people whose rights we were trying to defend.

I learned a lot from our Legal and Policy Director Jim Ross in New York. Jim had zero tolerance for fools, was gruff, highly intelligent and a workaholic. He also cared deeply about our work and had a dry sense of humour. Jim schooled me on human rights law and indoctrinated me into Human Rights Watch's more direct style of writing – Active not passive voice! What should the government actually do about this? – now whenever I write or edit anything I have Jim's voice in my ear.

The other person who got me through that first year at Human Rights Watch was my husband, Cam. We met on a white-water rafting trip through Northern Thailand, when we were both living and working in Bangkok, and we married at New York's City Hall in March 2008. In many ways we were opposites, we had completely different tastes in things like music, sport, and film but as Cam liked to say, 'It would be boring if we were the same'. Cam was passionate about politics and we shared an adventurous spirit, a desire to right the wrongs of the world, and we deeply cared for each other. In New York, he would stay up late, helping me prep for television interviews on topics like the elections in Thailand or the assassination of Benazir Bhutto in Pakistan. When your day-to-day work is stressfully navigating the crises of Asia, having a supportive partner at home makes all the difference.

Apart from adjusting to a new work culture, we were very happy to be in New York. We picked out an apartment in Chinatown – a fourth floor walk-up. After years of living in Bangkok and Hong Kong, I felt at home in Chinatown, and I wanted to be in Manhattan, at least in the beginning. We already had an eclectic group of friends in New York – mainly people I had met over the years in Bangkok, Hong Kong, London, Nottingham and Perth who had gravitated to the city. Many of them had nothing to do with the world of human rights, but they were fun and creative, thoughtful and cheeky. Friends who helped to keep me grounded. And took me out for cocktails, music, or dancing, especially if I was starting to take myself too seriously or feeling overwhelmed.

If Nepal was my introduction to a country at war and wartime abuses like the use of human shields, Sri Lanka was the country where I witnessed the horror and carnage when a government and armed group blatantly and repeatedly commit war crimes and thumb their nose at accountability. When governments fail, our job was to take matters to other governments who have leverage and also to the UN. At the UN, we pushed for international monitoring and reporting, as some form of accountability and deterrence. But sometimes it takes a lot longer than you'd think.

In the 1980s, long-simmering ethnic tensions in Sri Lanka erupted into a full-blown civil war. For years, the armed group, the Liberation Tigers of Tamil Eelam (also known as the Tamil Tigers or LTTE) occupied territory in the predominantly ethnic Tamil north and east of the country. The town of Kilinochchi was their self-proclaimed capital from 1998 to January 2009 and saw some of the heaviest fighting during the war. The Tamil Tigers fought for an independent Tamil state. But in the end, they lost. A remarkably different ending to a civil war, compared to the Maoist victory in Nepal.

Working on Sri Lanka, I learned about the crime of enforced disappearances and other war crimes. At Human Rights Watch from 2007 to 2009 we put a lot of the organisation's energy into a strategy to minimise abuses by both sides in Sri Lanka and to hold perpetrators of war crimes to account. In the end, it felt like we had little impact. Sometimes human rights work is like that. Sometimes we don't have the wins we crave. We don't save the lives that perhaps could have been saved. Sometimes things go from bad to worse. And governments just don't care. That's what happened in Sri Lanka. But I also learned that we don't give up, and one needs to be persistent, patient and in it for the long haul. If we and other groups hadn't been there, things might have been even worse. And for the relatives of those who were killed or disappeared, our documentation work mattered.

In the decades of conflict between Sri Lankan forces and the LTTE, horrific human rights violations were carried out by both sides, costing tens of thousands of lives. The Tamil Tigers terrorised civilians, whom they killed, captured, tortured, and used as human shields. They forcibly conscripted children to join their ranks. They deployed suicide bombers to blow up human targets. Their victims included a Sri Lankan president, an ethnic Tamil foreign minister, and an Indian prime minister. The LTTE pioneered the suicide vest and often used women to carry out explosive attacks because they could get closer to targets undetected.

The violence and brazen attacks on primarily Sinhalese and Muslim civilians made it easy for the Sri Lankan government to designate the Tamil Tigers as a terrorist organisation, and many foreign governments agreed, putting them on terrorism sanctions lists.

But the Sri Lankan government was also a brutal adversary. The military executed and massacred civilians. They disappeared, tortured, and displaced ethnic Tamils from their homes. The Sri Lankan government was deeply suspicious of Tamil youths presuming them to be either LTTE members or sympathisers. Journalists and activists who criticised the government were threatened, harassed and in some cases abducted or shot dead by security forces.

The Sri Lankan government that was instrumental in finally defeating the LTTE and ending the war was led by three brothers from the Rajapaksa family. Prime Minister Mahinda Rajapaksa was first sworn in as President in November 2005, in an election boycotted by the LTTE. He remained in power for a decade. When he won the presidency, Rajapaksa proclaimed at a news conference: 'I will bring about an honourable peace to the country, respecting all communities. Democracy will be strengthened, and law and order will be established in the country. For me, power is not an ornament, but a means to serve the people.'

He didn't mean it. Upon his election, he immediately appointed his brother, Gotabaya, as Defence Secretary. Another brother, Basil, served as a senior presidential advisor. The brothers ruled Sri Lanka as nationalistic strongmen, with no tolerance for dissent, and led a brutal war strategy of annihilating the enemy, whatever the civilian cost.

A few weeks after I started at Human Rights Watch, Brad gave me a report on disappearances in Sri Lanka to edit. Until that report, I didn't know a great deal about disappearances. I remembered in Nepal, my colleague Naresh had been fearful when the military came to his house in the middle of the night because lots of young Nepali men during the war disappeared. I knew that an enforced disappearance was when a government or militant group detained someone without officially arresting them. Their whereabouts became unknown – they just 'disappeared'.

Family members would file missing person reports at police stations or lodge writs of *habeas corpus* – a Latin term meaning 'show me the body' – requiring that a prisoner be brought before a court. Usually to no avail: sometimes those who were disappeared would wind up in prisons, tortured to confess to crimes. Many were simply killed, their bodies dumped or burned – or never found.

As a divisional editor, my job was to interrogate the facts presented, measure the alleged violations against international law, as well as more basic editing functions of style, structure, coherence and testing the logic and strength of argument. It was my first report, and he assured me it would be 'easy', though he neglected to mention that it was more than 200 pages long. It had been researched and written by Anna Neistat, one of Human Rights Watch's highly experienced Emergencies researchers, who had interviewed victims' families, lawyers, and activists.

The Emergencies Division was the crack team that Human Rights Watch deployed into crisis situations – war zones, massacres and disasters. Anna is Russian and studied law at Harvard. She's courageous, incredibly smart, and has a knack for getting into difficult places: she joked about travelling undetected to Jaffna – a city in Sri Lanka's north, tightly controlled by military and subject to a strict curfew – because the security forces presumed she was a Russian sex worker. And her report made chilling reading.

Thirty-year-old Kanapathipillai Ravindran lived in Colombo, Sri Lanka's capital, and owned a phone repair shop.[1] His mother described how on the night of 28 January 2007, he received a call from someone asking him to urgently repair a phone. The caller said he was waiting outside the house and kept ringing the doorbell. Neighbours reported that when Kanapathipillai stepped outside, two or three people were waiting by the door, while another two men were waiting in the street, near a white van. They accosted him and pushed him into a wall, bundled him into a van, and drove away.

Truck driver and father of five Vairamuththu Varatharasan was abducted from his home in Colombo on 7 January 2007. His wife described how a group of some twenty men surrounded their house – some in police uniforms, some in civilian clothes. An officer asked for their ID cards. She went into another room to get the documents, but when she returned, they were gone. She spotted a white van parked in a dark place on the road. By the time she got there, the van left.

Vairamuththu and Kanapathipillai were never seen again.

They were just two of the ninety-nine cases of men and women included in that report.

In every one, we had spoken to family members or eye-witnesses. We also had a longer list of nearly 500 cases of disappearances recorded by Sri Lankan human rights groups. Local groups and journalists documenting disappearances did so at great risk to their own personal safety. One of the most courageous was

Sunila Abeysekera, the executive director of Sri Lankan rights group INFORM: Human Rights Documentation Centre. Sunila passed away in 2013, but I remember her flowing long white hair, her casual and friendly demeanour, and her shrewd and articulate presentations. She faced threats for her outspoken criticism of both the Sri Lankan government and the Tamil Tigers, and for a time had to go into exile outside the country. Plenty of activists – Tamils, Sinhalese and Muslims – worked with us quietly behind the scenes passing us information.

The 'white vans' were a common feature of abductions, usually without licence plates, so families had no idea who had taken their loved ones, or where. In other cases however, they knew exactly which military unit detained their relatives, which camp they were taken to, and sometimes even the licence plate of the vehicle that drove them away. Those cases were no less frightening than the white vans – the captors didn't even bother to disguise their identity.

Even when it was clear who was responsible for the abduction, evidence often pointed to Sri Lankan security forces or pro-government paramilitary groups. The disappearances occurred in locations controlled by the government or close to military checkpoints, where it would be hard for groups of armed men to move about freely without the military's knowledge. The Tamil Tigers themselves didn't usually abduct people – they executed them on the spot.

In 2006 and 2007, not a single person in the security forces had been brought to justice for their involvement in 'disappearances' or abductions.[2] The government denied that their officials were responsible, blaming the Tamil Tigers or criminal gangs. At the same time, they passed new emergency laws granting security forces even broader powers to arrest and detain people – making it even easier to disappear them. At that time, and still as of 2021, Sri Lanka has had the second-highest number of enforced disappearances ever registered with the United Nations Working Group on Enforced or Involuntary Disappearances, all the more horrific given the small size of the country.[3]

The Human Rights Watch report was published in March 2008, and we called it *Recurring Nightmare* for two reasons. First, disappearing people was not a new phenomenon in Sri Lanka. In the late 1980s, security forces disappeared and killed thousands of ethnic Sinhalese in the south of the country, in the military's efforts to quell an armed insurgency. The military deployed these same tactics against ethnic Tamils from 1990. Secondly, disappearances are an especially egregious form of abuse: the suffering of family members can go on undiminished for years as they search for their loved ones, not knowing if they are alive or dead.

So what could stop the disappearances? We thought a UN human rights monitoring mission in Sri Lanka would help. It could do what we and local groups had done, by investigating and reporting on the abuses, but in an official UN capacity.

The Office of the High Commissioner for Human Rights (OHCHR) was the UN agency that specialised in human rights. The old UN *Commission* on Human Rights that I visited in Geneva all those years ago had been replaced by the UN Human Rights *Council* in 2006. The Council was made up of 47 governments elected by the UN General Assembly, selected by region, that served three-year terms. It could pass resolutions on specific themes or on individual countries. In both New York and Geneva, Human Rights Watch had hired skilled UN advocates to navigate the complex bureaucratic maze of commissions, assemblies and councils.

The UN already had a presence in Sri Lanka, represented by a number of their agencies working in the country, such as the UN World Food Program (WFP) and the United Nations International Children's Emergency Fund (UNICEF) but no dedicated UN human rights monitors on the ground. We wanted the Human Rights Council or the Security Council to authorise that. Not surprisingly, the Rajapaksa administration steadfastly rejected proposals for UN human rights monitoring, saying it would undermine Sri Lanka's sovereignty. They also claimed that their own national mechanisms and institutions were sufficient to ensure justice. This fallacy is regularly repeated by abusive governments to avoid accountability for human rights violations – and our report explained in detail how Sri Lanka's domestic accountability mechanisms were hopelessly inadequate.

The presence of UN human rights staff couldn't seriously be seen as an infringement on sovereignty, either. It was not an armed force like peacekeepers, just UN employees armed with pen and paper and the guiding principles of international law. But just their presence can be a very powerful promoter of peace, deterring abuses like killings, disappearances and torture on all sides.

So we spent countless hours briefing diplomats in Geneva, New York and elsewhere on our findings. Our targets were not only the Western countries that typically raise human rights concerns – such as the EU, US, and Canada – but also powerful regional governments like India and Japan. These two were among the largest foreign investors in Sri Lanka and consequently had a lot of sway with the Rajapaksa government. Peace and security in Sri Lanka was clearly in India's national interest– the Tigers had assassinated former Indian prime minister Rajiv Gandhi in 1991, and many Tamils were fleeing the conflict by boat to the nearby Indian state of Tamil Nadu, which had an ethnic Tamil majority and its state government had traditionally shown empathy for Sri Lankan Tamils. And Japan was Sri Lanka's largest international donor and had co-chaired a failed peace process. Its diplomats doled out large sums of money in development aid, but without the human rights strings that Western governments attached. Japan rarely raised human rights concerns publicly with other governments, but if it wanted peace and security in Sri Lanka, then we felt it needed to help press the case for UN human rights monitors with the Sri Lankan government.

While Western countries quickly came on board, India and Japan needed convincing. Our staff in Tokyo and Delhi met with diplomats and politicians, placed op-eds and briefed local journalists to try and raise the profile of the conflict and its civilian toll. They were up against the Rajapaksa administration stance that felt borrowed from Israeli diplomats, portraying themselves as 'innocent victims of terrorism', when the truth is much more complicated.

And then in September 2008, the Sri Lankan government ordered all UN and international humanitarian staff to leave the north and east of the country, signalling a serious escalation in the conflict. They had already banned foreign journalists and independent human rights monitors. The government was getting ready for their final offensive, and they did not want witnesses for what was about to occur.

The final months of the civil war in 2009 under the Rajapaksa government were barbaric. Several hundred thousand Tamil civilians who supported the LTTE or were forced by the Tamil Tigers to remain alongside their fighters, were trapped in the Vanni, the LTTE stronghold in the north of the country. As the LTTE suffered defeats, they deliberately herded the civilians with their forces inside an ever-shrinking strip of land on the eastern coast.

The Sri Lankan military unilaterally declared some areas 'No Fire Zones' – but 'Free Fire Zones' would have been more accurate. The military relentlessly and indiscriminately shelled these areas on a daily basis, killing civilians waiting in lines for food, at hospitals, or taking shelter. Under the laws of war, military forces can attack the opposing army, but it's unlawful to target civilians or conduct indiscriminate attacks that result in civilian deaths. The UN later estimated at least forty thousand civilians were killed in those final months of the war, mainly due to government shelling.

Those inside the zone faced severe shortages, and if they tried to escape, the Tigers shot at them. They held civilians as human shields, forcibly conscripting many, including children, as soldiers operating weapons or pressing others into forced labour as porters and cooks. Civilians who did manage to escape across to the government side were viewed with suspicion. After the fighting ended with the LTTE's complete defeat, the military detained thousands of Tamil families indefinitely in internment camps behind barbed wire.

The Sri Lankan government was so skilled at its advocacy that it had convinced international donors to pay for these internment camps. The UN agencies felt conflicted: on the one hand, the UN wanted people escaping the war zone to be treated humanely; but on the other, by propping up military-run prison camps it risked being complicit in imprisoning civilians arbitrarily.

Despite the government restrictions, we managed to get staff into Sri Lanka to document the atrocities during the fighting. In January 2009, I took a colleague who had recently been in Sri Lanka to meet with UN officials in New York to explain the humanitarian crisis and to urge agencies to speak out against the atrocities.

At one point we were in a UN office, with CNN playing silently on a television in the background. It was evident that the official was distracted. I looked over at the screen to see images of a plane that had landed on a river in New York.

'Did you see this? It's crazy!' the official said, catching my eye and turning the volume up.

I instinctively looked out the window over New York's East River, but the plane landed on the Hudson, on the west side.

'Miracle on Hudson, they are calling it,' he said.

As we made small talk about the incredulity of a planeload of passengers landing safely on a river in one of the world's busiest cities, I thought to myself that what we really needed was a Miracle in the Vanni to save the lives of Tamil civilians.

In those final months as the war raged on, I regularly took Human Rights Watch staff and activists from Sri Lanka to meet with UN officials and foreign diplomats. Most of the activists like Sunila came to New York in secret, lobbying at great personal risk to themselves and their families – the Sri Lankan government had already murdered and disappeared several journalists and activists.

When Japan joined the UN Security Council as a rotating member at the beginning of 2009, the stakes were raised again. One day I went to meet with Japan's Ambassador to the United Nations with two Sri Lankan activists. He took us to lunch at an upscale sushi restaurant in midtown. As we pushed slices of sashimi around our plates with chopsticks, one of the activists – a Catholic priest – described the shelling of Tamils inside the zone and the threats to activists who spoke up about the military's crimes. It was surreal.

Despite our efforts, there were no miracles. We couldn't even get an informal discussion on Sri Lanka at the UN Security Council, let alone a formal item on its agenda.

The Sri Lankan military may have been engaging in horrendous war crimes, but the conflict had minimal impact on the countries around it. Sri Lanka was not considered a threat to peace and stability of the world. There was little empathy for the Tigers due to their litany of atrocities. I often think Sri Lanka was a precursor to the war in Syria years later – it showed how bad things can get when the world looks away, and how willing the world can be to do just that.

But just because you're not making headway in your advocacy doesn't mean that the cries for help stop. We were listening to those suffering on the front lines. One hundred thousand people fled the war zone in April 2009. Conditions in the government-run camps were appalling, but circumstances inside the 'No Fire Zone' were barbaric. My office phone rang off the hook. Tamils living abroad called and left voicemails in tears desperate for someone, anyone, to do something for their loved ones back in Sri Lanka.

By late-April, the 'No Fire Zone' was a tightly packed twenty-kilometre patch of land where hundreds of civilians a day were being killed by the relentless shelling. We were in daily contact with doctors in makeshift hospitals inside the zone, grimly treating the wounded and counting the dead. The Sri Lankan government had ordered the doctors not to speak to foreign journalists or organisations, but they were fed up.

'We decided that we are beyond the point where we can just complain to the authorities,' one of the doctors told Human Rights Watch. 'Because we told them a hundred times and they have failed to take any proper steps to stop the attack on civilians and did not send in the necessary amount of medications. We have been reporting every day, every day providing reports to relevant authorities and to the international community, and still there are no real steps taken to save these innocent civilians.'

The Tamil Tigers were still opening fire on anyone who tried to escape.

Our team of researchers, advocates, lawyers, security and communication specialists around the world were meeting weekly on Sri Lanka, with many joining by phone or video. In one meeting in late April 2009, in our large conference room, our research team gave a grim assessment of what was happening on the ground. We went around the table and videoconference to hear what advocates around the world were doing: Brussels, Geneva, London, Tokyo, Delhi, Johannesburg. We racked our brains to identify every senior official and politician who might have sway with the Sri Lankan government to try and stop the slaughter; every point of leverage, every loan to the Sri Lankan government, every trade deal, every international institution, every manoeuvre in the book we could think of, to rein in the Sri Lankan military.

We tried to deploy all the tools at our disposal. Research. Communications. Advocacy. Led by our team at the UN, we worked hard to build support in Geneva and New York for a resolution to establish a commission of inquiry into allegations of war crimes by all parties.

But everywhere we went, Sri Lankan diplomats were already there, telling governments that their actions in the Vanni were humanitarian and that their military was only targeting barbaric terrorists, which was doing the world a favour.

The war ended on May 18, 2009, when the Sri Lankan government declared victory. That day, the political leadership of the Tamil Tigers attempted to surrender, in an event known as 'the white flag incident'.[4] But instead of a surrender, it was a bloodbath. The Sri Lankan government claimed the LTTE leaders and their families were killed in battle. A UN report, however, concluded that the rebels were likely executed. It was a brazen war crime at the end a conflict punctuated by acts of unconscionable and inexcusable barbarity.

As the Sri Lankan government declared victory, I and other staff at Human Rights Watch who had been working around the clock to try and prevent the slaughter felt numb. I remember the feelings of guilt and despair. We were all asking ourselves what more could we have done.

Incredibly, and to add insult to injury, a few days after the war ended the Sri Lankan government even succeeded in turning around a UN Human Rights Council resolution from condemning violations of the laws of war to congratulating the government for defeating terrorism.[5]

Just because the war was over, however, didn't mean our activism ceased. It simply shifted to a new phase – one of accountability. Our goal was to expose to the world the war crimes that had occurred, and demand justice for those who committed these crimes in Sri Lanka. UN Secretary-General Ban Ki-moon travelled to Sri Lanka soon after the war ended and signed a joint communiqué with President Mahinda Rajapaksa, in which the government promised to take measures towards accountability for alleged abuses.

Evidence of atrocities began to emerge, such as 'trophy footage' leaked by soldiers – videos and photographs showing the execution at close-range of blindfolded prisoners, or soldiers leering over the bodies of semi-clothed dead Tamil women raising questions about rape. As we confirmed details of more horrific war crimes and the extent of civilian casualties, we kept pushing UN mechanisms for action and accountability. UN staff also started to speak out, shamed by the organisation's inaction.

119

In June 2010, more than a year after the conflict ended, Ban Ki-moon seemed both concerned by the continuous flow of information about war crimes and fed up with the intransigence of the Sri Lankan government, who had of course made no progress on the promise to address accountability. Ban took the unusual step of establishing a UN panel of experts to examine accountability in Sri Lanka for allegations of war crimes.

Human Rights Watch shared the evidence we had collected with the three formidably accomplished experts: Marzuki Darusman, a former Attorney General of Indonesia; Yasmin Sooka, a South African judge and a commissioner of the South African Truth and Reconciliation Commission (TRC); and Steven Ratner, an American professor of law. These three were supported by a small team of UN professional staff. In March 2011, the panel produced its devastating report:

> The [Sri Lankan] Government says it pursued a 'humanitarian rescue operation' with a policy of 'zero civilian casualties.' In stark contrast, the Panel found credible allegations, which if proven, indicate that a wide range of serious violations of international humanitarian law and international human rights law was committed both by the Government of Sri Lanka and the LTTE, some of which would amount to war crimes and crimes against humanity.[6]

Bodies like the UN Human Rights Council or the General Assembly can only act when they have the support from most of the governments that make up their membership. The UN moves slowly (sometimes incredibly slowly) to ensure that it brings the international community along. The Secretary-General's panel was only an initial investigation into whether there were credible allegations: the next step, which the panel urged the Secretary-General to take, was to establish an international mechanism to investigate the allegations more fully, as well as to collect and preserve evidence for future prosecutions. It also recommended the Sri Lankan government take accountability for war crimes and urged the Human Rights Council to reconsider their resolution congratulating the Sri Lankan government on their victory.

Although it was only a first step, at last we had a UN document that was a vindication of what we and others had known for years. Many leaders had failed to respond to our lobbying, but a UN expert panel's findings of war crimes would not be so easy to dismiss. A few months later, in June 2011, Britain's Channel Four screened a powerful documentary film by director Callum Macrae, *Sri Lanka's Killing Fields*, about the bloody end to Sri Lanka's conflict. The film used the raw, horrifying 'trophy' footage by soldiers, and was shown in parliaments around the world. I flew to Ottawa to speak at a screening at Canada's parliament in September 2011. After watching real-life executions unfold on screen, there was actually little for me or the other MPs to say. I told the Canadian MPs:

> The Sri Lankan government needs to know that after two and a half years of denying abuses and taking no genuine accountability efforts, time has run out. Canada should lead the way in pushing for an international independent investigation into alleged war crimes in Sri Lanka, and this means shoring up support from like-minded countries ahead of the next Human Rights Council session.

A few weeks after the screening, I was invited to testify before Canada's House of Commons about Sri Lanka's war crimes and what the Canadian government should do. At the next session of the UN Human Rights Council in Geneva in March 2012, Canada co-sponsored a resolution calling on Sri Lanka to fulfil its legal obligations for justice and accountability, and to address violations of international law. The Canadian government was especially invested in accountability because they were on the Council in 2009 when efforts to pressure the Sri Lanka government failed, and had voted against the subsequent resolution that passed congratulating the Sri Lankan government.

The 2012 resolution instructed the UN Human Rights Office to report back to the Council on progress. Finally, nearly three years after the war ended, we had a mandate for the UN Human Rights Office. It was obviously not the monitoring mission we had called for in 2008, but it would provide a thorough reporting on human rights violations throughout the conflict. It had taken the intervention of the UN Secretary-General, a hard-hitting report by a panel of experts, a documentary film as well as relentless lobbying by both Sri Lankan and international nongovernmental organisations. It was a win. It meant Sri Lanka's human rights record was now literally on the agenda of the Human Rights Council – there would be future reports, and further scrutiny.

But while we considered this a hard-won success, it was not going to bring back the dead and disappeared from the Vanni.

*

Eight years after the end of the war, I sat in a ramshackle shelter outside Kilinochchi in Sri Lanka's northern Vanni region, a former stronghold of the Tamil Tigers, with mothers still desperate for answers about their children. '217 days' said the sign in Tamil script with the date in the corner: 28/9/2017.

I could only read the numerals of course. It was hand-written on a white piece of card, clipped with pegs to a wire. The shelter by the side of the road looked like a street stall, but there was nothing for sale. It was a wooden platform, open on three sides, raised about half a foot off the dirt. The roof was corrugated tin with bits of cardboard lining the inside. Several woven straw mats lined the floor of the platform. There were a couple of pillows for comfort. But what drew my eye was a row of framed photographs of faces, mostly young men, neatly lined up on the floor. The frames were different shapes and sizes. More photos unframed were strung up pegged to a wire, hanging from the roof of the little shack.

Everywhere I turned, there were photos of young men. Some smiling, some solemn, some moustached, some cleanshaven. A few of the photographs were young women. In the middle of the platform, three Tamil women dressed in brightly coloured saris sat together, barefoot on the mat.

The shack was a haunting roadside vigil to those who have disappeared.

I slipped off my shoes and stepped onto the mat, nodding to the women and greeting them with that most universal of South Asian expressions, 'Namaste'. The women motioned for us to sit. I was with several Human Rights Watch colleagues, as well as a Tamil translator.

As we sat down cross-legged, the women reached into their bags for more photographs and sat with them resting on their laps.

It was the 217th day of the mothers' roadside protest. They were waiting for passing motorists to notice them. They were waiting for justice.

One of the women, Priya (a pseudonym), started talking:

'I have been coming here every day since the protest began. They got my son in May 2009. The last I saw·him he was loaded onto a bus.'

Priya's voice started to crack.

'The military said they would release him, but . . . I never saw him again.'

Her voice trailed off as she looks at the photo of her son, her long fingers tracing the outline of his face. I could see Priya was still yearning for her son intensely, even though it had been eight years since he had been gone.

When Priya's son disappeared in May 2009, the war was ending – the Tigers surrendered. I had seen gruesome videos of Sri Lankan security forces executing blindfolded Tamil prisoners by shooting them in the head at close range. Priya, too, must have known her son's likely fate. Together we looked at the photo she held of the young slim man staring at the camera, dressed casually in a white shirt, jeans, and black sandals.

My memory was jolted back a decade – to that very first report I edited in 2007 about enforced disappearances of young Tamil men in Sri Lanka. The cover image was a woman's hands holding a photograph of her son.

It was well after that report that I discovered an enforced disappearance in our own family – my Amah's first husband and the father of her three children had also suffered this fate. He was disappeared during the Japanese occupation of Singapore, in 1942. The family had recently immigrated to Singapore from China, Japan's enemy. The Japanese military ordered the whole family to go for an 'inspection', including their children and Laumah, Amah's mother. Women and children were then allowed to leave, but the men had to remain behind. Afterwards, Amah said that her five-year-old son and Laumah went looking for him at every police station, but he was never found. They presumed he was executed and the story passed down from other family members was usually 'he was killed by the Japanese'. I had always wrongly presumed that was in combat.

It's a shock when you've been researching atrocities for years, interviewing families about what they've endured, to discover those stories exist in your own family too — just something so very terrible that no one ever wanted to speak of it.

Meeting those mothers in Sri Lanka was a stark reminder that our reports documenting abuses or disappearances were not just about driving accountability for violations. The victors of war often seek to re-write history and hide the facts. But the role of independent organisations like ours was to expose the truth, centre the experiences of victims and their families and provide an accurate historical record.

As we got up to leave, one of the mothers, who had not spoken the entire time, told our translator she wanted to say something.

'Thank you for listening. I also am a mother of a son who disappeared. The only progress we have seen is due to the international community. With that small piece of hope, we are sitting out here on the street. We are expecting a solution for our tears.'

She wiped away the tears that fell down her cheeks. I didn't know what to say to that.

I replied that we would continue to fight for justice.

I had another grieving mother to meet in Kilinochchi.

Shortly before coming to Sri Lanka in 2017, I'd travelled to meet refugees on Manus Island, in Papua New Guinea. This was where Australia had sent men seeking asylum, ostensibly for 'processing', but in reality for years-long detention. One of the refugees I interviewed in Manus was a shy and kind Tamil man in his twenties,

Thanush. After I left Papua New Guinea, he started sending regular messages and updates via WhatsApp. When I told Thanush I was going to Sri Lanka and would be visiting Kilinochchi, he asked if I would like to meet his mother, which of course I did.

Thanush's parents lived on a quiet unpaved street, outside the town centre, in a simple house with a cement floor, whitewashed walls, and big windows. It was spotlessly clean, larger than I had imagined. Thanush's mother Chitrani (pseudonym) was tiny, and wore a pretty green dress, her slightly greying hair tied back in a bun. She told me she had two children, her son Thanush and a daughter.

I showed her photos of Thanush on my phone and told her about our exchanges. Her tears started flowing freely and she said, 'Through you I feel like I am talking to my son, again. It's been so long.'

Chitrani explained to me why Thanush had left Sri Lanka: when he was still in high school, the Tamil Tigers had come door to door looking for young recruits and forced him to join them. After a week, he managed to escape and to avoid recapture went to stay with his sister in Puttalam. She found him some work in an auto-repair business, but that seemed to attract government suspicion. Soldiers followed him, and even detained him for two days, but his brother-in-law got him released. Then others came asking for him. He felt he had no choice but to escape: in 2008 he flew to Malaysia, where he worked in a textile shop.

It was the story of so many young men, caught between the Tamil Tigers and the Sri Lankan army, and viewed with suspicion by both. It was like the stories of the young men in our report, who had disappeared without a trace. Thanush was lucky.

After several years in Malaysia, though, he became frustrated at being in limbo: he had no papers to stay or work in Malaysia and faced long delays for the chance of resettlement to a third country. Eventually he saved up money, got on a boat to Australia – and wound up on Manus Island.

'I worry about him constantly,' Chitrani confided. 'For five years, I haven't eaten rice. It's a promise to the gods, I won't eat rice until he is safe,' she whispered.

As any Asian person knows, giving up rice is like giving up food.

As we were leaving, and I complimented the home, she told me that it had been paid for by Thanush, with money sent back from Malaysia. But now that he was detained, his mother had had to rent the house out – the tenant wasn't home. I asked her where she was living. She motioned around the back where there was a basic one-room hut.

'We didn't willingly send our only son away. We didn't want him to leave. We wanted him to provide for us. It's very hard to live separately from him,' she said, through her tears.

Chitrani should have been one of the happy ones. Her son did not disappear. He managed to escape from the Tigers and the government. He survived. Yet he was stuck on a remote Pacific island because he had the temerity to seek asylum in Australia.

The privilege of easy international travel is afforded only to those who hold certain nationalities. My Australian passport allowed me to travel to Papua New Guinea and to Sri Lanka, to meet two halves of a family that didn't know when they would ever see one another again.

I was reminded again of my grandmother's story – a story she told me via my uncles or cousins countless times. After the deaths of her other children and husband, my great-grandmother Laumah went to Singapore to look for Amah, her last living child, who'd been taken there by the opera troupe who'd bought her.

She couldn't find her. I'd heard Amah and Laumah tearfully tell the story of their eventual reunion. At age fifteen, Amah was sold to another troupe and taken back to China where she quickly became a popular Teochew opera singer. One evening when she was seventeen, she was on stage in the city of Shantou when a woman weeping in the audience irritated her. She asked for the woman to be removed. Later, someone brought the woman backstage: only then did Amah realise it was her mother. They reunited and did not lose one another again. My great-grandmother lived with my grandparents right up until she died, even sharing the tiny bedroom in their small Singaporean public housing apartment.

For many of the women I met, the pain of separation from their children was not yet over. For some it would never be. That was the agony of the mothers of the disappeared.

In 2015, Mahinda Rajapaksa lost the election and for a brief time it looked like progress under a new government. Civil society breathed a sigh of relief, and it was during this period that I visited the country. But it didn't last long. The Rajapaksas returned to power when former Defence Secretary Gotabaya Rajapaksa was elected president in November 2019. Gotabaya appointed his brother Mahinda, the former President, as Prime Minister. Fear returned to Sri Lanka, especially for journalists, human rights defenders, and victims of past abuses and their families. In the Vanni, families of the disappeared have bravely kept up their daily roadside vigils, more than 1900 days since the protests began in January 2017. The pathway to justice through UN mechanisms is long and agonisingly slow, too slow for some of the families of the disappeared. Since the protests started in 2017, 115 parents of the disappeared have passed away without finding out the truth of what happened to their loved ones.[7]

In May 2022, following widespread protests and an economic crisis, Mahinda Rajapaksa was forced to resign.

Sadly, Sri Lanka was not alone in its achingly slow progress towards justice and accountability for atrocities. I was soon to see how killings with impunity can form a pattern serious enough to amount to crimes against humanity, and that can spark the attention of international prosecutors, as I was to witness in the Philippines.

CHAPTER 5

'YOU CAN DIE ANY TIME' IN THE PHILIPPINES

'Hitler massacred three million Jews.
Now, there are three million drug addicts.
I'd be happy to slaughter them.'[1]

So said newly elected Philippine President Rodrigo Duterte in September 2016. He was speaking in a matter-of-fact tone to a packed press conference in his hometown of Davao City, on the southern island of Mindanao. Duterte stood at a lectern in front of a Philippine flag, dressed casually in black. In the audience were journalists, police and military in uniform.

'If Germany had Hitler, the Philippines would have . . . you know . . .' He paused and pointed to himself, declaring: 'My victims, I would like [them] to be all criminals, to finish the problem of my country and save the next generation from perdition.'

The comments went viral. I imagined journalists and diplomats around the world mouthing in collective unison, *Did he really just compare himself to Hitler? And pledge to murder three million people?'*

While Duterte's words were a new low, they followed a pattern of bombastic speeches during his election campaign, where he had promised to wipe out the drug trade by exterminating those involved. He wasted no time in acting on those promises. From the moment he was elected, police started killing drug suspects. The UN estimates that since 2016, tens of thousands of people have been killed in the so-called 'war on drugs'.[2]

One month after 'the Hitler comments', the President doubled down on his approach, defending the rising body count when challenged by journalists in a TV interview. Duterte told them: 'I don't care what the human rights guys say . . . If it involves human rights, I don't give a shit. I have to strike fear.'[3]

As President, Duterte was taking nationwide tactics he had honed as the mayor of Davao City in the late 1990s and 2000s. They were tactics I knew well, because in 2009, I was there with Human Rights Watch to document it.

Davao City is the Philippines' third-largest city, located on Mindanao, a large island at the southern end of the Philippines archipelago with some areas racked by lawlessness. Mindanao has long been home to armed groups opposing the government in Manila, from the Communist New People's Army (NPA) to various Islamist militants including the Moro Islamic Liberation Front (MILF) and more extreme groups like Abu Sayyaf and Jemaah Islamiyah.

The Philippines military and police had struggled to contain the violence in Mindanao. Government forces, paramilitaries and militants committed abuses against civilians including killings, forced displacement, arbitrary detention, and torture. In 1985, the *Washington Post* ran a story headlined, 'Davao Known as Philippines' "Murder Capital"' which documented numerous killings of insurgents, government security forces and civilians in Davao City by unidentified gunmen.[4] Back then, the NPA controlled parts of Davao City. In the 1980s, the government supported vigilante groups such as the Alsa Masa (Masses Arise) to fight the NPA and other militants in Davao and other places. But the solution became the new problem – the vigilante groups themselves grew powerful and started committing killings and other serious abuses for payment.[5] The random acts of killing and lack of accountability made the city very unsafe indeed.

Duterte, a former lawyer and prosecutor, was elected mayor of Davao City from 1988 to 1998, and again from 2001 to 2010. Many residents credited him with bringing peace and order to the city. He cut deals with militants which made the city safer from insurgent attacks. In his second term, he talked tough about combating illegal activities and making the city a 'dangerous place' for criminals and street gangs. Rumours began that he was co-opting armed militias to murder alleged gang members, drug suspects and criminals.

I first saw Rodrigo Duterte in Davao City in 2009. I had no idea back then that the tough-talking mayor would one day become the country's president. In fact, I had a ringside seat to an epic showdown between two strong-willed and outspoken personalities who would both make their mark on the Philippines.

Duterte's challenger was a small, fearless and tenacious lawyer from Manila, Leila de Lima. She was the chairperson of the Philippine Commission on Human Rights. In 2009, she was the first Filipino official to seriously confront the mayor about targeted killings in Davao City. Sadly, de Lima would pay a heavy price for her courage in challenging Duterte.

From 2007, as Deputy Asia Director at Human Rights Watch, I was supervising our Philippines work. Our researcher covering the Philippines was a former journalist, Kay Seok, based in Seoul. The Philippines was easy to travel around, and many people were happy to talk to foreigners – including lawyers, police and officials as well as those experiencing human rights violations. But there was also a disturbing nonchalance about the value of human life, which went hand in hand with widespread gun ownership and the high rate of killings. Back then, when investigating abuses in the Philippines, there was always a small risk of being shot dead because someone didn't like what we were doing or the questions we were asking.

Over the following years, I became very familiar with the nature of extrajudicial killings. I saw what happens when a violation by state actors is left unchecked and abusers not only get away with their crimes but become even more powerful and replicate those abuses nationwide. I learned about the importance of working in partnership with local groups and engaging with domestic mechanisms. In Manila, I saw our Executive Director Ken Roth in action for the first time and I learned from him lessons in effective advocacy. And while we did our best to minimise security risks for staff and those who interacted with us, I also witnessed the severe consequences for courageous high-profile journalists and politicians who spoke up against the 'drug war' killings. And when domestic mechanisms fail, I saw how justice through the International Criminal Court (ICC) can play a role in holding those who commit crimes against humanity to account, though it can take a very long time.

*

Extrajudicial executions are effectively killings carried out outside of any judicial process. Summary executions are carried out by militants or governments (usually police, military, or paramilitary forces), or can be state-sponsored (where someone is paid to kill on behalf of the state or an associated militant group). With an extrajudicial killing, it's totally illegal – it's simply state-sanctioned murder – whether a bullet in the head or a butcher's knife in the back.

Like enforced disappearances, extrajudicial killings become more common in armed conflict. Soldiers sometimes try to justify it by claiming those killed are combatants, that the killings are in self-defence, or in 'the heat of battle'. But if the police or the military shoot someone who is in their control or custody, and poses no imminent threat to life, then it may be an extra-judicial killing.

Human Rights Watch released a report in 2007, entitled *Scared Silent: Impunity for Extrajudicial Killings in the Philippines* which focused on executions of left-leaning political activists by the military.[6] For years, Filipino soldiers had fought skirmishes with the New People's Army. When the government killed those associated with the NPA, who were labelled as 'leftist sympathisers', it was a way of sending a message to communities – 'Don't support the Communist rebels, or you'll wind up dead too.'

In 2008, when I travelled to Manila to follow up on our *Scared Silent* report, Filipino civil society activists and journalists asked us, sometimes in a whisper, 'What about the killings of petty criminals in Mindanao?' They told us that the mayor of Davao City was openly bragging about the executions, saying that it made the city safe for residents.

Mayor Duterte already had nicknames such as 'The Punisher' or 'Dirty Harry of Mindanao'. He liked to pose with guns. He said publicly that drugs users and criminals were 'a legitimate target of assassination'.[7]

Meanwhile, in the slums of Davao City, people were being murdered – stabbed or shot to death – and no one was being held accountable. Local police claimed it was gang members or drug dealers knocking each other off.

But evidence started to emerge about the existence of a death squad – dubbed the Davao Death Squad. It was believed to be a group of hitmen, including former police officers, who were being paid by the police to kill targets. Davao City police failed to investigate the unresolved killings which increased to hundreds per year. Many of Davao's middle- and upper-class residents merely shrugged their shoulders at the killings. They were happy to repeat Duterte's claims that he had cleaned up their city, making it safer to walk the streets at night.

But Davao City was not safer if you were poor and living in the slums.

Allegations about a death squad in Davao City had been reported in the media, but came to international attention in April 2008 when the executions were mentioned by the UN expert on extrajudicial killings in his report on the Philippines.[8] No international human rights organisation had produced a detailed report investigating the matter, so in late 2008 we decided to examine the pattern of killings in Davao City and several other cities in Mindanao where bodies were also piling up. Things seemed to be spiralling out of control. We sent Kay Seok and Anna Neistat, our highly experienced Emergencies researcher who worked on the Sri Lanka disappearances report.

A couple of local groups had thoroughly documented the killings for years and provided support to families of the victims. These included the Tambayan Center for Children's Rights and the Coalition Against Summary Execution (CASE) – a ragtag group of local activists – including lawyers, Catholic priests, journalists and family members of those killed. These organisations came under intense scrutiny and pressure from the police. They were keen to share their work with us, an international organisation that could bring a greater profile to the issue, and also take the heat. They helped us to find families and witnesses to interview.

We hired a local lawyer Teddy (pseudonym) as our fixer – helping arrange interviews and translation. As a resident of Davao City, he also provided invaluable advice on the local context, security, and advocacy strategy, and he reviewed the draft of our report. Because of the security risks involved, he conducted his work for Human Rights Watch in secret.

Another helpful source was Carlos Conde, a journalist from Mindanao working for the *New York Times* who had previously reported on the killings in Davao City. Carlos was one of the first journalists to write about the Davao Death Squad. He spent a lot of time with families of the victims, building up their trust and encouraging them to speak up. Later, in 2012 Carlos would join Human Rights Watch as our dedicated Philippines researcher.

Kay and Anna investigated twenty-eight killings across three cities and interviewed nine people with 'insider' knowledge of the so-called Davao Death Squad. This helped us understand the modus operandi of the killings. But it was the testimonies from the family members of the victims that made for the most harrowing reading. For me, one case stood out for its utter heartbreak.

The Alia family, Clarita and her eight children, lived in a cramped shack next to a dump in a slum area of Davao City. Clarita was a single mum, separated from her husband. To make ends meet, she pushed a vegetable cart around the nearby Bankerohan Public Market. The market was crowded with vendors selling all manner of fresh and cooked foods, meat, and dried fish. It was also an infamous meeting place for thieves and criminals.

Clarita was the mother of four sons who were killed, one-by-one, over several years from 2001 to 2007. Each was stabbed to death. Clarita believed it was the work of the Davao Death Squad.

Clarita's second-oldest son, Richard, was a gang member and had already been arrested several times for petty crimes. He'd survived a murder attempt – the gunman was unknown. In July 2001, police tried to arrest him at Clarita's home, but Clarita pushed the policeman back out the door.

'Okay, if you don't want to give your child to me, then watch out because your sons will be killed, one-by-one,' the policeman threatened her. And that is what happened.

A few weeks later, Richard was stabbed to death. Clarita didn't know who killed her son, but she was shocked and terrified for her other children. She was too afraid to go to the police to report it. Three months later, Christopher was killed in the Bankerohan Market. When Clarita reached him, Arnold, her eldest son, was cradling Christopher's limp body in his arms. Clarita learned that Christopher was not the target, Arnold was – people at the market told her that two men had been following Arnold around that morning, but they lost him. Those men stabbed Christopher instead. Police came to the market and asked Clarita what happened. She recalled, 'I was hysterical, and kept telling them, "Why are you asking me? You are the policemen – ask the witnesses around here."'

After that, she filed a case with the local office of the Commission on Human Rights about the unresolved killings of her two sons. She was still too scared to go to the police directly. She did not know whether the Commission took any action on the cases, they never got back to her. Arnold left Davao soon after for his own safety, relocating to another city. Clarita said neighbours and *barangay*[9] (local) officials warned her too, 'Watch out for your sons or move away from here!' But Clarita was poor, she had nowhere else to go.

Two years later, in November 2003, in the same market, Bobby was stabbed in the back with a butcher's knife. This time, witnesses said they could identify the killer – he was a known hitman, allegedly with close ties to the police. Police had arrested Bobby a few days earlier, for supposedly stealing a mobile phone. Clarita managed to secure his release. Now, two days later, he was dead.

Clarita tried her best to protect Fernando, her youngest son. She sent him away from Davao to a boarding school. Even there, strangers would approach him saying things like 'You're next.'

The death of his brothers weighed heavily on Fernando, who would sometimes get into trouble with the police and, like other teenagers in the slums, he sometimes sniffed a chemical solvent used as an adhesive, called Rugby. Fernando came back to Davao for a while in 2006. He was attacked near the market by another teenager, who plunged an ice pick into his back. Fernando went to hospital to have it removed, but it stayed in his back overnight because the doctors said they were too overwhelmed with patients. Clarita struggled to pay Fernando's medical bills. 'I think I was sold', Fernando said quietly afterwards to a journalist covering the attack – using the Visayan term referring to the practice of hitmen targeting victims for money.[10]

For a while, it seemed Fernando was lucky. But then on April 13, 2007, unknown assailants stabbed him to death on a bridge near the market.

So this is the story of Clarita's boys:

Richard, eighteen years old.
> Killed on 21 July 2001.

Christopher, seventeen years old.
> Killed on 20 October 2001.

Bobby, fourteen years old.
> Killed on 3 November 2003.

And Fernando, fifteen years old.
> Killed on 13 April 2007.

Clarita is now sixty-eight years old. She remains living in the same slum near the market. She is still poor. She has her daughter, Vanessa and her son Arnold who lives far away, I'm not sure what happened to her other two children. But she still aches every day for her murdered sons and the fact that their killers have never faced justice.

I met Clarita in 2009 in Davao City when we both testified before a hearing on the Davao Death Squad. Kay and Anna investigated the killings and wrote up Human Rights Watch's report, but my role was to oversee the project, interrogate the evidence they had collected, and lead the advocacy strategy on our findings. We soon discovered we weren't the only ones concerned about the rising death toll in Davao.

Leila de Lima, who chaired the Philippines Commission on Human Rights, visited Davao City in late January 2009. According to CASE, that month saw an even higher number of murders than usual – thirty-three targeted killings in Davao City. Eight men shot or stabbed to death on 20 January alone. De Lima heard about the killings and civil society groups in Davao whispered to her about the existence of a death squad, and the alleged involvement of police and local government officials.

She was disturbed enough about the allegations to announce a public hearing by the Commission on Human Rights. The hearing would be an opportunity to question officials, victims and experts about the spate of hundreds of unresolved killings over the last decade. It was slated for late March.

In the course of our research, we wrote to the Commission (and several other government agencies), seeking answers to questions, and Kay met with de Lima to discuss our preliminary findings. De Lima asked Human Rights Watch if we would testify about our report even though it was not yet public. Neither Kay nor Anna was available, so I went instead.

I'd travelled to the Philippines probably a dozen times by then, for work and for fun, but I had never been to Mindanao before. I only knew the island by reputation. And it's not often that you get invited to testify about killings in the exact place where you are alleging a 'guns for hire' death squad has been organised by the police, with the approval of the mayor. So yes, I was a little nervous.

In my luggage, I had twenty printed copies of Human Rights Watch's embargoed report entitled, *You Can Die Any Time': Death Squad Killings in Mindanao*.[11] The words were a direct quote from one of Duterte's rousing speeches:

'I said henceforth Davao will be very, very dangerous for criminals. I've been telling criminals it is a place where you can die any time. If that's a cue for anybody, that's fine.'[12]

It was a chilling warning that rang in my ears when I touched down at the airport.

Obviously, I wasn't one of the 'criminals' in their sights, but the Philippines was well known for trigger-happy gunmen putting bullets in the heads of local activists who dared to criticise the government or security forces. As a foreigner and someone working for a well-known international human rights group, the risks for me were much lower, but I'd still weighed up the security implications of the trip with my colleagues. Local activists welcomed the hearing but were anxious about participating in such a public event due to the risks of reprisals. They were happy for Human Rights Watch to come and say things on the public record that they could not. This can be a practical way of working with local organisations on sensitive topics that implicate security forces – they help us to collect and corroborate the facts, but we make the noise and take responsibility.

With my colleagues at Human Rights Watch, we agreed some basic security protocols. These included checking in with New York at certain times each day, providing my colleagues with a list of contact numbers of diplomats and senior Filipino officials 'just in case' anything went wrong. And then the week after the hearings, Ken Roth, would come to Manila to launch the report. Before joining Human Rights Watch, Ken had been a stand-out federal prosecutor in the US. The plan was that his involvement would draw global attention to what was happening in Davao City, but we couldn't move the launch date forward because of his busy travel schedule. I'd preview some of the findings in the hearing but not speak to journalists on the record – we would save the media interviews until the release.

I arrived in Davao the weekend ahead of the hearings starting on Monday. On a whim, I decided to go out scuba diving on the Sunday – a hobby I enjoyed but rarely got to do now that

I was living in New York. Somehow, there was a mix-up at the port, and I wound up on the wrong boat – only discovering my mistake after the second dive of the day and an enthusiastic discussion with my fellow divers about how Mayor Duterte had singlehandedly cleaned up the city to make it safe to walk the streets at night.

After realising my mistake, I remembered someone had mentioned casually that they worked for the local government.

Paranoid thoughts suddenly ran through my head. Was I diving with cops?

I fell silent, chastising myself: *What sort of idiot goes scuba diving alone in Mindanao the day before a hearing on death squads?* I began imagining that my next dive would feature more than a faulty regulator, *'Oh, she drowned,'* they'd say. It took me a few minutes to put a brake on my overactive imagination.

Lucky for me, the paranoia was misplaced. The third dive was uneventful. Still, I kept the conversation light and avoided any more questions about murders or Duterte.

That night for dinner I met with Teddy, and other local activists, including a priest, a lawyer and a children's rights activist. All of them were too scared to attend the hearing the next day. Indeed, the local activists and some witnesses wanted to brief the Commission on Human Rights in private, and they asked me to repeat the request quietly to de Lima. Clarita, the mother of four sons who were killed in Davao, would still testify. She seemed to have nerves of steel, and nothing more to lose.

Teddy was concerned about me returning to Davao City for the report release the following week. He told me, 'Your profile is going to go up after you testify on Tuesday. It'll be all over the news. Duterte is unpredictable. Stay in Manila – it's better for you to be there.'

On Monday morning the public hearing commenced at a nondescript hotel conference room. People milled about drinking coffee and eating snacks. There were plenty of uniformed police and a press pack in tow. It reminded me of anti-trafficking conferences with that weird mix of police and activists.

I wasn't testifying until the Tuesday, but I wanted to hear Mayor Duterte speak. I couldn't see any other foreigners attending and I tried to blend in, hoping that people would think I was a *mestiza* (half-Filipino half-Caucasian) from Manila.

I introduced myself to de Lima and she impressed me immediately with her sincerity, and genuine concern for local activists and witnesses. She had a lawyer's manner of asking questions directly and succinctly.

Duterte was smaller than I expected. Because of all his incendiary speeches, somehow I expected him to be larger. He was casually dressed in a white polo shirt and as the long-reigning city mayor immediately commanded the room. He had a haughty arrogance. I didn't like him one bit.

As part of his opening remarks, he said theatrically, 'If there is one iota of evidence of the existence that I, the military or the police are behind the killings, then I will submit my resignation as mayor . . .'

He paused for effect to the crowded, silent room and then looking straight at de Lima repeated, 'Before you leave for Manila, you will have my resignation as mayor of Davao City.'

It was clear he was marking de Lima as an outsider in 'his city'.

Duterte went on to respond to de Lima's questions with a condescending smugness, like a cocky teenager showing off in front of his friends. He acknowledged there were unresolved killings in Davao, 'Yes, but summary? I don't know,' he said smiling. He emphatically denied the existence of any death squad or that the killings were backed by the state: 'If any government employee is involved in the killings, they are doing it on their own, there's no policy of the military or police to kill.'

De Lima asked Duterte, 'Isn't it your job to solve the killings, to stop people from being killed?'

Duterte responded, 'Yes, it is. I take full responsibility.'

In the next breath, he continued smugly, 'But if you have a DDS [Davao Death Squad] suspect then why don't you take him to the police station and question him and if you still do not get an answer, torture him.'

He was clearly deriving pleasure from trying to rile de Lima. But she kept her nerve and continued grilling him on his pattern of disturbing statements that advocated for murder. She asked Duterte if he had made a promise when he assumed the mayoralty 'to make the city the most dangerous place for criminals'.

'Yes, I said that . . . I am a hardliner against crime. I have to maintain order in the city,' Duterte responded matter-of-factly.

He then started rambling. 'Our legal system is failing. If you commit a crime as a minor, you are out the next day. What is the city to do to prevent drug use . . .? I arrest him and if he resists violently and if I think my life is in danger, then yes, I have to shoot him, what is wrong with that?'

It seemed like he was trying to show he knew the line between lawful use of force and not. It sent a message to the cops in the room that so long as the incident was framed as killing someone resisting arrest or someone who drew a weapon, then they wouldn't have anything to worry about.

I thought de Lima was extraordinarily brave. For Duterte, the hearing was a show, he was using it to play to a base of adoring supporters. He finished by reiterating his offer to resign.

'I am available until midnight tonight. If anyone wants to confront me, if police want to come and arrest me.'

While Duterte was playing it cool, I could see that his jaw was clenched, and underneath all the bravado, he was seething. He didn't like being challenged, especially not by a smart female lawyer from Manila on his home turf.

I didn't approach Duterte after his testimony. He was surrounded by an entourage, but I couldn't see anything good would come from introducing myself and alerting him to our appearance. It was better to remain low profile: they would learn soon enough the next day.

But the more I saw Leila de Lima in action the more I liked her. She was impressive in how she handled the mayor, outspoken, and had no qualms about making fun of him. This hearing was the first time Duterte and de Lima had sparred publicly. But it wouldn't be the last. Years later, as a senator, de Lima would remain one of Duterte's most outspoken critics – both while he was running for the presidency and after he became president. She didn't forget about the killings in Davao. And she made sure people in the Philippines would not forget either. She was one of only a handful of politicians who seemed concerned that a man who advocated mass murder was now running the country. She was brave enough to take him on.

The Davao City police chief and prosecutor both gave evidence later in the day. Clarita Alia spoke about the agony of losing her sons and being too terrified to report it to the police. As I listened to the witnesses, I sent updates by text to the local activists. They were tuning in to the hearings via radio and the Commission had agreed to hold a private briefing for them.

The next morning, it was my turn. I took my seat at the front of the room where Duterte had sat barely twenty-four hours before. I began my testimony by reading out some of Duterte's own words, from just a few months earlier:

'If you are doing an illegal activity in my city, if you are a criminal or part of a syndicate that preys on the innocent people of the city, for as long as I am the mayor, you are a legitimate target of assassination.'[13]

While our report did not implicate Duterte directly, his repeated statements condoning the killings made the killers feel protected. And it gave comfort to police who were not apprehending the perpetrators.

I explained how our investigations into twenty-eight targeted killings showed a pattern. The victims were street kids, drug users, petty criminals. In most cases, victims had been warned that their name was 'on a list' of people to be killed if they didn't stop their illicit activities. The warnings were delivered by police officers or local officials.

The assailants arrived in twos or threes, often on a motorbike without a licence plate. They wore baseball caps and buttoned shirts or jackets, apparently to conceal their weapons underneath. They shot or stabbed their victims, often in daylight and in public places, in the presence of multiple witnesses. And then, just as quickly as they appeared, the killers rode off, almost always before the police appeared. Witnesses were afraid to come forward, fearing that doing so would result in them becoming a target.

The death squad killers were organised by handlers called an *amo* (boss), who were usually police officers or ex-police officers. The *amo* would provide information on the target and pay between 5,000 to 50,000 pesos (about US$104 to US$1,041) – the price for the 'operation' depending on the target, and the amount split between those involved.[14]

I expressed our concern that if the killings were left unchecked, then the perpetrators would start to feel empowered to broaden their targets, killing anyone for money.

We urged the Commission to go beyond these public hearings and launch its own investigation into the death squad.

Once my testimony was over, it was time for me to leave Davao City. I travelled to Manila to meet Kay and make arrangements for advocacy meetings when Ken would join us the following week to launch our report.

We met up with de Lima in Manila. She was deeply troubled by the killings and wanted to get as many facts on the record as possible. We also briefed diplomats, the Philippine National Police chief, and the Ombudsman on our report findings and urged them to take action. We sought a meeting with then-President Gloria Macapagal Arroyo, but given we were working with Ken's limited time, we accepted a meeting with her Executive Secretary and spokesman Eduardo Ermita instead. Ermita was an experienced political operator – a former congressman with an extensive military background, who previously served as the Secretary of Defence and Vice Chief of the Defence Force.

Predictably, Ermita began by trying to deflect attention away from the killings in Davao by calling out the US's record on human rights concerns.

'How many murders are there in New York every day?' he bristled. This was a common tactic which I have heard deployed time and again in opposition to Human Rights Watch. Attack the country where the organisation is located and call them out as an interfering foreigner rather than engaging with the substance of the allegations.

As a former US prosecutor, Ken wasn't having a bar of it. He patiently explained how US criminal justice works, and acknowledged it was imperfect. He mentioned that Human Rights Watch published reports in the US devoted to problems in the criminal justice system there, but we weren't here to talk about that, we were here to discuss the Philippines.

Ken ran through the findings of the report. He explained how impunity in Davao City was leading to copycat killings elsewhere. The fact that President Arroyo had handpicked Duterte as a consultant to advise her on peace and order, effectively gave Duterte cover for his abuses.

Ermita tried to insist that the murders were random killings by feuding gangs rather than an organised hit squad. He tried to explain away the lack of accountability by focusing on the challenges that law enforcement face in the Philippines, including inadequate staff and funding for police investigations.

Ken was succinct, diplomatic but firm – a tone I have tried to emulate myself in my advocacy meetings. He said if Human Rights Watch can spend a few months and identify twenty-eight cases, and find death squad insiders to talk to, then surely the Philippine government could conduct its own investigations – if it had the political will to hold the perpetrators to account. That of course was a big 'if' – especially under President Arroyo, who was close to Duterte, and who herself had been president during a spate of political killings of leftist activists.[15] He concluded the meeting by urging Ermita to ask the president to establish an independent investigation.

To mark the launch of the report, we held a press conference at a hotel and flew up Clarita Alia to speak – colleagues in New York and Teddy felt it was too risky for me to return to Davao, as originally planned. They were probably right.

Clarita talked about her sons and the gaping hole left in families' lives when there was no justice and nowhere to turn for accountability. She cried – it had been a big week of talking about her experiences and I was worried about the toll on her mental health. But she was strong, and she wanted to do this for the memory of her sons.

The report got a lot of media attention from local and international press. Duterte tried to shrug off our findings, claiming they were 'unsubstantiated allegations'. Local police meanwhile challenged Human Rights Watch to name the names of the police involved in the killings.

We'd been worried that the Commission's hearings might overshadow our report, but in actuality it helped to amplify the message all the more strongly. And the fact Ken had travelled to Manila was a big deal. Our local sources told us that the hearing and report combined to enrage Duterte about all the negative attention he and Davao City were getting. It was unclear what he and the police would do next.

I knew our report gave some comfort to the victims' families we had interviewed, mothers like Clarita. It validated their anguish, and together with the Commission's public hearing, it gave more visibility to their stories. Sometimes I think that's one of the best things that an international group like Human Rights Watch can do – blow open the space to talk about sensitive and controversial issues. We take the heat, and this can create more space for local activists to speak about issues in the open.

That's what happened with our report on the killings in Davao. Previously, local activists had been too scared to talk in public about the killings; three months later, a prominent lawyer in Davao City asked us to send 250 copies of the report to disseminate at a public forum on the killings. The report gave local activists like CASE a useful and credible factual document for their own advocacy efforts.

For a while, it felt like we made some progress. The Commission's hearing morphed into a longer investigation. They even dug up a grave site on the land of a former police officer.

Various Philippine government institutions announced new investigations into the allegations of killings, including the national police and the ombudsman.[16] The President's office offered to put those who came forward in a witness protection program and directed local government and the police to 'get to the bottom of the alleged extrajudicial killings by determining the actual existence of such death squads, and by bringing perpetrators to account for their actions before the bar of the law.' But their statement also had the feeling of a whitewash, rather than a serious investigation.

Talking to de Lima in the years afterwards, the lack of sufficient protection for witnesses was one of the major obstacles she encountered. Witness protection meant giving up your life to be relocated to a 'safe house', which in reality was more like being placed in detention with twenty-four-hour surveillance and no real guarantees of safety.

There was also a backlash among local authorities in Davao against perceived outsiders from Manila and abroad 'meddling in local affairs'. The Davao City officials effectively closed ranks around Duterte. Later, de Lima said that the entire city seemed to be under Duterte's spell, hampering their investigations.

Then barely six months after our report release, another terrible and unexpected atrocity unfolded elsewhere in Mindanao.

On 23 November 2009, gunmen shot dead fifty-eight people by a roadside near the town of Ampatuan in the province of Maguindanao, about 200 kilometres from Davao City. The dead included the wife of electoral candidate Esmael Mangudadatu, his other relatives, about thirty journalists and media workers, as well as lawyers, drivers, and motorists. A rival candidate from a powerful family in the region, the ruling Ampatuan clan, was believed to be responsible for the killing. This massacre was the worst mass slaughter of journalists anywhere in the world. Attention to the death squads in Davao faded as global media turned their attention to the Maguindanao massacre. At Human Rights Watch, we also started investigating the mass killing, and other abuses committed by the Ampatuans' 'private army'.

After presidential elections in May 2010, Benigno (Noynoy) Aquino III succeeded Gloria Arroyo for a six-year term. Aquino clearly saw great potential in Leila de Lima – he tapped her to become his Justice Secretary. Over the next six years in that role, she turned her attention to addressing corruption in the country. But the new Chair of the Commission on Human Rights did not follow through on the investigations into the death squads. This reflected a weakness of the Commission as an institution, but also captured the mood in the Philippines towards the killings, which was one of apathy. As our Philippines researcher Carlos Conde explained it to me:

> With these killings, the victims were poor people, labelled as criminals, so there was no political constituency to care about them. Before de Lima came along, no one in the Philippines did much about this. It took external actors like Human Rights Watch, and Philip Alston [the UN Special Rapporteur on Extrajudicial, Summary or Arbitrary Killings] to make us care, and while local NGOs and media raised it, there was never any political will to address this issue.

Media interest in the Davao Death Squad killings dwindled. But when a serious abuse is left unchecked, it can grow into something far worse.

In late 2015, Duterte announced that he would be running for president. He ran his campaign on law and order, using exactly the same tactics he had used in Davao City – specifically encouraging the killing of drug users and criminal suspects as a deterrent and to strike fear. He proclaimed a 'war on drugs' manufacturing claims that the Philippines is in the midst of a 'drug emergency' and using questionable data about the number of drug users in the country. He said he would end the scourge of drugs by killing drug lords and drug users.

In May 2016, he won the election by a landslide. I couldn't believe it.

US President Donald Trump and Duterte were elected the same year. Duterte was often described by journalists as a mini-Trump. Both were populists and openly flaunted their disregard for international law.

Duterte's 'war on drugs' campaign enjoyed tremendous support from Filipinos. Many liked that Duterte projected strength, that he wasn't from the establishment, the Manila elite, or dynastic political families, some of whom had been accused of corruption. They felt that he was a straight shooter and spoke to them.

Leila de Lima also ran for office in 2016, and was elected to the Senate, where she would become an outspoken critic of the new government.

By the time of the Duterte presidency, I was no longer supervising our Philippines work. But as the murderous tactics from Davao City began to take hold across the rest of the country, our Philippines and Emergencies teams leapt into action, scaling up our work in documenting extrajudicial killings across the country.

The result was our 2017 report *License to Kill: Philippine Police Killings in Duterte's 'War on Drugs'*.[17] In that report, we documented how the killing of thousands of drug suspects in a pattern systemic and widespread could amount to a crime against humanity, effectively enabled and effectively encouraged by the long history of Duterte's public comments.

Again, Senator de Lima was one of the few prominent voices inside the country that spoke out against Duterte's 'war on drugs', and in July 2016, in her capacity as Chair of the Senate Committee on Justice and Human Rights, she announced an investigation into the killings.

Incredibly, a former police officer and self-confessed death squad member from Davao City, Edgar Matobato, came forward to testify with explosive allegations, including alleging Duterte's direct role in ordering the killings.

In one of the more sensational allegations, he claimed that in 2009, Duterte ordered him to ambush de Lima when the Commission was investigating death squad killings in Davao City.[18] The plot failed, he said, because she hadn't gone to the spot where the ambush was meant to take place.

Philippine media were captivated by the revelations. Duterte began a brutal campaign to tarnish de Lima's reputation, starting with accusations about her sex life, followed by ludicrous allegations of drug trafficking during her time as Justice Minister. Convicted felons were hauled out of prison to testify against her. Her reputation was shredded.

The vile campaign had severe consequences. De Lima has been in police detention since February 2017. Police initially spoke of charging her with sedition, but instead they settled on three drug offences. In February 2021, a court acquitted her of one of the three drug charges due to lack of evidence. Because the other cases are pending, she remains in pre-trial detention.

Putting de Lima behind bars was a way to send a message to anyone in the Philippines with the courage to challenge Duterte. If he can do this to a former minister and a sitting senator, then imagine what he can do to you.

Five years of imprisonment at Camp Crame, the Philippines Police National Headquarters, has not cowed de Lima into submission. She's not allowed a phone, computer or foreign visitors. She has been held incommunicado for long periods. However, through her Senate staff she has continued to issue handwritten statements (she has issued more than a thousand 'Dispatches from Crame'). She sponsored legislation, and makes her views known on various issues. She remains one of Duterte's fiercest critics and one of my human rights heroes.

From her cell, de Lima ran again for the Senate in 2022. She lost. But it was not just about trying to win the seat, but as her way of reasserting her identity, and not letting the Duterte administration define her. Through her unrelenting actions, de Lima is inspiring a new generation of younger Filipinos and activists around the world. Despite her incarceration on politically motivated charges, and despite the personal attacks, she won't be silenced.

Unfortunately, de Lima is not the only victim.

Another woman with the audacity to challenge the Duterte administration is Maria Ressa, journalist and founder of news website Rappler.com. Despite a crackdown against independent media, Rappler reported fearlessly on the Duterte administration's 'drug war' killings, and in retaliation both Ressa and her company have faced a string of politically motivated charges, from libel to tax evasion. In 2021, Ressa won the Nobel Peace Prize for her courageous journalism.

But like the end of the conflict in Sri Lanka, the international response to thousands of killings in the Philippines has been muted. It is viewed as a 'domestic matter' that is not affecting global peace and security and thus Duterte has not been sanctioned. Neighbouring Association of Southeast Asian Nations (ASEAN) member states have not spoken up, justifying their passivity in the face of atrocities with the excuse of 'non-interference in the affairs of another member'.

Under Duterte, the Philippines moved away from the West and closer towards China, worrying some democratic governments like Australia which were less willing to criticise Duterte's policies. Also, because he was such a loose cannon, they feared their words might not have much impact.

I was astounded when Australia's Foreign Minister Julie Bishop travelled to Davao City to meet Duterte in 2017 – it felt like she was going to kiss the ring of a mafia boss. The public statements were anodyne and made no mention of the killings. Instead, Bishop posted a smiling photo of the meeting. That led Duterte to say publicly, 'We never discussed human rights. They are so courteous.'

Bishop was then forced to contradict Duterte and claimed extrajudicial killings were raised during the meeting. For me, this diplomatic fracas underlined why public statements matter: Filipinos should have no doubt what the position of the Australian government is.

Conversely, the actions of Iceland over the killings showed how even smaller countries can make a significant difference if they have the courage and determination. For years, Human Rights Watch worked with other civil society organisations to get the UN Human Rights Council involved, efforts which paid off when Iceland led three joint statements and then a UN resolution on the Philippines at the Human Rights Council. The 2019 resolution mandated a report by the UN Human Rights Office into the killings. As a result, a damning UN report released in 2020 found 'credible allegations of widespread and systematic extrajudicial killings in the context of the campaign against illegal drugs, there has been near-impunity for such violations.'[19]

But that was as far as it went. The UN report scared the Philippines government enough that it softened its defiant tone, introduced some cosmetic measures, including announcing fresh domestic inquiries and investigations into several of the killings by police. These were largely designed to get the international community to butt out.

It was a charade, and we didn't think the international community should buy it.

Once again, an abusive government was let off the hook because their diplomats said the right things in Geneva and made shallow promises to investigate the abuses.

*

When governments fail to investigate very serious crimes – such as crimes against humanity, war crimes, genocide or the crime of aggression, there is a court of last resort that can investigate and bring a prosecution, the International Criminal Court (ICC).

The ICC was established in 2002 through its founding treaty, known as the Rome Statute, which has been signed by more than 123 countries including the Philippines. Sri Lanka never signed on, meaning for the court to have jurisdiction over war crimes in Sri Lanka, it would require a referral from the UN Security

Council (unlikely due to the veto powers of China and Russia), but the Philippines had ratified the Rome Statute in 2011 under President Arroyo.

In October 2016, ICC prosecutor Fatou Bensouda warned the Philippines government that these cases of extrajudicial killings could fall under the court's jurisdiction. She stated that 'anyone who incites or engages in acts of mass violence by ordering, requesting, or encouraging or contributing in another matter to the commission of crimes within the jurisdiction of the ICC is potentially liable to prosecution before the Court.'[20]

President Duterte responded angrily, threatening to withdraw the Philippines from the Rome Statute. Undeterred, in February 2018, the ICC announced a preliminary investigation into extrajudicial killings in the 'war on drugs'.

The very next month, Duterte formally announced the Philippines government would withdraw from the Court saying, 'It is apparent that the ICC is being utilised as a political tool against the Philippines.'

But the former prosecutor from Davao City did not understand the Rome statute. The process of withdrawing from the ICC takes a full year to come into effect, and because the Court's prosecutor had already launched its preliminary investigation, it was too late to stop the process. Three years later, in June 2021, there was a decision from the ICC's preliminary investigation. Bensouda stated: 'I have determined that there is a reasonable basis to believe that the crime against humanity of murder has been committed on the territory of the Philippines between 1 July 2016 and 16 March 2019.'[21]

This was big – the prosecutor was acknowledging the killings could amount to crimes against humanity, just as we had stated in our report in 2017. These two dates marked the start of the

Duterte presidency and when the Philippines' withdrawal from the ICC came into effect, but Bensouda announced her investigation would go back even further to 2011 when the Philippines joined the ICC and when Duterte was mayor of Davao City. Bensouda noted that in fact the killings started much earlier than 2011, but she was bound by the period of the ICC's jurisdiction.

After so many years of obfuscation, delay tactics and denials, reading Bensouda's statement I felt an immediate wave of satisfaction and vindication. I called Carlos Conde who told me he was at home jumping for joy when he saw the announcement. He told me in a bright voice: 'This gives me hope. This has been a long time coming, there's still a long way to go, but it's a start. I've been monitoring this for so long, to get this result, it really means something to know that the ICC will pursue this.'

For all of us at Human Rights Watch, who had been working on the Philippines for many years, the ICC decision to push forward and expand the scope of its investigation felt like a significant victory. It is these moments that sustain us, and keep us pushing for accountability, even when sometimes it feels hopeless.

Carlos was still in touch with Clarita Alia. He called her soon after the ICC ruling to explain it to her and gently break it to her that because the ICC jurisdiction only started in 2011 – after the murders of her sons (and indeed after all the twenty-eight cases in our 2009 report), the cases of her children would not form part of the case. It was sorry news. As Clarita said, 'We've been looking for justice for a long, long time. Are they not important? Why can't our cases be investigated? What will happen to us?'

I hoped Clarita took some comfort in knowing that, even if the cases of her children were not included, an ICC investigation was the best opportunity for justice that the Philippines had had in a very long time.

From her cell in Camp Crame, de Lima was quick to welcome the ICC announcement in one of her 'Dispatches from Crame'. She filed a communication with the court, sharing information she had gleaned through her investigations, and handwrote a note to the president which was shared on her social media channels the day after the ICC's announcement: 'That's why it is called the rule of law. You can't just play with the law of humanity and use your own set of rules. So, the international criminal court is now at your door, behind it are thousands of victims of your bloodbath.'

In a separate note, she wrote: 'The days of Rodrigo Roa Duterte are coming to an end . . . All power, no matter how absolute is always fleeting. Only justice is permanent.'

CHAPTER 6

CONTROLLING WHAT WOMEN WEAR IN INDONESIA

At around 3.45 pm, the sound of the call to prayer suddenly drifted from the loudspeakers at Minangkabau International Airport in Padang, the capital of Indonesia's West Sumatra province. A low male voice warbled 'Allahu Akbar'.

The arrivals area was a sea of *jilbab* (headscarf) wearing women. Women and girls cloaked in Muslim headscarves of various colours and lengths were interspersed with the odd Western surfer in t-shirt and boardshorts, towering above the locals with badly tousled hair, juggling multiple surfboards. The Mentawai Islands, just off the coast of Padang, are a world-famous surf spot.

There were also Muslim pilgrims returning from the Hajj pilgrimage to Mecca, dressed head-to-toe in white. No one seemed to pay much attention to the call to prayer, because everyone was fixated on getting their hands on their luggage.

Padang is a city of just under a million people about halfway down Sumatra Island on the west coast, 900 kilometres south of the city of Banda Aceh, and about the same distance north of Indonesia's capital, Jakarta.

Hearing the call to prayer at any Indonesian airport outside of Aceh is unusual. Indonesia is a Muslim majority country, and most follow Sunni Islam, but it is not the state religion. There are many Christians, Hindus, Buddhists, and practitioners of other smaller religions living throughout the archipelago. But West Sumatra's population is about ninety-eight per cent Muslim and its major ethnic group, the Minangkabau or Minang people, are known to be especially devout.

I'd flown to Padang from Jakarta with Human Rights Watch's Indonesia researcher Andreas Harsono to see for myself how West Sumatra's religious conservatism affected women and girls. I wanted to understand the impact of local regulations that compel them to wear the headscarf known as the *hijab* in Arabic, or the *jilbab* in Indonesian.

Andreas is Indonesian, of ethnic Chinese background, and lives in Jakarta. We've worked closely together since 2008, and we've become good friends. Prior to Human Rights Watch, Andreas was a journalist and helped establish Indonesia's first independent journalists' union during the repressive Suharto era. He's covered crises and conflict from end to end of the archipelago and wrote a book about the myth of Indonesian nationalism and the influence of race and religion on politics.[1]

Andreas knew a lot about religion in Indonesia, including from personal experience – one of six authorised religions[2] must be listed on your national ID card. Andreas has had to officially change his religion more than once on his ID. Interreligious marriages are still not recognised. He was the perfect work travel buddy who knew all the important stuff – from who was connected to who in the military and state politics, to where the best *nasi padang* restaurants were.

Since 2009, on our many work trips together around the country or in Jakarta's gridlocked traffic jams, I asked Andreas random questions about Indonesia, shamelessly exposing my ignorance. He reminded me of a passionate university professor, clearly and patiently explaining the historical background of events, peppering me with ever more idiosyncratic facts, and making me even more curious about the country.

Indonesia is an intoxicating and complex mix of ethnicities, religions, and political factions. It has a deeply troubling past of mass atrocities – a topic that is still taboo. On every trip, I met smart and passionate local human rights activists who were working on issues ranging from land to LGBT rights, accountability for torture or killings by security forces to the rights of asylum seekers.

One of the worn-out talking points Western political leaders like to say when they visit Jakarta is that Indonesia is the model Muslim democracy – 'a model of religious tolerance'. Barack Obama, Malcolm Turnbull and David Cameron all said it. True, freedom of religion is written into Indonesia's constitution, but that freedom is limited to choosing one of those six state-recognised religions. In practice, women and those from non-Sunni religious minorities do not always enjoy religious tolerance. Far from it. In conservative parts of the country like Aceh, gender discrimination based on religion is obvious, but elsewhere it is often more subtle.

After advocating about war crimes in Sri Lanka, and extra-judicial killings in the Philippines, you might wonder if women's rights were the most pressing concern in Indonesia. In my years supervising our work on the country, we worked on a range of human rights abuses from Aceh to West Papua. And what

I liked about Human Rights Watch is that we also invested time and energy in addressing not only atrocities, but more hidden violations that affected a substantial portion of the population and which left unchecked, opened the door to more abuses.

Where Islamist organisations and conservative politicians bullied local governments into making concessions, such as introducing Sharia-inspired dress codes for women, too often further restrictions and repression followed. It also showed the disinclination of the national government to fully protect rights guaranteed under Indonesia's constitution, and the limits of an international organisation when acting on sensitive matters such as religion. It underlined why Human Rights Watch supporting local efforts mattered and why lasting reforms ultimately must come from within.

In his three decades of authoritarian rule, from 1967 to 1998, President Suharto stifled any social movement that might pose a threat to his rule, including religion. From 1982 until 1991, Suharto's administration implicitly but effectively banned wearing the *jilbab* in state schools – the *jilbab* was simply not part of the regulation uniform, and anyone wearing one risked expulsion, clearly violating their rights to freedom of religion and free expression.[3]

Then in 1991, the regulation on school uniforms was changed to allow 'special clothing' or religious attire.[4] Around that time, as Andreas explained it, Suharto was trying to demonstrate his Islamic credentials, going to Mecca, and embracing political Islam in order to 'balance the power of the military and neutralise pro-democracy forces'.[5]

Post-Suharto, as Indonesia transitioned to democracy, Indonesians of diverse backgrounds were emboldened to speak out. Both liberal and conservative values squared off in a new more

164

liberal regime, with human rights lawyers calling for greater freedoms, and Islamists agitating for stricter religious policies. The year 1999 was pivotal, as Indonesia changed from a highly centralised model of governance to a more decentralised one where local provinces, regencies and cities were given autonomy to pass their own laws and regulations on certain topics. That same year, the province of Aceh gained especially broad powers including the right to implement Sharia.

At the far north tip of Sumatra, Aceh was on the ancient maritime trade route between the Middle East, India and China and historically a stronghold of devout Islam. A fiercely independent sultanate prior to Dutch colonial rule, after Indonesia's independence, central authorities fought Aceh separatists in an escalating armed conflict, which had its roots in the desire to establish an Islamic State (Darul Islam). From 1976 to 2005, the militant group Free Aceh Movement (*Gerakan Aceh Merdeka* or GAM) led an armed resistance to Jakarta. In 1999, the Indonesian government of President Abdurrahman Wahid offered the province a new status – 'special autonomy' – with the ability to impose Islamic Sharia in Aceh as an additional 'gift from Jakarta'[6] to sweeten the deal.

Even though GAM did not call for Sharia, they could not refuse it – to do so would be political suicide. Offering up Sharia was a way of weakening GAM's power in Aceh as well as appeasing Islamists, who were increasingly finding their voice in post-Suharto Indonesia.

Aceh's Sharia meant that local regulations (called *qanuns*) could be introduced and enforced on matters of religion. The *qanuns* covered issues including charitable giving, gambling, regulation of Islamic rituals and 'proper' Islamic behaviour.

Sharia is not necessarily incompatible with human rights. But at least two of Aceh's *qanuns* passed in 2002 discriminated against women and violated women's rights to free expression and privacy. One was a law that mandated dress codes and the other prohibited *khalwat* (seclusion), making it a crime for unmarried men and women to be together unchaperoned.

The Islamic dress requirement required all Muslims in Aceh to wear Islamic attire, defined as clothing that covers the *aurat* (for men, the area of the body from the knee to the navel, and for women, the entire body except for the hands, feet, and face). In practice, this means that Muslim women are required to wear the *jilbab* in public and are prohibited from wearing clothing that reveals the shape of the body.

I visited Banda Aceh in 2010, and I still have a little photocopied booklet that I picked up on the street called *Islamic Dress Codes for Women*. It defined *jilbab* as 'a thing that prevents, debars, conceals or hides, because it prevents seeing or beholding.'

'Partition' is another definition of *jilbab* – because in effect a veil or headscarf is a barrier between men and women to protect them from 'sin'.

Of course, several Islamic countries across the Middle East have compulsory *hijab* laws, like Saudi Arabia and Iran. But few of these countries are democracies and in Indonesia, adopting such laws marked a dramatic shift towards conservatism.

In 2003, Aceh set up a new court system and specific Sharia police (known as the *Wilayatul Hisbah* or WH) to enforce the Islamic regulations. The new laws emboldened local communities to take matters into their own hands and enforce Sharia against suspected violators. Vigilante groups violently assaulted women who did not wear the *jilbab* or unmarried women in the company of men, at times breaking into people's homes.

The Indian Ocean tsunami in December 2004 devastated Aceh and led to a lasting peace agreement between Jakarta and GAM, but Sharia in Aceh was there to stay.

Between 2008 and 2010, my colleagues and I deliberated about whether to tackle the discriminatory impact of Sharia in Aceh on women as a research project. Media reports covered it from time to time. Part of our reluctance was whether Human Rights Watch – as a perceived 'Western' human rights organisation – should be the messenger on this issue. We worried it could backfire, inflaming a delicate situation with Acehnese and Indonesian authorities dismissing us as foreigners who did not understand Islam, and doubling down in the face of international criticism.

Human Rights Watch had looked at the reverse issue of countries banning headscarves in the West. This was also a human rights violation. In 2010, France banned the *niqab* (full face veil) during a heated public debate about secularism, women's rights, and security, and several Western European countries followed.[7] Human Rights Watch condemned another French law in 2004 banning Muslim headscarves for teachers and students at public schools.[8] The ban applied to wearing 'conspicuous religious attire', items of clothing such as the *hijab* for Muslim women, turbans for Sikhs, and large crucifixes for Christians (apparently ordinarily-sized crucifixes were totally fine).[9] Despite its vague wording, the law seemed squarely aimed at preventing Muslim women and girls from wearing the *hijab*. Both laws that mandated or banned the *hijab* were matters of the State interfering with religious freedom and with women's autonomy over their own bodies.

In Aceh, female Muslim activists we spoke to wanted pressure on the government but confided that they were afraid of vigilantes and blowback from Aceh officials. Eventually, we decided to do the research with their help, but without local activists speaking publicly due to security concerns. We would make the case, and Acehnese activists would be protected.

The involvement of domestic civil society organisations is a key consideration when Human Rights Watch staff are deciding which topic to focus on in a country. We ask ourselves, what impact will it have? Are local groups already covering this issue? Will we as a global human rights organisation bringing international attention help or hinder the efforts of local groups?

In this case, we were not convinced that our report would have the desired impact of curbing the abuses or revoking the discriminatory laws, but local groups wanted our help and in the absence of international pressure, things were getting worse. In September 2009, Aceh's regional parliament passed a new *qanun* that allowed married 'adulterers' to be punished by stoning to death, while those engaging in same-sex relations and sexual relations outside marriage would be flogged – 100 lashes each.[10] This barbaric law amounted to sanctioning the torture of consenting adults.

To his credit, the Governor of Aceh at the time – Irwandi Yusuf, a former GAM militant leader – refused to sign the *qanun* into law, fearful perhaps of the international fallout. Still, it was a worrying sign. (Irwandi, by the way, is now in prison, convicted of corruption.)

By late 2009, we moved ahead with the project to document abuse in the implementation of Sharia in Aceh. I was supervising our Indonesia work at the time. Andreas was our Indonesia researcher, but the project was led by a fellow, Christen Broecker.

Fellows at Human Rights Watch are like junior researchers, brought on for a year to learn the ropes of investigating and advocating on a discrete human rights project. Christen was a young American lawyer, a whip-smart recent graduate. She researched and wrote the report collaborating with a female Indonesian fixer and translator and consulting with Indonesian women's rights groups over a period of six months.

Our research documented how the laws discriminated against women, but also between women. They were enforced selectively – rarely, if ever, applied to wealthy or politically-connected individuals. Instead, it was poorer women, riding on motorcycles or using public transport, who were stopped at checkpoints by the Sharia police, not women in cars.

For example, Sharia police stopped Dewi (pseudonym) while she was riding her motorbike near Banda Aceh. Dewi was wearing a scarf on her shoulders rather than a veil. Two female Sharia police officers asked her to dismount. Dewi described what happened:

> The officers took my ID card, they took down my name and my ID number and asked me to sign the book and write down the 'bad thing' I'd done. I asked, 'What have I done?' They said, 'Your clothing. You're not wearing a veil . . . There's a regulation in Islam about that.' I said, 'It's my choice to wear the veil – it's my business with God.' Their answer was, 'No, there is a rule in Islam that regulates it.' Then they gave back my ID card and told me that if I did the same thing three times, I would be whipped.

Dewi, a journalist by profession, later told me, 'I might want to use a veil, but not because I'm forced by the WH, because I want to.' She was right, wearing the *jilbab* should be a choice, not something imposed by the state.

In December 2010, we published the report, entitled *Policing Morality: Abuses in the Application of Sharia in Aceh, Indonesia*.[11] Christen and I travelled to Banda Aceh ahead of the release and met with the Deputy Governor Muhammad Nazar, as well as the Sharia police, regional police, women's rights groups, and local journalists.

The head of the Sharia police was a big bulky man with a moustache who did not speak English. I wondered if him sitting down with three young women in his office was considered *haram* (unlawful). Our translator wore a *jilbab,* but she was from Jakarta and clearly her clothes did not satisfy the Sharia police standards of modesty. He immediately chastised her for showing the patch of skin from her wrist to her mid-arm where her three-quarter-length sleeve ended. I couldn't understand what he had said, but I could see the discomfort on her face, so I asked her to translate their conversation. I told her to ignore him and was irritated that he had offended our translator. I couldn't refrain from rolling my eyes.

We briefed him on the abuses we had documented by the Sharia police. He asserted the reason Sharia police targeted women, more than men, is because 'women made more mistakes'. There are times when you just know it is not worth the time to try and persuade someone based on facts – we left shortly after, giving him an embargoed copy of our report. I hoped that he would soon face a deluge of calls from journalists and officials once we released it.

That afternoon, we asked our taxi driver to follow a Sharia police truck around. Having read the stories of women in our report, I wanted to see officers in action for myself.

The Sharia police set up a checkpoint and stopped numerous women for wearing what they deemed to be improper attire.

I didn't see them stop a single man. The Sharia police especially targeted women on motorcycles wearing practical clothing like pants or jeans. Most of the women we saw were wearing *jilbabs* (which seemed redundant under motorcycle helmets anyway), but it was the perceived tightness of their trousers that seemed to be the problem. Everything I saw confirmed what was in the report. Later, in 2013, a city in Aceh would ban women from straddling motorcycles altogether, forcing them to sit side-saddle because straddling the seat 'violated Islamic values'.

From Aceh we flew to Jakarta to discuss the report with officials in the Ministry of Home Affairs and Law and Human Rights. Lamely, they said they could not do anything to interfere with Aceh's special autonomy, and it was a matter for Aceh's government alone. Only *Komnas Perempuan*, Indonesia's National Commission on Violence against Women, enthusiastically welcomed the report and joined us in speaking at the Jakarta press conference to inform the public and journalists about the issue.

In our meetings and the press conference, I made the point that Human Rights Watch not only advocated against compulsory Islamic dress requirements, but also called out governments that stop women from wearing Islamic attire. I do not know if it helped, but it was important to show we were consistent in calling out these violations whether in Indonesia, Iran, or Western Europe.

The report got significant media attention. Much as we feared, the Acehnese government largely dismissed it as the product of a Western organisation that did not understand Islam. But privately, women's rights groups in Aceh thanked us. One of the female activists from Banda Aceh said to me: 'When Human Rights Watch says these things, it is like a bomb going off.

You can say it, we cannot. But it does help us later to have a dialogue with the government on these issues.'

In the months after the report, I felt conflicted. On the one hand, it felt like we didn't have impact in abolishing the dress codes. But I felt comforted that our report opened up space for women in Indonesia to talk about these issues. At least we were able to put the experiences of women on the record, just as we had done with the disappearances in Sri Lanka or extrajudicial killings in the Philippines.

And as time passed, sadly, we saw even more rights-abusing Islamic regulations proposed. In 2014, the Acehnese parliament passed a *qanun* criminalising same-sex relations and pre-marital sex and extending these laws to non-Muslims, punishable by lashes or imprisonment.[12] Even though Aceh was the only province authorised to implement Sharia, what happened in Aceh quickly influenced other parts of the country. Religious conservatives became emboldened to agitate for Sharia-inspired laws in their own communities. West Sumatra passed local Sharia-inspired regulations that mandated the wearing of Islamic attire for Muslims, and West Java, Banten, and Riau provinces and several regencies within South Sulawesi province soon followed.

While local Sharia-inspired dress code regulations were multiplying, in 2014, the Indonesian government approved a new nationwide regulation for state school uniforms. It showed an illustration of the *jilbab* as part of the school uniform for Muslim girls. The regulation didn't explicitly say that the *jilbab* was mandatory, but given it was the only uniform option presented for Muslim girls, many officials across Indonesia inter-preted it that way. Local Education offices in Muslim-majority areas started making the *jilbab* mandatory from primary school through to high school.[13] This didn't happen in Jakarta, Surabaya or Bali. But it was occurring in more conservative areas.

Komnas Perempuan identified thirty-two regencies[14] and provinces across the country where the *jilbab* was now required in state schools, the civil service, and some public places.[15] Failure to comply meant civil servants, including teachers and university lecturers, could lose their jobs. It encouraged '*hijab* bullying' – the harassment of people who don't wear headscarves. Some girls who failed to wear the *jilbab* to school were even expelled or suspended.

Komnas Perempuan called on the national government to revoke the local decrees based on Indonesia's constitution, but to no avail – it was a fight the government didn't want to have. Andreas explained: 'The *jilbab* has been weaponised by Islamic conservatives. And it is difficult for Muslim women to speak up about it because their own religious piety is questioned.'

Our report on Aceh may not have had the desired impact, but it cast us as a critical voice on this issue. From 2013 onwards, Andreas collected interviews of women and girls forced to wear the *jilbab* in provinces besides Aceh. We worked with female Indonesian consultants to conduct the interviews. I spoke to one university lecturer in Jakarta who broke down in tears describing the social pressure on women to wear the *jilbab* at her former university:

'I'm a Muslim. I lived in the United States after 9/11, so I know very well what religious intolerance feels like. But to be here and have my faith questioned constantly just because I don't wear the *jilbab*, it hurts. I couldn't do it anymore. I left that university.'

In an example of how sometimes research on one topic can unexpectedly steer you from one human rights violation to another, our interviews on the impact of mandatory *jilbab* decrees led us to expose the practice of forced so-called 'virginity testing' in the police and the military.

In January 2014, I was visiting Jakarta and Andreas arranged for me to meet three young women to talk about their experiences of being forced to wear the *jilbab* in high school. One of the women was a fresh police cadet. We were at a bustling Chinese restaurant in a modern shopping mall in downtown Jakarta. I asked, 'So what has been your worst experience?' thinking it would be related to the *jilbab*. One of the women who was nineteen years old gave a long answer about an experience as part of the examinations to get into the police force:

> I was told that there was a health examination as a prerequisite to enter the police force – an 'internal examination'. We were told to enter a room and to lie down. The medical staffer, a female, then carried out a test – inserting her fingers into my vagina. It was painful. I felt humiliated and scared. Later, I understood it was to check if I was a virgin.

I was shocked. I checked with the translator a couple of times to make sure I had understood it correctly. I had heard of forced 'virginity testing' in countries like Afghanistan and Pakistan – in India, Human Rights Watch had written a damning report about how unmarried rape victims were forced to submit to a 'two finger' test by doctors after the rapes to determine if they were virgins or not.[16] (Apparently, consensual sex before marriage does not happen.)

These tests were discriminatory, degrading and had no scientific basis whatsoever. They were traumatising for women. I struggled to understand why the police would require such tests to get into the force. Andreas was less shocked. He was aware of the practice and said it had been going on a long time.

'The police here are still very conservative, Elaine. They think only virgins can be good police, they'll say things like they don't want sex workers in the force. But of course, it is discriminatory, they don't test the men!'

Andreas explained the test was for younger, unmarried female recruits. I felt we should document the practice and expose it. Sustained international and local pressure from women's groups could help end this practice. Andreas agreed. Later he told me sometimes it takes someone outside the country to cast fresh eyes on an issue and show how long-standing practices are wrong. Andreas kept working away at it, unravelling the thread, corroborating, and gathering interviews from different locations.

In November 2014, we released a report and video with eight cases of police cadets from six cities who confirmed they and their female classmates were forced to take a 'virginity test' as a requirement to enter the force.[17]

We learned that female police officers had tried internally to stop the practice. While some police officers tried to brush us off, saying the test was no longer applied, a senior police general responded to the report not denying the practice but doubling down, saying the test was essential for cadets to ensure their 'good morals'. He responded defensively, 'It's not just us doing this – it's the military too.'

That admission then led Andreas to research 'virginity testing' in the military. We put out a follow-up statement in May 2015. Later in 2015, at a meeting at police headquarters of senior generals and police about virginity testing, some of the generals scolded Andreas. They told him it was not discriminatory, that if there was a virginity test for men, they would do that too!

But the media attention and pressure from civil society worked. It came from Human Rights Watch, *Komnas Perempuan* and women's rights activists, especially women inside the police force or those who had recently retired. In late 2015, the police ordered an end to virginity testing. There were some issues with compliance – particularly in more remote islands far from Jakarta – but overall, it was a huge shift.

And finally, in August 2021, the army finally issued its own order banning 'virginity testing' with consequences for those who disobey. Andreas led this work for years, painstakingly documenting and advocating for these tests to stop. It was both a success of public shaming and advocacy (involving Indonesia's international defence partners such as Canada, the US and the EU) and spearheaded domestically by *Komnas Perempuan*.

Besides the public advocacy, there was behind-the-scenes lobbying by military daughters, military wives, and retired doctors who once administered the tests, asking their respective husbands, fathers and supervisors to end the unscientific practice. It was a lesson in both the power of building coalitions and in sticking with an issue long-term to achieve change.

In 2019, we came back to the mandatory *jilbab* policies, after our work on forced virginity testing, religious violence and abuses in West Papua. Andreas and I went to West Sumatra because it was a province where *jilbab* regulations were strictly enforced – we knew of several cases where even non-Muslim girls were forced to wear a *jilbab* to school. We travelled with a female translator who spoke Bahasa Indonesia and Minang (the local dialect), as well as a filmmaker to record interviews and shoot 'B-roll' – background footage for a short video to accompany the report.

The day we arrived in Padang, we met nineteen-year-old Lestari (pseudonym) at a restaurant inside a hotel. The sun was setting, and a group of Australian men was drinking beer nearby outdoors. We sat inside the restaurant which was chilled to refrigerator temperatures. The service was slow, there was hardly any clientele, so it was the perfect quiet spot for an interview.

Lestari had moved to Padang from her small village, a couple of hours drive away, to attend university. She was studying engineering and loving it. Lestari is Catholic, but she had to wear the *jilbab* to school. Through our translator, Lestari told me:

'I had to wear it since primary school every day. I was forced to wear it. I felt I didn't have dignity, because they know I am a non-Muslim, but they forced me to wear the *jilbab* anyway.'

Lestari said her Catholic parents didn't want to make a fuss. They said that it was part of the school rules, so they encouraged her to comply. She said the teachers enforced it strictly: 'Once, one of the male teachers at my high school said to us, "you cannot show your hair, if I see your hair, I will cut it."'

Lestari hated wearing the *jilbab*. She doesn't wear it anymore. Her university did not require it for non-Muslims. She told me: 'Now that I'm in college, sometimes I want to show high school photos to my friends, but I'm embarrassed. It is not my religion. And then they'll wonder why I wore it, and why I'm not wearing a *jilbab* now.'

She connected us with other Catholic girls in her town who were still forced to wear the *jilbab* to school, and the next day we drove the two hours from Padang to visit them.

On the way there, we stopped on a bridge and got out of the car to admire the view of a river. A friendly policeman noticed us, or rather noticed I was a foreigner. I thought I would blend in in Indonesia – after all Padang is less than 500 kilometres from my mum's home of Singapore – but in this conservative part of the country, my Western clothes (black skinny jeans and a button-down shirt) were a dead give-away.

The cop stopped his car in the middle of the bridge and wanted to take photos together. I was more amused than anxious so agreed. I wasn't thrilled about it, but in Indonesia, it's often easier just to go with the flow and I was with my colleagues. I now have a photo memento with two soldiers in full military uniforms, the smiling cop from the bridge, and some other random guy who was just hanging around the police station. Later, I wondered to myself, if walking around with a bare head in West Sumatra, was like the equivalent of walking around downtown Sydney in a bikini. It was time to go incognito.

I had brought a *jilbab* with me but hadn't worn it yet. It felt strange, knowing Islam wasn't my religion – like wearing someone else's clothes without their permission. But since we were going to a small town and I didn't want to draw any more attention to myself, I got changed at the next restaurant stop. I put on clothes I had bought in a Jakarta department store – a long baggy shirt and a long skirt – and a navy blue *jilbab* which our translator helped me with.

I thought of what my Human Rights Watch colleague Anna Neistat used to say about wearing a full *niqab* when she was travelling for us in Syria, 'It's my invisibility cloak', she joked. She was right. I certainly wasn't sneaking across borders into war zones like Anna, but now that I had it on, no one paid us any attention.

In the town, we met two high school students and got permission from their parents to interview them. Fifteen-year-old Annisa (pseudonym) was Catholic. She was shy, but excited to meet a foreigner. Like Lestari, she had been forced to wear the *jilbab* to school since first grade. (For our interviews, I of course did not wear the *jilbab* – that would have been odd.)

Annisa spoke in Indonesian, with Andreas translating,

'I don't like wearing the *jilbab*. I am Catholic. But when I wear *jilbab*, people assume I am Muslim. I feel like I deny being a Catholic because I must wear it.'

I asked her if she had ever refused to wear it.

'I often think about complaining. But it's impossible. My mother does not have a *jilbab*. When I had to register for high school, she was not allowed to enter the school grounds. So, I registered by myself. My parents asked about it then, but their complaint was rejected.'

Like Lestari and the other young women we interviewed, Annisa said her parents convinced her to comply with the rules. She said there were about ten non-Muslim female students at her school. They all wore *jilbabs*. Annisa said it was some of the Muslim students who sometimes rebelled, by showing their hair, or wearing *jilbabs* that are too thin or too short and got penalised for it.

I asked Annisa if she had a message for the government about the *jilbab*. She thought about it for a moment: 'I just want to tell the government to respect my privacy. I am not a monster! Please respect my privacy.'

Thirty minutes after our interview, Annisa had tracked me down on Instagram and sent me a follow request. There was no hiding from tech savvy teenage girls, even in a small town in West Sumatra! Between Annisa and the friendly policeman, I realised this part of the country did not have many foreigners passing through. And that fact was starting to make Andreas a little nervous, particularly given the size of our videographer's camera. It was not exactly discreet. While we were indoors talking, she was outside shooting B-roll from the car. It's not illegal to shoot video in Indonesia but in these small villages it certainly could cause problems with the authorities if they mistook us for journalists.

We decided to get out of there quickly to avoid any potential misunderstandings.

On our last day in Padang, Andreas and I went a university campus to meet Ibu Siti (pseudonym), a former high school teacher now working for the Department of Education.

As Ibu Siti spoke good English, she and I went and sat outside on a bench together under the shade of a tree. Ibu Siti was middle-aged, wore a bright orange *jilbab* and colourful batik top. She spoke at a million miles an hour and did not hold back. She explained that she herself never wore the *jilbab* as a student and so found it perplexing that it was now a requirement for her own daughters.

'Since I grew up in Jakarta, it seems to me this mandatory *jilbab* regulation is not suitable with the Indonesian condition. Why? Because we have many religions in Indonesia. And children have the right to go to the school. So why should public schools have a *jilbab* regulation?'

I asked her how the *jilbab* rule affected the students that she taught, and how it made them feel:

'For Muslim students, let them choose it. If they want to wear it, wear it! But once you force students, then it becomes like a role play. Put it on for school but take it off outside. If putting on the *jilbab* is only ornamental, then it's no longer about the Muslim identity.'

Ibu Siti told me that she herself only started wearing the *jilbab* at university.

'I still remember the date – it was the 15th of September 1989, a Friday at 7 o'clock. I felt my religion called to me. I made the decision to wear it. And I have ever since.'

180

Compelling women and girls to wear a *jilbab* is obviously not the worst human rights abuse to endure, but it was a more subtle form of oppression. It impacted women's mental health. And it paved the way for further restrictions on women – such as mandatory curfews for women. As always, paternalistic restrictions that were supposedly introduced to uphold Islamic values and 'protect' women took women's freedoms away. As Indonesian feminist and writer Julia Suryakusuma wrote in the Jakarta Post, 'The targeting or neglect of women's rights is the first indicator of the overturning of democracy into authoritarianism.'[18]

In October 2020, in finalising our report, Andreas reached out to the Indonesian Ministers of Education, Culture and Home Affairs with questions about the mandatory *jilbab* regulations. In response, ministerial staff called Andreas and asked him to provide a briefing on our draft report. The staff recognised this was a problem – they wanted to know details of which schools, where, and how extensive the practice was. That seemed encouraging, I thought. And then just as we were finalising the report for release, a video from Padang shared on Facebook went viral.

In January 2021, a Christian man named Elianu Hia turned up at his daughter's school in Padang to challenge the requirement that his daughter wear the *jilbab*. The father met with the school's vice-principal and streamed the conversation on his smartphone using Facebook live. The video was poorly shot, often at weird angles cutting off the subjects. It wasn't particularly exciting; but it recorded the conversation between the two men.

The vice-principal confirmed the school regulation was based on a local decree by the Mayor of Padang and that Elianu's daughter should comply with school rules. Elianu refused to accept the school's response and asked for the Department of

Education and the National Commission on Human Rights to intervene.

Within hours the clip was shared widely on social media. Many Indonesians were shocked that non-Muslims outside of Aceh could be required to wear the *jilbab*. There was also something about the way the principal dismissed the father's complaint in such a nonchalant fashion, as if to say that the daughter will wear the *jilbab*, like it or not, or else she will be kicked out of school.

National media reported on the video, noting that this was not an isolated case nor was it unique to West Sumatra. Netizens (Indonesian internet users) started to protest to the school and the local Ministry of Education office. Elianu's clip went viral with more than 840,000 views. Elianu wrote in a comment on his Facebook page, 'Friends, I am fighting, not for my own children but for our children in the future . . .'

From there, things moved very fast. Two weeks later, on 24 January 2021, Indonesia's Minister for Education Nadiem Makarim responded to Elianu's video saying that the mandatory *jilbab* regulation at that school, or at any state school in Indonesia, was against the constitution, against the education law, and against the 2014 public uniform regulation. Makarim told the Padang local government to change its policy. This was the first time any senior official had publicly clarified that the 2014 national regulation did not make the *jilbab* mandatory for students.

On 3 February 2021, ministers[19] signed a new decree to allow students to wear a uniform of their choice 'with or without religious attributes'.[20] The government ordered the removal of more than sixty mandatory *jilbab* regulations in all state schools and government offices across Indonesia saying they had thirty days to comply with the order.

As a small child, at home in Blacktown in the late 1970s. From left to right: Mum, Dad, my sister Chris (holding me), my brother Nigel and his girlfriend Cheryl, my sister Jill.

With my maternal grandparents, Amah and Akong in Singapore.

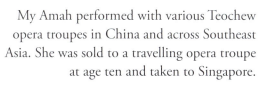

My Amah performed with various Teochew opera troupes in China and across Southeast Asia. She was sold to a travelling opera troupe at age ten and taken to Singapore.

With women activists attending the United Nations Working Group on Contemporary Forms of Slavery consultation on human trafficking, by that chair sculpture at the entrance to the UN, Geneva, June 1999. I'm on the far left, next to me is Meena Poudel from Nepal.

On my first trip to the UN in Geneva, June 1999.

On the streets of Bangkok's red-light district with women from EMPOWER, 2000.

Handing out condoms with EMPOWER in Bangkok, 2000.

UN advocacy in Bangkok, 2000.

Bruno and I visiting Edo State officials working on trafficking in Nigeria including Eki Igbinedion, founder of the NGO Idia Renaissance (to my left), Benin City, 2002.

Meeting Amina Titilayo 'Titi' Atiku-Abubakar, the founder of Women Trafficking and Child Labour Eradication Foundation, in Abuja, Nigeria, 2002.

Meeting women in rural Nepal.

Left: Shortly before my arrest
in Kathmandu, April 2004.
© Devendra M Singh/AFP via Getty Images

Below: Human Rights Watch
headquarters at the Empire State
Building, New York.

A protest shack for the disappeared on the road to Kilinochchi, Sri Lanka. The '217' marks the 217th day of protest.

Middle left: Meeting mothers of those who disappeared in Sri Lanka's civil war, near Kilinochchi.

Middle right: With Thanush's mum in Kilinochchi, 2017.

Bottom left: Walls of photographs of people who disappeared during Sri Lanka's civil war.

Clarita Alia at her home in a slum area of Davao City in the Philippines. Clarita was the mother of four sons all murdered from 2001 to 2007. Clarita believes it was the work of the Davao Death Squad. © Carlos Conde

Clarita, seen here holding Christopher, with (from left) Richard, Vanessa, and Bobby. The three boys were all stabbed to death in Davao City.
© Carlos Conde

Philippines Senator Leila De Lima has not let her detention stand in the way of running for the Senate. A screen projecting an image of De Lima at a campaign rally for Presidential candidate Leni Robredo in Makati, Manila, May 2022. © Carlos Conde

With a high school student in Indonesia's West Sumatra.

With the police in West Sumatra.

Interviewing students in Jakarta, 2014.

Touching down on Manus Island, Papua New Guinea, 2015.

Daily protest by asylum seekers and refugees at the Lombrum detention centre on the naval base, Manus Island, 2017.

Interviewing Kurdish Iranian writer Behrouz Boochani, Lorengau, Manus Island, 2017.

With Rohingya refugee and writer Imran Mohammad, Lorengau, Manus Island, 2017.

Interviewing Tamil refugees Shaminda Kanapathi and Thanush Selvarasa, Lorengau, Manus Island, 2017.

Meeting Imran again in Chicago, 2019.

Meeting Thanush again at Parliament House in Canberra, 2021.

Meeting Abdul 'Aziz' Muhamat in Geneva, 2020.

Jailed Bahraini footballer Hakeem al-Araibi arrives at court in shackles, Bangkok, 2019. © Athit Perawongmetha/Reuters

With Human Rights Watch's Senior Thailand researcher Sunai Phasuk and the unstoppable Craig Foster at Carriageworks, Sydney, 2019.
© House of Cameo

Celebrating Hakeem's freedom, at Human Rights Watch's Voices for Justice dinner in Melbourne, 2019.
© Zoe Twomey-Birks

Saudi teenager Rahaf Mohammed barricaded herself inside her hotel room airside at Bangkok airport to avoid being deported to Kuwait, 2019. © Sophie McNeill

Australian journalist Sophie McNeill, Rahaf Mohammed, and author Mona Eltahawy celebrating Rahaf's freedom in Canada, 2019. © Sophie McNeill

Meeting Shukri Shafe at Human Rights Watch's Sydney office, 2016.

Shukri holding Human Rights Watch's report on crimes against humanity in Ethiopia's Somali Regional State.

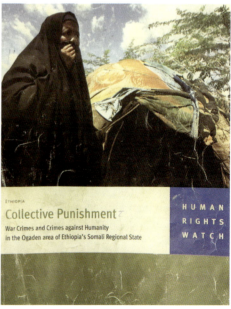

The battered copy of Human Rights Watch's 2008 report on crimes against humanity that Shukri carried with him from Kenya to Australia.

The family of Mr Jackamarra in Broome, Western Australia, 2019. From left to right, Shaquille Jackamarra (brother), Zarack Teh, Georgette Jackamarra (mother), Lorraine Dodd, and Phyllis Teh. © Nicole Tooby/Human Rights Watch

The immense boab tree outside Broome Regional Prison is a momentary distraction from the imposing steel fences and razorwire. The prison is in the centre of town, opposite the courthouse.

With Damian Griffis, CEO of First Peoples Disability Network Australia, and Kriti Sharma, Human Rights Watch researcher, launching our report, '"I Needed Help, Instead I was Punished": Abuse and Neglect of Prisoners with Disabilities in Australia' in Sydney, 2018.

With Australian Chinese artist Badiucao in Sydney, 2019.

Andreas called me as soon as he heard the news. We couldn't believe it! We were amazed that it all happened so fast and excited. Of course, part of me wished that we had put our report out already but getting the progress on women's rights was what mattered.

And it happened because of one courageous family in Padang. It showed the power of social media to ignite change. And it illustrated that mandatory dress codes were an issue that Indonesians cared about. Clearly, many people still had no idea how prevalent these rules had become.

Despite the positive announcement, we were still worried about pushback from religious conservatives. As Andreas said, 'This is just the beginning. This is going to be a long battle. Controlling women's bodies is always political.' When we finally released the report in March 2021, it was more important than ever to give context to the live discussion on compelling women and girls to wear headscarves. Elianu Hia's video exposed the problem, our report showed the impact of the policies on women and girls and how pervasive it was.

The mainstream media attention to the mandatory *jilbab* issue awakened a new movement of courageous women and girls, who, once silent, were now determined to speak up. At our online press conference to launch the report, we had a renowned activist Alissa Wahid and psychologist Ifa Hanifah Misbach join us on a panel. Alissa heads the Gusdurian Network, a grassroot organisation focused on religious freedom. She is the daughter of former Indonesian president Abdurrahman Wahid, nicknamed Gus Dur. The irony is not lost on Alissa that her father was the president who offered 'the gift' of Islamic Sharia to Aceh as a bargaining chip with GAM. Alissa herself wore the *jilbab*.

Ifa Hanifah Misbach told the audience how she counselled more than thirty women and girls who faced mental health issues due to bullying and pressure to wear the *jilbab*. Two of her clients had even tried to take their own lives. She said: 'The impact of religious pressures, especially to wear the *jilbab*, when you're young, it makes it feel like you have no breathing room.'

Our online press conference was unusual – it went on for nearly two hours and was attended by some two hundred people, in Indonesia and throughout the world. There was a collective spirit amongst the women and men who joined that this was an important moment. Someone asked a question about what young, more privileged Indonesians could do to help. Alissa Wahid responded to the question by talking about social media: 'Netizen engagement is key. Those who are more aware of their rights and have the opportunity to speak up, should do so. Whatever social capital you have, use it to your advantage.'

It felt like a real turning point in terms of solidarity and getting people to understand the politics behind governments making decisions about women's bodies.

But it didn't take long for the predictable backlash to begin. By the end of February 2021, a group in West Sumatra[21] petitioned the Supreme Court in Jakarta claiming the new ministerial decree was not in accordance with 'customs of the area' and that it contradicted several laws. Their challenge was largely on jurisdictional grounds, arguing that education should be a matter for regional not central government. Unfortunately, they won. In May 2021, three male judges of the Supreme Court cancelled the ministerial decree that allowed girls and women the freedom of choice to wear a *jilbab* to school. The judges accepted the petitioner's argument that the decree violated laws dealing with regional government, child protection, and the national education system. It was hard to follow their reasoning, but they claimed the decree put girls 'at risk'. The court's unanimous decision was a blow; we were devastated. Indonesia is a democracy, but its institutions are weak and at risk of capture from powerful interests.

Indonesian activists and lawyers have questioned the ruling. *Komnas Perempuan* organised a forum with leading lawyers which cast doubt on the legality of the verdict. Public figures including celebrities, intellectuals, women's rights activists and even a former Religious Affairs Minister signed a petition to Indonesian President Joko Widodo rejecting the Supreme Court ruling.[22]

Back in that sleepy little village in West Sumatra, Annisa is at high school, and she still wears the *jilbab* to school, her life has not changed.

The galvanising of a women's movement in solidarity against mandatory *jilbab* laws was something beyond our expectations. As a result of our report, on the last Friday of every month, women and girls meet online in a Zoom 'survivor forum'. It was the idea of Ifa and one of the mothers interviewed in our report. It's a space for women to speak freely and share their experiences. The forum is not advertised, it's passed on by word of mouth. Initially it was for the women and girls we interviewed in the report to have an opportunity to connect with one another. But it has grown well beyond that, showing how pervasive the problem of forced veiling has become. The forum now has a WhatsApp group where survivors discuss how to counter the mandatory *jilbab* regulations and how to deal with rising Islamic conservatism. Slowly, women are connecting with one another and finding solidarity and support. As Ifa said in our press conference responding to that question on what privileged women can do: 'Replace noise with voice! They have been making noise in our spaces for too long. And we have been silent for too long in theirs.'

That comment would resonate with me as I witnessed how marginalised people, long repressed by their governments, began to find their voice and turned up the volume.

PART III

SEEKING SAFETY ABROAD

CHAPTER 7

BANISHING PEOPLE TO AN ISLAND PRISON IN PAPUA NEW GUINEA

For six years, a rugged remote island in Papua New Guinea became the site of a horrible experiment in human suffering. Manus Island is part of the Admiralty Islands archipelago, some 300 kilometres north of the Papua New Guinean mainland, across the Bismarck Sea. It is more than 800 kilometres, or two plane hops, north of the capital, Port Moresby.

I visited Manus twice – in 2015 and 2017. My lasting memory of the place is of tropical rainstorms, mountainous jungle, and the haunted look in the eyes of the men I met there, banished by the Australian government.

Much of Manus Island's 2,100 square kilometres is uninhabited. The main town, Lorengau, with an estimated population of 6,000, hugs a northern coastal bay. There is a bustling local market, a clinic which serves as a rudimentary hospital, a police station, several shops, and a few guesthouses. Small fishing villages dot the rest of the coastline.

About 20 kilometres from Lorengau, near the airport, is an old naval base, called Lombrum. That's where the Australian government built a facility to detain people seeking asylum. Between July 2013 and December 2014, more than 1300 men were sent there.[1]

These men were not criminals. Nor – despite the Guantanamo-like set-up – were they suspected terrorists. They came from countries such as Afghanistan, Iran, Iraq, Myanmar, Pakistan, Sri Lanka and Sudan. Most of them had fled persecution or conflict at home. They all travelled to Australia by boat from Indonesia, thinking the government would protect them. But Australia sent them either to Manus Island or to the remote Pacific island nation of Nauru, as part of a punitive, mandatory offshore detention regime that was designed to deter future boat arrivals.

This was the second time Manus Island's naval base had been used this way – a previous Australian government had sent asylum seekers there from 2001 to 2007.

That was in response to the 'Tampa affair', when ahead of the 2001 federal election, the Howard government refused to let a Norwegian freighter MV *Tampa* dock – the captain had rescued hundreds of asylum seekers at sea. 'We will decide who comes to this country and the circumstances in which they come,' said former Prime Minister John Howard in an infamous election speech that aimed to galvanise Australians against people seeking asylum.

In fact, the prime minister who ended the offshore policy in 2007, Kevin Rudd, was the same one who re-introduced it in July 2013, making it even harsher, again in a last-ditch attempt to win an election. He failed, but the policy endured.

The naval base itself had an unusual history. During World War II, Manus and the Admiralty Islands were the site of a ferocious contest between Japan and Allied naval forces. The Japanese occupied Manus from 1942 and built the airstrip that is still used today. The US invaded two years later, and in a sheltered bay, American forces built the Lombrum naval base.

Australian forces took over after the war and established a war crimes court on the base between June 1950 and April 1951 to try Japanese soldiers accused of war crimes.[2] When Papua New Guinea gained independence in the 1970s, Lombrum was handed over to the PNG navy. With their permission, Australia intermittently used part of it as an immigration detention facility. It is tragically ironic that the venue of trials for atrocities would later see serious human rights violations committed by the same government that orchestrated those trials.

Australia's government claimed this harsh system of detention was necessary to deter asylum seekers from undertaking dangerous voyages and losing their lives at sea. Media outlets and successive governments have sought to demonise people seeking asylum as potential terrorists, economic migrants, and 'queue-jumpers'. The tough border protection policies seemed to win votes. And as far as Papua New Guinea and Nauru were concerned, they were eager to enter the partnership, knowing it meant opportunities for additional revenue, jobs, and funded infrastructure projects.

Because Manus Island and Nauru were so remote, going there meant navigating a challenging research and security environment, with both governments preventing access to the main detention centre. By the time I went to Manus, I'd interviewed many migrants, asylum seekers and refugees in places like Thailand, Malaysia, Indonesia and Nepal. But seeing this system of manufactured cruelty and detention by a wealthy country like Australia shocked me. And so did the outcome when some of the asylum seekers' stories began to emerge. I learned how exposing the facts and sharing people's stories are sometimes not enough to change a situation that is politically toxic.

On the other hand, I witnessed how the refugees became strong advocates for themselves. For me, this reinforced the central tenant of human rights work: that our aim is to support the participation and self-representation of affected groups and that those with lived experience are best-placed to tell their stories – especially when their lives have been controlled by others for so long.

*

After five years in New York as Deputy Asia Director at Human Rights Watch, I wanted to take a step back. I craved some time and space to think more deeply about how to successfully challenge abusive governments. From July 2012 I commenced a Master in Public Policy at Princeton University's School of Public and International Affairs.

Cam and I moved into graduate student housing in the woods on the outskirts of Princeton. I rode my bicycle to classes every day. After more than a decade of working nonstop on human rights violations, now I got to learn, think, and debate ideas with classmates fulltime.

The classes were extraordinary. I was studying the economics of the welfare state with Nobel Prize-winning economist Paul Krugman, debating the laws of war in a course on 'the military and diplomacy' led by the former chairman of the US Joint Chiefs of Staff, Admiral Michael Mullen, and learning the skills of investigative journalism from Pulitzer Prize winner Jo Becker.

While I was there, Human Rights Watch started recruiting for an Australia Director for our first-ever office in Sydney. I hadn't thought about returning to Australia. But jobs like this didn't come up all the time and establishing a new office for Human Rights Watch sounded like an exciting challenge. Plus, on the home front, my father had been diagnosed with Alzheimer's. He was going downhill fast – I'd made a few trips back to care for him to give my mum a break. After being away from Australia for fourteen years, it felt like the right time to move home.

Cam was up for it; he'd never lived in Australia before. He insisted on one thing – that he got to plan our cross-country road trip from New York to Los Angeles as we left the US – and I happily ceded control to him on that one.

Opening the Australia office was part of a global move by Human Rights Watch to expand our advocacy beyond the traditional targets in the United Nations, the US and Europe. We wanted to influence 'middle power' countries – besides Australia, we also opened offices in Japan, Brazil, Kenya, Lebanon and South Africa.

Our objective was to target Australian politicians, officials, media, and the public to raise awareness about human rights violations, especially in Australia's 'sphere of influence' in the Asia-Pacific. We hoped that increasing the visibility of egregious human rights situations would help make the government more proactive and accountable in protecting human rights. Australia already had strong organisations and institutions focused on local human rights problems, but I felt that to have credibility, we should have a voice on some domestic concerns too. I arrived back in August 2013, just as mandatory offshore detention on Manus and Nauru resumed. It seemed like a serious human rights violation that deserved more international attention.

*

When I went to Manus Island in 2015, it had been almost two years since the mandatory offshore detention policy was in place. Some 900 men detained were now on Manus – men, women and family groups were sent to Nauru, but only men were sent to Papua New Guinea.

In the months leading up to my visit, about forty refugee men moved out of the Lombrum detention centre to a different facility – the East Lorengau Refugee Transit Centre – on the outskirts of the main town. Unlike on the naval base, the men at East Lorengau could come and go from the guarded transit centre though they could not leave the island. The transit centre was so-named because it was meant to be a temporary place before refugees resettled elsewhere in Papua New Guinea once they found employment. I knew if I got to Manus, I could at least try to interview these men in the town. Getting to Manus was expensive and a logistical challenge, but it was not impossible.

The small Air Niugini plane from Port Moresby flew to Manus three times per week. The flight stopped briefly in the town of Madang, on the north coast of Papua New Guinea's mainland, and then across the sea to Manus Island.

There weren't many people on my flight. Most of my fellow passengers were Papua New Guinean men of varying ages, with a few burly Western males, bearded and tattooed, who I presumed were Australians working at the detention centre or in construction. There were various Australian-funded infrastructure projects on the island. The Australian government was building a new market in Lorengau and a new road to the airport to sweeten the deal.

There were a couple of youngish Westerners on the plane, keeping a low profile. I found out later that they were staff of the International Committee of the Red Cross (ICRC), which has a

194

mandate to visit people in detention anywhere in the world to ensure conditions are humane. But they never report publicly on their visits. I didn't make eye contact with anyone on board, putting on my headphones and flicking through the Air Niugini inflight magazine. There was a feature promoting Manus's white sandy beaches, claiming it was the intrepid traveller's next hot tourist destination. It didn't seem like any of my fellow passengers were going on a beach holiday.

Approaching the airstrip, we flew over dense mountainous jungle in endless shades of green and landed near a terminal that was little more than a shed. But at least it was shelter from the rain sheeting down.

A minivan from the hotel had come to collect me and some of the other passengers. It quickly became clear why a new road was a big incentive: we bounced through potholes and mud for the forty-five minutes to Lorengau as the windscreen wipers struggled madly to keep up with the rain. We didn't see the detention centre on our way in, but looking up at the concrete-coloured sky, I thought about the detainees – did they welcome the respite from the tropical heat, or feel suffocated by even the sky conspiring against them?

Before arriving, I had tried my best to convince Papua New Guinea's Immigration Department to let me into the detention centre. Before leaving Australia, I dutifully followed all the steps on their website, filling out forms, but the email bounced, and the fax number didn't work – almost like they didn't *want* people applying. In Port Moresby, I turned up at the PNG Immigration and Citizenship Service Authority (ICSA) several mornings in a row asking each time to speak to the Chief Migration Officer, who approves visits to the detention centre. The officer was never there. I left my business card and my printed forms. Eventually, a kindly secretary seemed to take pity on me and gave me the mobile phone number of another immigration official to argue my case.

After a week of getting no response, I went to Manus anyway.

I picked one of the two hotels in Lorengau, called the Harbourside. It had a modest restaurant, a bar that could get rowdy at night, and a pleasant grassy garden which would become the backdrop for many of my interviews. As its name suggested, the Harbourside backed onto the waterfront with palm trees swaying in the breeze; but we were separated from the sea by a mesh fence topped with barbed wire that ruined the ambiance. As did the rubbish floating on the water.

It was overpriced, but there were few alternatives. At least the staff were friendly. They told me the best rooms were the demountable units, known as the 'dongas', which according to the manager were gifted from the Australian Immigration department. The dongas were small individual rooms – each with a single bed, a desk, and a tiny bathroom cubicle. Mine seemed fairly clean, though the bathroom smelt faintly of urine and the air conditioning chilled the room to refrigerator temperatures. I'd seen similar demountable units at a women's prison in Western Australia, and they are commonly used on mining sites. It would do.

The other hotel was nicer, but I figured any visiting Australian government officials would stay there, so it was better to avoid it.

Once I arrived, I called the Papua New Guinean immigration official again to check if they had made a decision about granting me access. I could tell she was taken aback that I was already there. When she called me back, a few hours later, she held her line: I was free to visit the transit centre, but not Lombrum.

No reason was given for denying the visit. No matter – I got straight to work.

When conducting interviews in a foreign country, it's best to choose somewhere discreet and keep a low profile. The hotel is not ideal – in case people you are interviewing are under surveillance and because interview subjects then know exactly where you're staying. You don't want to do interviews in a very public place as you may attract the authorities' attention. It should be somewhere where you and the interviewee feel comfortable and safe – often a quiet restaurant or another hotel.

On Manus, it was impossible to find a location that met all these criteria – the only cafés and restaurants were attached to the two hotels. Anywhere I went, as a female foreigner I was going to stand out. Blending in – my usual trick across so many Asian countries – was not going to work in Papua New Guinea. So – the hotel it was.

My first interview was with a refugee from a Middle Eastern country, Rahim (pseudonym) who was living at the transit centre. I got his phone number from a journalist. He was about thirty years old, handsome, neatly dressed, and spoke good English. Like many of the men I met on Manus, he was incredibly proud – he wouldn't even let me buy him a meal.

Rahim was an engineer, well-educated and middle class. He told me he had to leave his home because he had uncovered corruption in some contracts between his company and the government. When he reported it, his safety was at risk. He fled to a different city, but then he and his wife had to leave. They flew to Indonesia, registered there with the UN refugee agency and waited. But his wife had medical issues; she couldn't get treatment in Indonesia. After several months, in early 2013, she got on a boat to Australia.

Rahim told me: 'I'm someone who does everything by the book. I just wanted to wait; I didn't want to get on the boat.

But she wanted to go, so we agreed she should go first. She made it to Christmas Island where she was detained.'

Rahim's wife found it difficult to cope in detention without him. She pleaded with him to join her. Rahim eventually agreed, and he took a boat to Australia in late July 2013. What he and other asylum seekers did not know was that Australia's immigration policy had changed – instead of detaining him with his wife, authorities sent Rahim to Manus Island. His wife's asylum claim was eventually approved and she was transferred to mainland Australia on a bridging visa. When I spoke to him in 2015, they had been apart for more than two years. He later confided that they were getting divorced. Family separation was all part of the Australian government's strategy of deliberate cruelty designed to make conditions so difficult that people would give up and go home.

By 2015, Papua New Guinean authorities were finally processing asylum claims and many of the detainees were granted refugee status. To move from detention to the transit centre, one had to sign a paper accepting resettlement in Papua New Guinea.

Rahim was one of the first to move. Some detainees refused to participate in the refugee determination process altogether because they did not want to live in Papua New Guinea. Others who were recognised as refugees refused to leave the detention centre because they were afraid of locals, especially after a night of horrific violence in February 2014 where an Iranian-Kurdish man was beaten to death by a local security guard and dozens more were badly injured. But Rahim was impatient to get his life back – he wanted to start work and earn money however he could. Due to the absence of a formal government resettlement policy, refugees were not yet entitled to work in Papua New Guinea. So the 'transit' part was somewhat of a misnomer.

198

Rahim was determined, but frustrated. He showed me his new Papua New Guinean identity document, which looked like a passport. He said he'd lined up a job interview in Port Moresby in March 2015. He booked a domestic flight, but immigration officials refused to let him board.

'The documents are just for show – they don't mean anything,' he said bitterly.

For six months, he'd been sitting around waiting at the transit centre, pestering immigration officials but to no avail.

After a day or two on Manus, I was joined by Daniel Webb – a lawyer and friend with another NGO, the Human Rights Law Centre (HRLC). He had been working on refugee issues for several years and was challenging the lawfulness of the Australian government's offshore detention regime in the Australian High Court. By coincidence, we had discovered we were both planning trips to Manus Island at the same time. Since we were seeking similar information, we decided to join forces and work together.

Once Daniel arrived on Manus, we used the access I secured to interview others at the East Lorengau transit centre, as well as staff working there, and Papua New Guinean officials. The centre was about three kilometres from our hotel at the top of a hill, behind a guarded checkpoint to keep non-residents out. The friendly Manusian driver who gave us a ride there was curious to see what was behind the gate, since locals were not allowed to visit. He seemed disappointed to find it was just several new two-storey buildings in blocks, built to accommodate about 300 people. They looked far sturdier than a lot of the shacks around Lorengau.

When we arrived, I was surprised that most of the refugee men did not want to meet us. They sat outside smoking in groups. Rahim came over, 'I told them you were coming, but they said, what's the point? We've been here two years, we talk to the UN, the Red Cross many times and nothing changes, so why should we talk to Human Rights Watch?'

I didn't have a good answer. We introduced ourselves and our organisations. I said to the group honestly that I couldn't promise anything would change as a result of our visit, but at least our reports would be public and help people around the world know more about what is happening on Manus Island. Eventually, curiosity (or perhaps it was boredom) prevailed and several of the men agreed to talk.

One was an older barber from Iraq, who smoked constantly. He told me he tried to strike a deal with a local hotel owner to cut hair on Manus.

'Cutting hair is my skill. I just want to do my job. I don't want to be a barber on Manus for the rest of my life, but it would at least help me to pass the time.'

But the immigration authorities would not allow it because refugees were to be resettled in other parts of Papua New Guinea, not Manus Island.

A twenty-two-year-old Rohingya man from Myanmar told me tearfully how he was too ashamed to tell his mother that he didn't make it to Australia. His family had sold their gold jewellery to pay for his journey. He pretended in calls with his family that he was in Australia. But he was lying every time he spoke to them to try and keep his family's spirits up. It was taking a huge emotional toll on him. He barely went outside.

Ahmad (pseudonym) in his twenties from a Middle Eastern country stood out because he had a big smile and a laidback positive attitude towards life – both things in short supply amongst the other refugee men, who appeared sad, worried, and despondent. Ahmad said he moved from the detention centre to the transit centre because he felt suffocated in detention, where everyone was living on top of each other. He said at least here in the transit centre it was calm. He could appreciate the small pleasures of being on an island, like swimming in the sea. In detention, it was like prison.

'Many of the guys are afraid to swim in the sea, but after everything we've been through, I'm not scared of crocodiles or sharks,' he shrugged.

Most of the men were exhausted physically and mentally. Despite being able to leave the centre, most didn't bother. They smoked. They sat. They were glued to their phones communicating with loved ones back home. They felt the stress of being in limbo and far away from their families.

I asked Ahmad how he felt. He paused for a moment, then tried to explain:

'In detention, you become domesticated. Like an animal inside a cage – you think they are fine, they look fine, they seem healthy, but mentally, they are not fine. The mind doesn't work very well. They read, but they can only read a page and they forget. They have lost the ability to live.'

Even though we couldn't visit the main detention facility on Manus, a driver took us to the naval base to at least get a visual of the outside of the detention centre. It was forty minutes from our hotel. As we passed through the checkpoint to enter the base, manned by Papua New Guinean navy personnel, they recognised our driver and simply waved us through.

The detention centre complex was a ramshackle bunch of buildings, sheds and shipping containers packed tightly together – all behind high steel fences. The buildings looked weathered, even though some were new: the jungle and heat had taken a toll. One of the compounds was the infamous 'P block' – an aged

World War II hangar with a curved corrugated iron roof where more than a hundred men slept in crowded, inhumane conditions in the tropical heat.[3] Someone had written 'Hell' in large letters on the wall of one container. Locked gates with uniformed guards manned the entrance to stop people from going in or out. That was as close as we could get.

I had managed to get phone numbers for a couple of refugees inside the detention centre. One of them was a young Sudanese man, Abdul 'Aziz' Muhamat. He spoke perfect English in a deep voice with a slight American accent. Aziz did not show much emotion about his circumstances, but he spoke quickly with urgency and determination. He patiently answered my questions – we spoke for three or four hours in total. Because his mobile phone was contraband, he would speak with his head and the phone hidden under a blanket, and sometimes would hang up suddenly if a guard was approaching. Just like a prison, the guards subjected the detainees to random shakedowns and searches of their rooms looking to confiscate mobile phones.

We stayed in contact after I returned to Australia. Aziz sent me WhatsApp audio files because the wifi was not strong enough for international calls. Aziz and several others in detention would become trusted sources to verify facts when we heard about breaking events occurring at the detention centre.

Following the trip, Daniel and I published a short report based on our interviews describing life in detention and at the transit centre. We released it ahead of the second anniversary of offshore detention and called it *Australia/Papua New Guinea: The Pacific Non-Solution*, noting that more men had died on Manus (two) than had been resettled (zero) in the past two years.[4] The report got a lot of international and domestic news coverage and Daniel and I later testified before an Australian senate inquiry examining human rights violations in offshore processing.

Both in the report and at the Senate inquiry, we urged the Australian government to shut the facilities on Manus down, and transfer everyone to Australia for processing and resettlement. But Australian authorities simply said that the detainees were now the responsibility of Papua New Guinea. Shamefully, Australia was hiding behind the sovereignty of a developing country that was struggling to look after its own people, let alone those fleeing persecution.

*

Two years later, in September 2017, I returned to Manus. By that time, most of the detainees had been there for four years and the number of deaths on Manus Island had reached five; from inadequate health care, violence, suicide, or drowning. Authorities had transferred about a hundred or so detainees to Port Moresby for medical treatment. Health services on Manus were extremely limited and prolonged detention in a tropical climate caused a range of health issues, not to mention the acute mental health problems.

The Australian and Papua New Guinean governments had announced they were shutting down the Lombrum detention centre by the end of October, and I felt it would be strategic to go back and report on current circumstances. By then, several things had changed.

In May 2016, the PNG Supreme Court ruled that detaining asylum seekers was unconstitutional. The Lombrum detention centre was then declared 'open'. But just like the transit centre was an inaccurate and misleading description of reality, so was this. Because the detention facility was on an active naval base, with restricted access to navy personnel, 'opening' the centre did not mean tearing down the fences and unlocking the gates. It only meant detainees were now allowed to take scheduled buses between the detention centre and Lorengau. It was a slight improvement to their conditions, but it was nowhere near enough. The guards and fences remained.

Then in 2017, the Australian government said it would formally hand over all responsibility for services to Papua New Guinean authorities. PNG officials intended to transfer everyone from the detention centre to the transit centre or other new facilities on the island – repossessing their naval base. Simply shunting the men from one facility to another would not provide the freedom or safety that they deserved after four years of detention and mistreatment.

The other major development was that in November 2016, on the eve of the US presidential election, Australia announced a resettlement agreement with the United States. The US government agreed to screen and accept an unspecified number of refugees from Papua New Guinea and Nauru. In return, Australia would accept some Central American refugees from the US. But when I went to Manus in September 2017, while interviews for US resettlement had commenced, not one person had departed yet for America.

Meanwhile, resettlement for those who agreed to stay in Papua New Guinea was tediously slow. Only about a dozen refugees had obtained work and moved to other cities. Several experienced problems such as violence or homelessness. Rahim and Ahmad, whom I met on Manus in 2015, had both returned to their home countries.

I had stayed in touch with Rahim for a couple of years. In 2016, he finally was allowed to move to the city of Lae on the mainland to take an engineering job. He rented a house and got a car. It was okay for a while, but in the end, Rahim just couldn't make it work.

He was lonely. It was tough – Lae has a very high crime rate. It was difficult living in Papua New Guinea as a foreigner without the safety net and high salary of most expatriates but also outside the traditional 'wantok' system of tribal and familial bonds. After a year, Rahim made the decision to go back to his home country. He was still worried about reprisals, but he decided it was a risk worth taking.

By September 2017, several refugees had become prominent advocates themselves, speaking, writing and filming the conditions in detention, and developing public profiles in the Australian and international media. They broadcast developments on Manus Island in real time through Facebook, Twitter, and encrypted messaging apps like Telegram.

Aziz was part of an award-winning podcast produced by The Wheeler Centre and Behind the Wire – an oral history project documenting asylum seekers' voices – called The *Messenger*. He worked with a Melbourne journalist who put together thousands of Aziz's voice memos to tell a story about life in the detention centre.

Although more journalists, politicians, and activists had now travelled to Manus, there were still few visual images of the island. So when I went back in 2017, we decided to record video as well as document conditions in a report. We asked the refugees to speak about their situation in their own words. We hired a cameraman to shoot high quality footage. I hoped the video would help to humanise the stories of the men and generate more media coverage and empathy.

On my second visit, I travelled with my Australian colleague, Georgie Bright. It was her first research mission for Human Rights Watch and her first trip to Papua New Guinea.

It got off to a troubled start. We had been in Port Moresby for a few days of meetings but got to the airport a bit late for our flight to Manus Island. It was PNG Independence Day: chaos at the terminal meant the check-in queue took forever. We finally got to the front, and the check-in attendant handed back only one boarding pass with Georgie's name on it.

'Sorry, flight is full. You are on waitlist,' she told me.

'But that's impossible. I have a confirmed ticket,' I shot back.

'Yes, but it's the weight of the plane, sorry.' She gestured for us to move away.

Georgie's eyes widened in shock. I knew there was no way she wanted to go to Manus Island alone. Georgie whispered: 'Do you think they know who you are?'

I had faced no questions at immigration when I entered Papua New Guinea. But now, we were both a bit freaked out. Maybe it wasn't about the weight of the plane. What if I was about to be PNG'd (declared *persona not grata*) from PNG?! I wondered if I was on a Manus blacklist. I thought about all the media interviews I had done following my last visit to the island.

I tried again with the check-in attendant, smiling but pressing a bit harder:

'We're travelling together, we really want to go to Manus, and we don't have much time here. We booked this flight weeks ago.'

'Just wait, miss' was her curt reply.

We waited anxiously as our departure time approached.

Miraculously, I was handed a boarding pass at the last minute. The check-in attendant told us we had to run to the gate as the plane was about to take off.

Weirdly, once we got on the plane, it was only half full.

We were seated apart, in different rows. I heard squeaking noises coming from two rows ahead, the same row as Georgie. I wondered, was someone sick? Was it a baby? A puppy? I craned my head forward. A young guy was trying to hide a tiny black piglet from the flight attendants. He had wrapped it up in a t-shirt in his lap. After all the stress of the airport, the piglet made us both laugh.

Piglet left us in Madang, and we continued on over the Bismarck Sea in a nearly empty flight. Upon arrival in Manus, I immediately noticed one change – the road from the airport was now sealed and smooth. I commented on it to the driver who picked us up.

'Oh, the road is from the Australians,' he replied.

Offshore processing had brought one tangible benefit to Manusians after all.

Returning to the Harbourside Hotel was comforting and familiar. Not much had changed, though a refugee from Pakistan now manned the reception desk – he lived at the East Lorengau transit centre.

Since we arrived on Independence Day, a number of locals were celebrating by getting drunk at the Harbourside's small bar. It reminded me of how some Aussies celebrate Australia Day. By evening, several occupants of neighbouring rooms were still drinking and listening to music in the open area directly outside our rooms. I put my noise-cancelling headphones on and went to sleep.

The next morning, Georgie told me that in the middle of the night, a man had used a key to enter her room just after midnight. Georgie said he appeared drunk and surprised to see her.

'Wrong room!' he said to his friend laughing.

She shut the door and locked it again but was understandably terrified. She did not sleep a wink knowing that a stranger somehow had the key to her room. Meanwhile I slept soundly with my headphones on, oblivious to the commotion next door and did not see the text message she had sent me about the incident.

We reported it to the front desk. It turned out it wasn't some random guy with a key, but the hotel security guard. He'd had too much to drink, wanted somewhere to crash for the night, and thought that Georgie's room was vacant. I appreciated the hotel staff's candour, but God help us, I thought, if we have any security problems here! I could imagine our Human Rights Watch security adviser telling us the right thing to do now would be to change hotels immediately, but there was nowhere else for us to go.

This trip was also more complicated because of our plans to make a video. Besides the Harbourside, we weren't sure where else would be safe to film. One cameraman had already pulled out of our shoot because of security concerns. We had arranged another to fly from Port Moresby at short notice.

The first people we met with on Manus were Aziz and Kurdish Iranian journalist Behrouz Boochani. They caught the bus from the Lombrum detention centre where they lived to meet us at the hotel. I'd never met Aziz in person, but after so many phone conversations, texts and voice memos, it was like meeting an old friend. Both Aziz and Behrouz were strong advocates for the other detainees. From the moment they arrived at the hotel, they didn't waste time with small talk, they filled us in on everything that had been happening on the island.

It was my first time meeting Behrouz, although we had already been corresponding via text. In Iran, Behrouz was a journalist.

He fled the country when the Revolutionary Guard raided the offices of the Kurdish magazine where he worked and detained several of his colleagues. In Iran, Kurdish people are a minority that have long faced repression. Efforts to promote the Kurdish language are often considered as 'separatist' and subversive by authorities. Behrouz thought Australia would be a country where his rights would be protected. But of course, he was wrong.

By the time we met, Behrouz had quite a profile in Australia. He worked with an Iranian filmmaker, to co-produce a film shot on his iPhone, *Chauka, Please Tell Us the Time*, about life in the detention centre. Behrouz defied the label 'refugee' or 'victim' or 'prisoner'. He channelled the horrible experiences on Manus Island into his work. He collaborated with Australian and international media and human rights groups to help document abuses on Manus Island, wrote for *The Guardian* and several other publications and was regularly quoted by the rest of the press.

When we met, he looked exhausted. His blue t-shirt hung loosely on his gaunt frame. It had a picture of the Statue of Liberty on it, and the words 'Keep calm and stand still'. He smoked constantly, and his long dark hair and bushy beard give him a 'castaway Jesus' vibe, which seemed fitting with the surroundings.

'The big torture here is, we don't know when we will leave this island. We cannot imagine our future and where we will go. We didn't do anything wrong. We don't know why we are in prison. It's been more than four years,' he said with a solemn urgency in his voice.

Aziz and Behrouz were natural leaders among the detainees. As the date for the closure of the detention centre approached, they organised a daily protest amongst the detainees. While largely symbolic, it gave the men a sense of unity.

Aziz and Behrouz described how the atmosphere on the island had become more hostile in the weeks before our visit, with several violent assaults on refugees by groups of young local men. Things had gotten so tense that many of the refugee men chose not to leave the detention centre at all, due to fear of being attacked. There were frequent robberies for cash or mobile phones. Aziz showed me photographs of some of the injuries. Someone slashed at the elbow with a machete. Another beaten on the head and injured so badly they were airlifted to Brisbane with a brain injury. They put us directly in contact with several men who had experienced violence so that we could interview them.

Behrouz worked non-stop, responding to messages on his phone and smoking as we talked. Keeping busy was a way for Behrouz to try and block out the misery of detention. At the time, he was also tapping out messages on his smartphone that would become passages in his award-winning book, *No Friend but the Mountains*, to be published in 2018. In the book, he writes:

'The only people who can overcome and survive all the suffering inflicted by the prison are those who exercise creativity. That is, those who can trace the outlines of hope using the melodic humming and visions from beyond the prison fences and the beehives we live in.'[5]

There was one other writer on Manus I was keen to meet. A twenty-three-year-old Rohingya refugee Imran Mohammad. I'd read some of Imran's articles in the *Sydney Morning Herald*[6] and we had been corresponding via WhatsApp.

Imran fled Myanmar's Rakhine state at the age of sixteen due to the Myanmar government's repression of ethnic Rohingya. He spent several years in Indonesia, and then the last four years detained on Manus Island. Sitting outside in the hotel garden on a humid morning, the clouds shifting above us with foreboding,

Imran explained to me the shifting dynamic between local Manusians and the refugee men. He paused for a moment looking down at the ground and then spoke:

This place is very isolated. The locals have no understanding of people from other countries. We are different. We are like exotic birds for them. We are walking around in our nice clean clothes with our mobile phones. They want what we have. While 'they' are scary for us. We are changing their culture; we are changing the way they live. It makes them want these things [he gestured to his phone]. It makes them feel bad. They don't know what is means to be a refugee. They don't understand it. They only know we are prisoners, and they were told we are bad people.

Imran spoke and wrote like a poet. His command of English was so strong, I was shocked when he told me he had only learned it while in detention on the island.

A sudden introduction of hundreds of foreign men into any small, isolated town anywhere in the world would trigger social and cultural unease. But it was particularly challenging in a place like Manus, an impoverished region unaccustomed to foreigners in an already poor and developing country.

Some Manusians were hospitable and empathised with the refugees, offering them work or befriending them. Others viewed them wrongly as criminals or freeloaders – getting free money and housing from the government. They resented the groups of young foreign men now milling about in the town.

The refugees had got a small taste of freedom they had long been denied. For some, this meant access to alcohol, drugs, and relationships with local women. Inevitably, tensions started to build with some of the locals, particularly young men. Incidents of violence became more frequent and more brazen.

Imran went on: 'I haven't left the centre since one and a half months ago. Many of my friends have been beaten, they have been robbed. There is no one here to protect us. It wasn't that bad in the beginning when we started to come out, but it is getting worse.'

As we sat, the rough ocean waves were visible through a rusty wire fence. Imran looked towards the water, he was contemplative.

The hardest thing here is not knowing anything about our future. Being stuck in limbo. But for me, we are Rohingya – we are born with fear, we live with fear all our lives. Why I fear being here is very hard to put into words. When I am away from the centre, I feel anxious. The fear is something intangible, it's a mental torture. One day I went to town and got the bus home to Lombrum an hour later. The guy on the bus [Australian staff escort] said to me, 'Why are you desperate to get back? You live in that bloody hellhole.'

Imran's comments reminded me of my first trip to Manus. When Ahmad described the impact of detention as being like a caged animal. Living for years in prison-like conditions had institutionalised the men. In a deliberate effort to dehumanise asylum seekers, the government assigned them numbers, instead of names – people were identified by a prefix of their boat number. On several occasions, when I started to interview asylum seeker men, some of them, by habit, introduced themselves by their boat number instead of their name. It was jarring and dystopian.

While I was on Manus in 2017, the Myanmar military was conducting a brutal campaign of killings, rape, and arson against the Rohingya in Rakhine state. The UN later called it as 'a textbook case of ethnic cleansing'. It added to Imran's stress, feeling helpless and isolated from loved ones at such a dangerous time. He spoke about his homeland with great sadness: 'If I had a choice to go back home, I would not have struggled for more than seven years in detention centres. The Rohingya people have been persecuted by the Burmese government for decades. Rohingya people want to be in their homes, but their homes are not there anymore. Everything is gone.'

Imran referred affectionately to his Australian 'parents' – a retired couple from the mining town Mount Isa in Queensland who started writing letters to him in detention. He commented how everything he owned – his shirt, his mobile telephone, his laptop – was due to the kindness of Australians who cared about people they had never met on Manus Island. Other refugees I interviewed also spoke about the generosity of Australian refugee advocates and church groups. The refugees recognised the difference between the Australian people and the government that had banished them to this place.

We interviewed several Tamil refugees. One of them was a shy man in his late twenties, Thanush and several weeks later I would have the surreal experience of embracing his mother Chitrani in northern Sri Lanka as mentioned in chapter four. Like Imran, Thanush did not want to move to the transit centre in Lorengau: 'It's not safe to move there. Guys have been beaten, robbed. Also, we have been here for four years. If we move to East Lorengau or Port Moresby that is not a solution for our life. It is temporary, we want a permanent solution.'

In the week I spent on the island, I noticed a significant deterioration in the mental health of people I had met two years previously. Suicide attempts and self-harm amongst the refugee men were escalating. They were different ages, religions, ethnicities, but shared the same frustration at being in limbo. Some had young children they dreamed of seeing and holding. Others spoke bitterly about wives who had left them. Or anxiously about family members back home who depended on them or loved ones who had passed away. The suffering of those parents, wives and children of the detainees was invisible, and yet it had gone on for four years.

Four years! I thought of everything I had done between July 2013 and September 2017. I had moved countries, changed jobs. Cam and I bought an apartment, we had been on overseas holidays. There had been sad and painful events too. We had to put my father in an aged care home. Then he passed away. And I had had a miscarriage.

All those experiences over four years, while these men had been locked up and living this shitty existence on a naval base on a remote Pacific Island. It was a horrible purgatory, every day the same.

A driver from the hotel gave us a ride to the airport. We got there in no time on the smooth sealed road. Georgie was deeply moved by our interviews and the predicament of the men which seemed so needlessly cruel. We felt a sense of guilt about flying away and leaving people behind, when we knew they so desperately wanted to have the freedom that we took for granted. We arrived, we interviewed, and we left, but they stayed behind.

As we sat at the terminal under the brooding sky, watching droplets of rain start to fall, this time, I thought the sky was crying.

*

After returning from Papua New Guinea, we got to work putting forty or so interviews together into a short report documenting violence against refugees, police inaction, and inadequate medical care. We used our footage to make a short video and longer 'B roll' to distribute to journalists. We released it on October 25, 2017, just shy of a week before the closure of the detention centre.[7] We wanted to provide journalists with facts from the ground, and to encourage media to travel to Manus to do their own reporting.

When we discussed our findings with Australian government officials, they didn't deny the violence had occurred, but they insisted that we 'didn't have the full context'. They blamed the violence on refugee men, as well as alcohol and drug use. But having just interviewed a middle-aged Bangladeshi farmer who had shown me his arm sliced nearly to the bone with a machete, I didn't think any 'context' could justify those actions.

As the detention centre closed, a handful of Australian and international journalists travelled to Manus to see it for themselves.

As promised, Papua New Guinean officials closed the detention centre and Australian contractors left the island. But several hundred refugees and asylum seekers remained – including Imran, Behrouz, Aziz, and Thanush. They refused to get on buses to take them to alternative accommodation in Lorengau. They did not accept being forcibly relocated from one facility to another, they wanted a proper solution – resettlement in a safe country. The power was turned off at the detention centre. The standoff was tense.

I briefed journalists and activists heading to the island. The men sent me regular updates, photographs, and videos. They were organised, they had solar batteries to charge their phones.

They had stockpiled food and dug wells to locate fresh water. The refugees described it as a siege – they lived without running water, electricity, or regular food supplies for three weeks.

But for once, these men had agency in their lives. It might seem strange that they clung to the place where they had been detained, where some of them had been beaten and shot at. But now there were no guards and no rules to follow. They themselves were in charge. It was their first taste of freedom in more than four years, and despite the physical hardships, that independence gave them strength and courage. Which made it all the more ridiculous when politicians like then Home Affairs Minister Peter Dutton started saying Australian activists were encouraging the men to stay in the detention centre. These men were determining their own fate, they weren't puppets being controlled by anyone else.

After some time, the Papua New Guinean police entered the facility to try and force the men to move. They threw garbage into the wells and slashed holes in their water supplies.

Back in Sydney, I felt stressed during the weeks of the standoff. I couldn't sleep. I felt anxious. I am usually good at compartmentalising my work – 'switching off' even when I work on traumatic issues. You have to be able to do it, if you're going to do this work long-term. But this time, it felt impossible.

Every day I woke up to messages of what had transpired overnight. Videos. Photographs. Texts. Missed calls. It was a constant flow of information from a place I had just visited. Trapped in the detention centre, they kept those of us outside informed. I did my best to talk to journalists, politicians, and officials. I wrote, I spoke, I posted on social media. But it felt hopelessly inadequate.

At Human Rights Watch, we have two counsellors who help staff to cope with mental health issues. For the first time ever,

I booked an appointment. I felt embarrassed. I wasn't the one being detained. I wasn't even there. I was safe in my home. But I was feeling enormous guilt, and I realised it was eating me up.

I think many activists go through this. We are stubborn. We don't want to ask for help. We bury our feelings in the work because any stress we feel seems insignificant compared to the experiences of those we interview.

It was a difficult conversation with the psychologist over Skype. I refused to turn my camera on. I didn't want him to see my tears, I didn't want him to see my weakness. Some things he suggested were just not practical. I couldn't suddenly stop checking my phone. I couldn't take a leave of absence. There was no one in my team to refer things to.

But some of the things he said made sense. I could impose limits. I could stop checking my phone for messages at all hours. I could put it somewhere away, out of reach. I could try and do a daily short meditation or distract myself with something enjoyable – a walk, a yoga class, or a drink with a friend.

Still, the guilt stayed with me for some time. It felt unfair that I could choose to switch off. I remembered something Aboriginal psychologist Dr Tracy Westerman once said about people hearing traumatic stories as part of their jobs, 'Our training teaches us there's a fine line between caring too much and burning out, and caring too little and being ineffective and compassionless.'

During the siege, my ruminating thoughts would sometimes go back to my grandparents – imagining how my grand-mother had finally left her situation of bondage, fleeing China for Singapore at age nineteen. She disguised herself as an old woman to escape from the opera troupe owner – she did not want to become his concubine. She travelled to Hong Kong and then Singapore. My grandparents met during the Japanese occupation. Singapore was then 'liberated' by the British, and eventually Chinese people were given permission to remain. But what if my grandmother had been sent to a remote island prison instead? How would she have coped?

Meanwhile my dad, an Englishman, and an economic migrant looking for a better life, was able to come to Australia by boat, for ten pounds from London to Sydney in the 1960s. He was welcomed to Australia, not banished. He made a good life in Australia, working for Qantas.

And I had this fortunate life of travelling, living and working in different countries with ease simply because of the passport I held. Luck, privilege and race determined one's fate. I had known this from my early days working on trafficking, but still found this inequity especially galling.

The standoff came to a sudden end after 22 days. Police and immigration officials finally moved the men by force from the detention centre to other facilities near Lorengau. Once again, the men had lost their battle for freedom.

After the siege, in Lorengau town, there were sporadic acts of violence. And some local community members who lived near the new facilities were upset at the lack of consultation. They tried to block access to the new centres due to disputes over land ownership. Once again, the refugees and asylum seekers were stuck in the middle of these disagreements. They waited, biding their time, hoping for US resettlement.

Gradually in dribs and drabs, some of the men departed for the US, including Imran Mohammad who left in late 2018. Others were rejected from US resettlement without explanation. Some were transferred to Australia for medical treatment, including under a short-lived Australian medical evacuation law, introduced in March 2019. Thanush was one of those: he had developed depression and anxiety from prolonged detention and uncertainty.

Moving to Australia was not respite: it meant going back into detention. Many of those transferred faced more than a year confined to hotels and onshore detention centres. I stayed in touch with Thanush while he was confined to a Melbourne hotel. In May 2020, he tried to end his life. He was rushed to hospital and then moved from the hotel to an immigration detention centre. Finally, in January 2021, Thanush was released. He posted this message on Twitter:

Thanush selvarasa

@Thanus79084726

#Heartwarming After 8years later I got very good news 2day that I will be free next week this such a wonderful time 4me my mother has been waiting year by year for only one message from me that 'hey mom I'm a free' I have been waiting 4that beautiful moment to tell that message

In February 2021, I was in Canberra. It was my first trip back there in over a year due to the COVID-19 pandemic. I was on the phone, waiting in line for a coffee at the café inside Parliament House, when I looked up and saw Thanush. It was a great surprise – the last time we had met was on Manus Island in 2017. Now he was in Canberra with refugee advocates to deliver a petition to the government and meet with Members of Parliament. Thanush has become a powerful voice for refugees and asylum seekers in Australia. I felt very happy for him.

Since 2013, more than a thousand people like Thanush have been transferred back to Australia from Papua New Guinea and Nauru for medical or other reasons. Australian lawyers have filed cases preventing their return to Nauru and Papua New Guinea. Most of those freed from detention are working. But they are still in limbo, with temporary visas that need to be renewed every six months, no rights to study or travel and no financial support.

In 2019, the PNG government shut down all facilities on Manus Island and transferred those remaining to other facilities in Port Moresby. In 2021, the Australian and PNG governments announced they were closing facilities permanently in Papua New Guinea altogether. The men who remained could either stay in Papua New Guinea or else move to Nauru. As I write this, about 220 refugees and asylum seekers remain in Papua New Guinea and Nauru.

Human Rights Watch is just one voice campaigning against Australia's abusive offshore detention policies. We work alongside the Human Rights Law Centre, Amnesty International, Refugee Advice and Casework Service (RACS), the Asylum Seeker Resource Centre (ASRC), the National Justice Project, the Refugee Action Coalition (RAC), the Kaldor Centre for International Refugee Law and many other individuals and organisations. I have much respect for activists and lawyers who have worked for years on refugee cases in Australia despite endless hurdles and despair.

But I especially admire the resilience of the men on Manus Island who fought for their rights. Imran, Behrouz, Aziz and Thanush all escaped the horrors inflicted by their governments and by the Australian government on Manus Island. They found new lives in different countries.

Imran lives in Chicago. I met him there in June 2019. He was dressed casually in a white shirt, jeans and sunglasses and he was happy and relaxed. We walked besides Lake Michigan on a summer evening and toasted to his freedom in a bustling restaurant on Chicago's north side. It felt like a parallel universe from our last meeting on Manus Island sitting in the garden of the Harbourside Hotel and staring at the sea through a fence. Now we watched the gentle waves of Lake Michigan under a big blue open sky.

Imran was upbeat. He had just completed his high school equivalency test and was looking forward to studying at a community college. He was working part-time. But he said moments of joy were always tinged with sadness: 'I'm happy of course, but I am also broken for those who are left behind. I think about them constantly.'

I introduced Imran to my Human Rights Watch colleagues in the US. I urged him to write about his experiences and we connected him to an editor at the *Los Angeles Times* who promptly published Imran's op-ed about his long journey to freedom from Myanmar to the US.[8]

After I left Chicago, Imran wrote to me on WhatsApp: 'Freedom allows us to do so many great things. We are really grateful to be free and safe in this country. I will do my best to get an education because it will open doors and will allow me to be a voice for others.'

Imran has become that powerful voice on behalf of Rohingyas, migrants, refugees, and students in the US. In 2021, he was elected a student representative for the seven City Colleges of Chicago. He graduated from Truman College, and is continuing with his studies, at Northeastern Illinois University, studying social work and journalism.

He is also a fellow at the Pulitzer Center, using his talents in storytelling for a global audience and wants to publish his autobiography.

Aziz won the Martin Ennals award – a prestigious international prize bestowed each year to a frontline human rights defender – in February 2019. He travelled from Manus Island to Geneva to accept, and initially planned to return after the ceremony; but thankfully he changed his mind and stayed in Switzerland where he was granted refugee status. He enrolled in university, where he is studying in a third language – French.

In February 2020, on my last overseas work trip before the pandemic, I met Aziz at a café in Geneva. He was smiling, he'd just finished his university exams and celebrated his twenty-sixth birthday. Aziz's first choice was to study law, but it was too difficult in French, he said. So, he was doing a Bachelor of Arts instead.

Aziz had just returned from visiting the refugee camps in Lesbos, Greece. He eagerly showed me photos and videos from that trip. 'I was really shocked,' he said. 'I was in tears when I went there. I know Manus was tough. But in Lesbos, at night women and children are wearing diapers because it's too danger-ous for them to go outside the tent to go to the toilet.'

I asked him why he went, and who he went with. Aziz just shrugged: 'I went on my own. No organisation. I paid for it. I feel it is my duty, I have to do it. I was [he paused] . . . just like them.'

As with Imran, Manus is never far from Aziz's mind. He told me, 'When I wake up, I think about it. When I go to sleep, I think about it. I get constant messages from the guys. I think about them all the time.'

In 2018, I was at a university conference on migration in Germany. Academics were discussing the work of famous detained Kurdish writer Behrouz Boochani, and quoting from his book, *No Friend but the Mountains.*[9]

'What did it mean, that someone could make award-winning art – films and literature that won worldwide acclaim – and yet still be punished in this exile?' a German academic pondered aloud, clearly horrified at Australia's policies.

Via WhatsApp, I sent Behrouz a photo of the lecture theatre and the power point slides which featured his face prominently. Still on Manus, Behrouz sent back a smiley face emoji and told me to tell them his book would soon be available in German.

In November 2019, Behrouz was invited to speak at a writers' festival in New Zealand, where he claimed asylum. Eight months later, and exactly seven years after Australian authorities first detained him at Christmas Island, New Zealand granted him refugee status. The New Zealand government had done in months what the Australian government should have done seven years earlier.

Behrouz is now living in Wellington. He is an associate professor at the University of New South Wales, he's working on a feature film about Manus Island and the *New York Times* magazine wrote a cover feature about his life. Behrouz's haunting portrait by artist Angus McDonald was a finalist in the 2020 Archibald Prize, Australia's most prestigious art competition. For a time, Behrouz's giant face was staring at me from bus stops all over Sydney advertising the Archibald. It made me smile. At the Sydney Biennale, I interviewed Behrouz and an artist from Ghana for an online event about art, migration and story-telling. Without ever setting a foot on the Australian mainland, I love that Behrouz looms large and ever-present in the Australian arts and literary scene.

I'm happy and relieved for these men who are finally able to get on with their lives and achieve their dreams. But I still feel disgusted by the policy of the Australian government that has robbed so many men, women and children of the best years of their lives through a deliberate manufactured state of cruelty.

After working for years to expose the plight of refugees transferred offshore with very limited success, little did I know that soon I would be working around the clock to help one refugee and somehow the Australian public found his story easier to connect with.

CHAPTER 8

BANGKOK AIRPORT, DETENTIONS AND PREVENTING FORCIBLE RETURNS

Every year, the Kingdom of Thailand welcomes thousands of newlyweds on honeymoon packages, promising a once in a lifetime experience. Couples can choose between the fine food and swanky hotels of cosmopolitan Bangkok, the white sand beaches of southern Thailand, or the thrill of riding elephants through mountainous jungles in the north. All the while, enjoying the legendary hospitality from Thai people in a country known as the Land of Smiles. What more could one ask for from a holiday destination?

On a Tuesday afternoon, 27 November 2018, a young couple in Melbourne were eagerly anticipating their first overseas holiday together. Twenty-six-year-old soccer player Hakeem al-Araibi and his wife Nani (pseudonym) got an Uber to the airport to catch their Jetstar flight to Thailand for a belated honeymoon. Hakeem, a refugee from Bahrain, was an Australian permanent resident.

When they landed in Bangkok nine hours later, their dreams of an idyllic honeymoon quickly turned into a horror show.

Uniformed Thai police were waiting at the gate. They entered the plane, went directly to Hakeem and Nani's seats, and promptly escorted them to the airport's detention area. The young couple didn't understand what was happening, but they were terrified.

Thai immigration officials told Hakeem they detained him because Bahrain had issued an Interpol red notice against him, due to his (politically-motivated) criminal conviction there in 2014. A red notice is an international alert to law enforcement. Not quite an arrest warrant, it provides a basis for police officers to apprehend fugitives pending extradition or legal proceedings. The Thai officers told Hakeem he would be sent back to Bahrain.

Hakeem was shocked. Returning to Bahrain would mean imprisonment and likely torture, both things he had already experienced. He tried to explain to the Thai authorities he was a refugee: 'I told them I am not Bahraini now. I am Australian. I have Australian travel documents.' But they did not seem to care.

Unlike the refugees on Manus Island, Hakeem made it to Australia without being detained. He thought he was free from Bahrain's persecution, he felt safe enough to book a holiday overseas. But our interconnected world that makes international travel for those from wealthy countries such a breeze, also makes it easier for authoritarian regimes to hunt down government critics across country borders.

Bahrain is a tiny island kingdom in the Persian Gulf, connected to neighbouring Saudi Arabia by a twenty-five kilometre-long causeway. It is majority Shiite, yet ruled by a minority Sunni royal family, the House of Khalifa. During the Arab Spring of 2011, the kingdom brutally crushed large protests for democratic reform. Yet Bahrain's repression goes largely unnoticed and unchecked by the international community.

Fears about Iranian influence have helped to shield Bahrain from international censure in the UN – the Sunni kingdom falsely claimed the protests were being orchestrated by majority Shiite Iran. And the US maintains a naval presence in Bahrain – an important strategic base for their Middle East military operations.

In 2018, my knowledge of Bahrain was limited. I knew that one of my former colleagues had once been pepper-sprayed and briefly detained in the capital, Manama. Back in 2012, our then-Washington director Tom Malinowski, now a US Congress-man, was observing a peaceful night-time demonstration when he was detained in a crackdown on protesters.[1] Tom left Human Rights Watch in 2013 to join the Obama administration as the State Department's top diplomat on human rights.[2] He returned to Bahrain two years later in that role, but was expelled by Bahraini authorities for meeting with an 'unauthorised' Shia opposition group, al-Wefaq.[3] Meeting with peaceful opposition groups is a standard part of any US diplomat's job anywhere in the world. It rarely leads to expulsion. But Bahrain had zero tolerance for anyone who spoke up about their human rights violations.

The kingdom had effectively outlawed all peaceful opposition groups and placed severe restrictions on media and civil society. Scores of activists and journalists were jailed for criticising the government; many of them alleged torture and mistreatment.

During the Arab Spring uprising, Hakeem, a Shia, was a football protege. He joined peaceful protests in Manama with other athletes three or four times. In November 2012, when Bahraini authorities were arresting thousands of peaceful protest-ers, they arrested Hakeem and he said that they tortured him in custody. Officers charged him with vandalising a police station, a crime Hakeem said was impossible for him to have commit-ted: he had been playing in a televised football match around the time the attack occurred. Authorities released him on bail in February 2013 and later that year he started travelling abroad to play soccer for the national team.

In January 2014, while Hakeem was with the national team in nearby Qatar, he was tried in absentia and sentenced to ten years' prison. Rather than returning home, he fled, and several months later made his way to Australia where he claimed asylum.

Hakeem travelled by plane, rather than by boat, so he was not transferred to Papua New Guinea or Nauru. Australian authorities granted Hakeem's asylum claim in 2017. He became an Australian permanent resident in 2018.

Refugees with permanent residency can travel internationally using an Australian travel document in lieu of a passport. When planning his trip to Bangkok, Hakeem says he checked with the Australian government's immigration hotline to make sure he could travel to Thailand and that everything was in order. He obtained his visa at the Thai consulate.

What he didn't know is that his travel to Bangkok was flagged in Interpol's system – at some point since he fled, Bahraini authorities had issued the Interpol red notice and so on the day of the flight, Australian Federal Police notified the Bahraini and Thai authorities of Hakeem's travel to Bangkok.[4] Interpol has a policy that red notices should not be issued or enforced against refugees by the countries from which they fled. This is to prevent refugees from facing politically-motivated charges. Shamefully, Australian police had neglected to check Hakeem's status as a refugee with the Department of Home Affairs. This was a massive cock-up and only revealed weeks after Hakeem's arrest.

Now, Hakeem was in Thai custody. Unable to leave the airport detention area, Hakeem and Nani panicked. They rang the Australian embassy in Bangkok as well as several Bahraini human rights activists exiled in Australia and the UK.

At 2pm on Wednesday, 28 November, about 13 hours after Thai authorities detained Hakeem, I was sitting at my desk in my office in Sydney when I saw an email come in, with the subject 'Very Urgent – Bahraini Refugee Facing Refoulement if Deported from Thailand.'

Lama Fakih, Human Rights Watch's then-Deputy Middle East and North Africa Director in Beirut had forwarded me an email chain from Sayed Ahmed Alwadaei.

Sayed was a former political prisoner from Bahrain, and now an activist working with the Bahrain Institute for Rights and Democracy (BIRD) in London. Although he'd never met Hakeem, the two had previously been in contact about human rights concerns. Sayed wrote a detailed email to UN officials in Thailand with precise information about Hakeem's arrest, his background, copies of his travel documents as well as links to press articles mentioning him.

Refoulement is a fancy French way of saying forced return. *Nonrefoulement* means governments should never force someone back to a country from which they fled if there is a substantial risk they will face persecution, torture or other mistreatment. The principle of *nonrefoulement* is recognised under customary international law, meaning it applied to Thailand even though the country had not ratified the UN's 1951 Refugee Convention.

Despite these international obligations, Thailand repeatedly forced people back to abusive regimes. At Human Rights Watch, we had tried unsuccessfully to stop several deportations from Thailand, including the return of ethnic Uyghurs to China, and Cambodian political activists back to Phnom Penh.[5] Amnesty International had reported on how Thai authorities had escalated the practice of forced returns since the military coup in 2014.[6] They did this in part, because in return, they wanted other governments to send back Thai political activists in exile.

I could see from the email chain that my Human Rights Watch colleagues in Bangkok and Beirut were frantically trying to stop Hakeem from being forced back to Bahrain. They had verified his story and were following up with UN contacts and the Australian embassy, urging them to intervene.

It is unusual for Human Rights Watch to get involved in an individual case like this – our focus is usually on documenting and advocating on patterns of human rights violations and making recommendations to governments. We are a small team – with only one or two staff per country covering a plethora of human rights concerns. Case work is intensive, and we lack the capacity to provide direct individualised support.

But sometimes, a person's life is in danger, or the event will set a worrying precedent, or there's just no clear referral path to others. Hakeem's case met all of those criteria.

His detention sparked an intensive few months for Human Rights Watch. Several of our staff around the world became closely involved in *two* separate cases of individuals who were facing deportation back to authoritarian regimes from Bangkok Airport – Hakeem al-Araibi and a Saudi woman, Rahaf Mohammed. I saw how authoritarian governments defy international borders and try to pressure weaker governments to force their citizens home, especially those who had spoken out or 'shamed' them. Having refugee status in a third country like Australia was no guarantee of protection.

The two cases had major ramifications beyond the individuals involved. They showed how 'people power' and how social media campaigns can make a difference. One person's story is often easier for people to relate to, making it easier to build empathy and outrage than a pattern of violations against nameless and faceless individuals. This was a story of collaborating with activists around the world and finding allies.

The two cases were successful in raising the stakes for abusive governments and finding points of leverage, be they foreign governments or institutions like sporting bodies. Finding the right point of leverage is especially important when dealing with an authoritarian regime that is otherwise difficult to influence directly.

Our Thailand researcher Sunai Phasuk is one of the most well-connected men in Bangkok. He knows everyone – journalists, diplomats, activists, the most senior officials in the Thai government and the military. Also in Bangkok, was our outspoken Asia Deputy Director, an American, Phil Robertson. He had lived in the city since the 1990s and spoke fluent Thai. His background was in the labour rights movement, and we'd been friends for years, from when I lived in Bangkok and consulted for the UN in the 2000s. Back then, we both worked on human trafficking, but Phil wasn't well suited to the UN bureaucratic straitjacket. He was about as subtle as a sledgehammer.

Lama and our Bahrain researcher, Aya Majzoub, were in Beirut and coordinating with Sayed in London. It was an 'all hands on-deck' situation – activists scrambling across different countries and time zones because the clock was ticking. I had a sick feeling in my stomach that Hakeem would be sent back to Bahrain with dire consequences.

Over email, we recalled how Thai authorities had sent back another peaceful Bahraini critic of the government in his early twenties, Ali Haroon, in December 2014. The UN human rights office in Bangkok as well as the UN refugee agency had urged the Thai government not to return Ali to Bahrain, but their pleas were ignored. At Bangkok airport, he was handed from Thai authorities to Bahraini police officers, also following an Interpol red notice. The Bahraini officers bundled him onto a flight, beaten, shackled and sedated. Amnesty International said that Ali's injuries were so severe that he had to be transferred to a hospital on his arrival in Manama.[7]

We did not want that to happen to Hakeem. We thought media attention might help. It might force the Thai government to back down and put pressure on Australia to prioritise raising his case through diplomatic channels. There was a risk that it could backfire, and cause the Thai government to double down, but given Ali Haroon's precedent, we thought the benefits of media coverage outweighed the potential risks.

Luckily, Hakeem still had his mobile phone and he agreed that we should make his case public. The key difference between the two cases is that Hakeem was an Australian permanent resident. If Australian diplomats pressured the Thais, then we reasoned it should be harder for them to ignore both the Australian government and UN officials.

Sayed quickly drafted a press release on behalf of his organisation, BIRD, and we did the same, though ours took longer to get it through our internal vetting process. We shared the statements with journalists in Thailand, Australia and internationally, and also on social media.[8] Meanwhile, I alerted contacts in Canberra at the Departments of both Foreign Affairs and Home Affairs, and the Foreign Minister's office. I asked Australian officials to press the Thai government to release Hakeem and allow him to return to Australia.

At that stage, none of us knew that it was the Australian authorities who had informed the Thai police about the red notice.

We were puzzled as to why the police had been there waiting for Hakeem's flight. We presumed that either someone in the Thai consulate had tipped off the Bahraini authorities, or that Hakeem's emails were being monitored. Electronic surveillance is a common tactic by authoritarian regimes to track dissidents, even those who are outside the country. But we didn't spend too much time debating how the Thai authorities knew, we had to resolve the immediate problem of Hakeem's safety.

The story got picked up by Australian and international news outlets. On Friday morning, I was attending an address by then-Foreign Minister Marise Payne at a Sydney thinktank, the Lowy Institute. An ABC journalist asked her about Hakeem's case. The Minister was caught off-guard and seemed unusually vague, 'I am aware of the matter. The issue has been raised with the Thai authorities and our post is following up.'

In Canberra, at 3.03pm on Friday, the federal police emailed Interpol headquarters in France confirming that Hakeem was a refugee on a protection visa.[9] Interpol cancelled the red notice within 24 hours. We know this from a Freedom of Information request, which also revealed that it was in fact Interpol headquarters who first wrote to the Australian police inquiring about breaking media reports stating that Hakeem was a refugee.

Australian diplomats often tell families of Australians detained overseas, like Hakeem, not to speak to the media, and that their circumstances will be best resolved through 'quiet diplomacy'. It is true that there is sometimes a window where targeted strategic diplomacy can be used to resolve things quickly and quietly. But in Hakeem's case, without the media coverage who knows otherwise how long it could have taken for the red notice to be withdrawn?

By Friday afternoon, several of us had heard back from our various contacts that 'things were looking encouraging' but no one could speculate further. Australian officials never want to speak with us about the specifics of cases, due to privacy obligations owed to the individuals involved.

Sayed emailed from London with some welcome news. 'I just spoke to Hakeem, someone from the Australian Embassy was in touch with him, they are trying to book a flight for him to Melbourne tonight. The next flight is at 7pm,' wrote Sayed.

That Friday night as I flopped on the couch after work, I felt a wave of relief. It had been a busy week, and I was about to depart to New York for a 10-day work trip. At least now it looked like this footballer would be home over the weekend.

Hakeem and Nani booked the first available return flight on Jetstar, but unfortunately, it did not depart until the Saturday evening. Nani and Hakeem were still in detention at the airport. By Saturday afternoon, they started to worry. Thai immigration officials were not allowing them to leave. Meanwhile, I boarded my flight from Sydney to New York.

On Sunday, 1 December, as I landed at LAX airport in transit, I picked up my phone and saw a flurry of worrying emails. Hours before Hakeem's flight was due to depart, Thai immigration took him out of the airport, and on a forty-five minute bus journey to an immigration detention centre in the city. They had changed their minds.

Phil called Hakeem and spoke to the Thai official escorting him, who confirmed the transfer from the airport to Suan Plu – Bangkok's notoriously crowded main immigration detention centre. Phil has spent more than a decade helping people navigate the Thai immigration detention system. He explained that Hakeem was a refugee and should be sent to Australia, not under any circumstances to Bahrain. The official listened but did not react.

Our Thailand team quickly notified UN staff and Australian diplomats in Bangkok. Sunai worked his contacts in the Thai government to try and find out more from their side. Sayed issued another press release about the worrying new developments. Phil spoke to Hakeem again on Sunday morning. For now, he still had his mobile phone and the immigration authorities let him and Nani stay in an office rather than the detention cells at Suan Plu. It appeared to be special treatment, but we later learned that Thai immigration officials did this because they were sorting out what to formally charge Hakeem with.

From the LAX transit lounge, I emailed Australian press contacts alerting them to Hakeem's transfer to Bangkok's immigration detention centre and urging them to contact my colleagues in Thailand for more information.

I boarded my flight to New York, feeling incredibly anxious.

Hakeem was going to need an experienced Thai lawyer to help fight the extradition to Bahrain. We contacted local organisations who suggested some lawyers, but representation would cost money. The Bahrain community in Melbourne were willing to help and set up a GoFundMe web page. They would also approach Hakeem's football team in Melbourne for support.

My colleagues in Bangkok were working the phones pressing the UN agencies and embassies – European Union countries, the US, Canada and New Zealand – all governments with influence in Thailand and solid records of defending human rights in urgent cases. We alerted them to Hakeem's situation and urged them to support the Australian government in pressing for Hakeem's return to Australia. From those conversations, I was surprised and irritated that the Australian government did not seem to be already doing this themselves.

We knew Hakeem's case would set a chilling precedent if he was sent to Bahrain. Thailand hosted large numbers of people fleeing oppression, especially from neighbouring countries like Myanmar, Cambodia, Laos, and Vietnam. If he was sent back, it would mean more abusive governments would try their luck in influencing the Thai government to hand over dissidents in exile.

The press coverage around Hakeem's case resulted in a response from the commander of Thai Immigration, a man by the name of Police Lieutenant General Surachet Hakpan – who goes by his memorable moniker 'Big Joke'. Most Thais have a short nickname, that starts from childhood because their actual names are often long. It is common for the word 'Big' to be adopted as a prefix if they join the upper ranks of the police or military, a form of playful, but clear, deference.

Big Joke said the Thai government had yet to receive an extradition request from Bahrain. 'He will be held until the 4th (of December) and if there is no letter from Bahrain seeking extradition then we will return him to Australia,' he said publicly, adding that there is no formal extradition treaty between Thailand and Bahrain.[10]

Big Joke's comment worried us. Despite the withdrawal of the red notice, it now felt like the Thais were biding their time, waiting for Bahrain to file the documents.

Then on Monday, December 3, six days after Hakeem landed in Bangkok, we got the email that we had been dreading from Sayed: 'Just received a call from his wife in tears. Thai authorities have taken Hakeem and she does not know where. He does not have his phone.'

Bahrain had submitted the extradition request.

Sunai quickly phoned around his police and immigration contacts. It turned out Hakeem was transferred from an office into the cells. By now, Amnesty International Thailand was also involved in helping Hakeem, which took some of the pressure off us.

Our team and Sayed kept discussing ways to elevate Hakeem's case to bring it to the attention of decision-makers with influence over the Thai government. It's all about exerting the right amount of pressure and finding people who can make a difference. Human Rights Watch spends years building up networks of contacts with people in and outside government to be effective. People often listen to us, because we share useful information, we do not exaggerate claims, we are independent, and we are as factually accurate as possible.

Hakeem's professional football status offered a unique point of leverage – the international football association, FIFA (Fédération Internationale de Football Association). If we could get FIFA, the Australian government and the UN to lean on the Thai authorities, then hopefully that would be enough pressure to get the Thai government to relent and send Hakeem back to Melbourne. Many Thais are soccer fans, and the country is a longstanding member of FIFA.

Our colleague in New York, Minky Worden, has a specialist expertise on the intersection of sport and human rights. Originally from Tennessee, with a relentlessly sunny disposition, she is energetic and a famously smooth talker with excellent contacts in the global football community and FIFA itself. In 2017, she managed to convince the international football body to introduce a human rights policy. We hoped she could work her contacts to get FIFA to issue a statement calling for Hakeem's release.

FIFA had skin in the game – part of why Bahrain's government wanted to punish Hakeem was payback for critical comments he had made about a member of Bahrain's ruling family who ran for FIFA's top job.[11] In 2016, Sheikh Salman Bin Ibrahim Al-Khalifa was a candidate for FIFA's presidency.[12] That same year, feeling safe from his new home in Australia, Hakeem was quoted in the *New York Times* calling for Sheikh Salman to be investigated over allegations that Sheikh Salman was involved in the arrest and detention of Bahraini athletes during the Arab Spring uprising. Sheikh Salman lost the bid to Swiss-Italian Gianni Infantino but he remained the president of the Asian Football Confederation (AFC). Our aim was to get FIFA to exert pressure on Sheikh Salman to get Bahrain to drop the extradition order.

Minky got to work, informing her contacts in sporting organisation to lobby FIFA for Hakeem's release. She alerted more international journalists to his plight, including the *New York Times*, who wrote a story on 6 December – now day eleven of his detention in Thailand.

'Al-Araibi's case is a true test of FIFA's new human rights policy: will FIFA stand with a football player and defend him against rich and powerful human rights abusers like the Bahraini government?' Minky wrote in an op-ed published in *The Guardian* that same day.

Meanwhile on 7 December, a Thai court recognised Bahrain's arrest warrant. This paved the way for authorities to transfer Hakeem to prison. It felt like a gut punch.

Thai prisons are notoriously bad, a Hollywood cliché for any nightmarish foreign jails – oppressively hot, overcrowded unhygienic group cells, with prisoners often forced to sleep on the floor. I could only imagine how frightened Hakeem must have been feeling.

Any slim hopes that we could resolve this quickly evaporated. Now that the courts were involved, the phase of frantic scrambling was over, and the next phase would be slower, sustained and strategic advocacy involving a variety of allies.

By now, Phil and I were both in New York for work meetings. In picturesque Tarrytown, an hour north of Manhattan, we were locked away at a conference centre with a dozen or so colleagues for tedious management training.

Hakeem's extradition hearing began on 11 December. His application for bail was denied. Meanwhile, Sayed at BIRD had obtained the court documents from Hakeem's 2014 trial in Bahrain. He said the documents proved the conviction relied upon a coerced confession and was riddled with factual errors and a lack of due process. I had never met Sayed (and I still haven't), but I was super impressed with him. He was like a machine, up at all hours working on Hakeem's case, cranking out documents and correspondence.

A week later and I was back in Australia, with Christmas looming, and the end of year summer holidays where nearly the entire country shuts down for several weeks – I myself would be on leave overseas for two weeks. The sense of urgency was gone, since we knew nothing was likely to happen until Hakeem's next court date.

But our efforts to highlight Hakeem's sporting credentials in the international media were paying off. Around this time, I noticed that a high profile television sports commentator, Craig Foster was tweeting daily about the case. On 22 December, Craig and the Professional Footballers Association (PFA) held a press conference about Hakeem in Melbourne. Craig was a former Socceroo and ex-FA Cup player for Crystal Palace who had carved out a successful career with Australian public broadcaster SBS. He was charming and articulate and I had watched him deliver the sports segment on the evening news for years, but I had no idea until that moment that he was passionate about human rights. I told Minky I would connect with Craig once I got back from leave.

Coming back to work in early January is usually dead slow in Australia. It's mid-summer and most people are still on holidays. But I was about to return to work with a jolt – as we became aware of another person from the Middle East stuck at Bangkok airport, at risk of being sent back to an abusive regime.

On Sunday morning, 6 January, I received a text from ABC reporter Sophie McNeill:

'Have you seen these tweets about a Saudi girl who ran away from her family in Kuwait and now is trapped at Bangkok airport? I spoke to her. She's terrified. Is anyone in your Thailand team able to help her?'

My heart sank. It sounded similar to Hakeem's situation; I couldn't believe it.

Sophie had been the Middle East correspondent in Jerusalem for the ABC, and now worked for their investigative program *Four Corners*. She was a gun reporter – bold, smart, and compassionate. We had connected many times for various stories, and she always impressed me with the depth of her coverage on human rights issues, her willingness to take up sensitive topics, and her ability to connect with people to tell their stories.

I clicked on the link to the tweet. A prominent Egyptian feminist Mona Eltahawy had translated several tweets by a young Saudi woman, Rahaf Mohammed, from Arabic to English.

@monaeltahawy

Translation of tweets from the #Saudi woman trying to flee into asylum who said she is being held at #Bangkok airport: 'I am the girl who escaped #Kuwait to #Thailand. My life is in real danger if I am forced to return to #Saudi Arabia.' https://Twitter.com/rahaf84427714/status/1081646654497964032. . .

This Tweet is unavailable.

8:00 AM · Jan 6, 2019·Twitter for iPhone

Jan 6, 2019

Replying to

@monaeltahawy

'My name is Rahaf Mohamed. I will publish my full name publicly if my family and the #Saudi embassy and the #Kuwaiti embassy man don't stop chasing me' https://Twitter.com/rahaf84427714/status/1081647421799755782?s=21. . .

It appeared that a young Saudi woman, Rahaf, had escaped from an abusive family while on holiday in neighbouring Kuwait. She purchased a plane ticket to Bangkok. She planned to stay a few days, and then proceed to Australia. After arriving at Bangkok Airport, a man who claimed he was there to help her obtain her visa-on-arrival instead seized her passport and documents – it turned out he was a representative of the Saudi Arabian Embassy. He spoke to Thai immigration officers who refused Rahaf's Thai visa-on-arrival application and told her she must return to Kuwait.

Saudi Arabia has strict male guardianship laws – meaning women cannot travel without the permission of a male relative, no matter their age. I knew this because Human Rights Watch had released a report on male guardianship in 2016. 'Every Saudi woman must have a male guardian, normally a father or husband, but in some cases a brother or even a son, who has the power to make a range of critical decisions on her behalf' read the opening lines of the report.[13] The Saudi system gives women a secondary status compared to men, their entire lives they are treated effectively like children, unable to make decisions for themselves.

I zoomed in on Rahaf's profile image on Twitter. She was an attractive young woman with dark hair and there was a filter on the image that gave her eyes a feline look. The account had less than a hundred followers. I felt chills reading her tweet:

'I am real, I exist, I am still breathing, but I am not sure I can continue or that I can stay alive unless the #Saudi embassy stops pursuing me.'

First Bahrain, now Saudi Arabia pulling people off planes to try to compel them back to their abusive regimes – I wondered what on earth was going on with Bangkok Airport. Hakeem was flying *from* Australia, and Rahaf flying *to* Australia. It was a bizarre coincidence.

Rahaf's detention at Bangkok Airport came three months after Saudi officials had murdered journalist Jamal Khashoggi in their embassy in Istanbul, where they dismembered his body to destroy the evidence of their horrific crime. We knew that the Saudi government did not respect international borders.

I clicked 'follow' on Rahaf's account and called Sophie back. She said had spoken to Rahaf briefly and said that she was terrified. Sophie had messaged Phil Robertson in Bangkok but hadn't heard back from him. Sydney is three hours ahead of Thailand.

'I keep thinking of what happened to Dina Ali in Manila,' Sophie said anxiously.

Dina Ali Lasloom was a 24-year-old Saudi Arabian woman intercepted at Manila airport in April 2017. She too had escaped

Saudi Arabia, travelling without the permission of her male guardian to escape a forced marriage. Dina's family came after her, all the way to the Philippines.

I remembered Human Rights Watch issued a statement about it at the time.[14] In a last-ditch attempt to save herself, Dina approached a Canadian passenger at the airport to borrow her phone – the passenger helped to film Dina speaking about her situation. The clips were later circulated on social media. In one video, Dina said, 'They took my passport and locked me up for 13 hours . . . if my family comes, they will kill me. If I go back to Saudi Arabia, I will be dead. Please help me.'

A witness said that airline staff and men of Middle Eastern appearance bound Dina's hands, feet and mouth with duct-tape, put her in a wheelchair and rolled her onto the flight. Dina's whereabouts after she returned to Saudi Arabia were uncertain.

With that in mind, I wrote a quick email to Phil and Sunai in Bangkok, as well as our Middle East colleagues working on Saudi Arabia. And since it was Sunday, I later messaged and called Phil on WhatsApp.

A few hours later when Phil woke up, he got on it straight away. He called Rahaf to ascertain the facts. She spoke basic English. She was determined not to return to Saudi Arabia and wanted to seek asylum. She described how family members beat her and locked her in her room – a punishment because she cut her hair. She said she had renounced Islam, which meant if she returned to Saudi Arabia she could be tried for apostasy.

The Saudi agent and airline staff escorted Rahaf to a transit hotel – where passengers can rent rooms by the hour if they have a long layover, without passing through immigration. A Thai security guard was stationed near her room to make sure she did not leave.

Phil and Sunai started working the phones again, alerting the UN refugee agency – United Nations High Commissioner for Refugees (UNHCR), journalists and diplomats. They put together a press release. As it was a Sunday, officials were slow to respond. UNHCR said they could not interview Rahaf without the Thai government's permission.

The urgency of Rahaf's case was similar to how we had felt six weeks ago with Hakeem. And now he was in jail. We were anxious about the precariousness of Rahaf's situation and worried that the Saudis would find some way to simply force her onto a flight.

Our team stayed in contact with her throughout the day and night. She may have only been eighteen years old, but she was smart, savvy and knew her way around social media. She bravely (and secretly) filmed the Thai officials who told her that she was going to be sent back on a Kuwaiti Airlines flight at 11.15 am the next day. She posted this video to Twitter and live-tweeted in English and Arabic, posting photos and videos to explain her situation. Rahaf was dressed casually in jeans and a t-shirt, looking like any other young person posting content to their socials. But Rahaf's social media posts were being amplified by human rights activists around the globe. They quickly started attracting mainstream media attention. Phil and Sunai had alerted Thai and international journalists. Detained in her hotel room, Rahaf made her case talking to journalists from the BBC and CNN about her situation. Overnight she started amassing tens of thousands of followers.

Meanwhile, my colleagues coordinated a game plan with Sophie McNeill in Sydney. Sophie, on leave from the ABC to write a book, took the huge step of secretly flying from Sydney to Bangkok. She managed to slip into Rahaf's room unseen. Now, with Sophie there, we had an extra set of eyes in the room to document Rahaf's situation and another line of communication to her. At worst, we feared Sophie would be there to film Rahaf's attempted deportation.

As the social media campaign gathered pace, a hashtag #SaveRahaf started trending. It went viral. People all over the world were horrified and captivated by the thought of a rebellious young woman at risk of being sent back to an abusive family in a country where women had no rights. It was like something out of *The Handmaid's Tale*. Within twenty-four hours, #SaveRahaf had been used more than half a million times.

I woke up on Monday morning to a barrage of media requests about Rahaf. By now, our Thai and Middle East teams were getting some sleep. I explained to reporters our fears for Rahaf, reeling off a list of precedents, context, and concerns for Saudi women. I explained the male guardianship laws – and why women like Rahaf were going to such lengths to escape. I reiterated Thailand's track record of cooperating with authoritarian governments to send people back and highlighted that an Australian permanent resident was also at risk, Hakeem.

All the while, I kept one eye on the clock and my email inbox, because we were anxiously counting down to Rahaf's supposed deportation flight at 11.15am Bangkok time.

'Don't answer the door under any circumstances!' Phil told Rahaf over the phone early that morning. Thai officials were pleading with her to come out, offering breakfast and coffee. She had barricaded herself in her room, putting furniture behind the door. If the authorities took her, they would have to use force. Only a small group of activists knew that Sophie was in there with her. People in Australia, Thailand and around the world were watching Rahaf live-stream every knock at the door and attempts to coax her out of the room. It was like voyeuristically watching an impending abduction about to take place on Twitter.

A press core had formed inside the airport. International reporters based in Bangkok were staking out the lobby of the transit hotel and the gate where the plane was to depart to Kuwait.

11.15am came and went. When the flight departed without Rahaf on board, social media users following Rahaf cheered online. *Thank god!* I thought, but I still felt nervous.

Then a sudden announcement from Immigration Commissioner, Big Joke (familiar to us from Hakeem's case). He promised not to send Rahaf back into harm's way because Thailand is the 'land of smiles' and 'we will not send anyone back to their death'.[15] Still, his assurance alone was not enough.

UNHCR staff told Phil they were headed to the airport, Rahaf waited for them to arrive. Throughout the day, many people had come knocking, claiming this or that, to try to get her to open the door. When they finally did so around 5pm Rahaf asked them to slip their identification cards under the door. She confirmed via phone with Phil that they were legitimate staff from UNHCR, and this was not a trick.

Once satisfied, she opened the door somewhat stunned to a large group of UN and Thai officials outside. Sophie surreptitiously emerged from the room and did her best to try and blend in with other Western UN officials milling about. The UN had agreed to hear Rahaf's asylum case in Thailand, and they would find her somewhere safe to stay. If her asylum claim was approved, she would be resettled to a third country.

What a twenty-four hours! Rahaf's determination and savvy internet skills, backed by Sophie and human rights activists on social media, may very well saved have her life. Rahaf's asylum claim was verified and a few days later she flew to Canada, after the Australian government refused to fast-track her application. Australia's then Home Affairs Minister Peter Dutton said Rahaf Mohammed would get 'no special treatment' continuing the government's political position on tough border protection. What Dutton failed to grasp is that Rahaf wasn't safe in Thailand – her brothers and father had arrived in Bangkok, were trying to speak to her, and demanded the Thai government help them to take her back to Saudi Arabia.[16] In stark contrast to Australia's approach, Canada made the decision to grant her a visa within hours of receiving a referral from UNHCR. The Canadian Foreign Minister at the time, Chrystia Freeland personally greeted Rahaf off the plane in Toronto. Finally, Rahaf was safe.

At Human Rights Watch, we celebrated the work of our colleagues – especially Phil, Sunai and our Saudi researcher Adam Coogle – it was a rare instance where social media and public pressure succeeded. Social media is often a cesspit of negative comments and trolling. But the quick amplification of Rahaf's predicament through social media had been highly effective in changing the position of the Thai government.

Now if only we could apply the same tactics to Hakeem's case. Already, we started to weave Hakeem's story into the global media coverage around Rahaf. We mentioned she was not the only person vulnerable in Thailand. There was another young man in prison at risk of extradition to Bahrain.

I'd been so absorbed in Rahaf's case and busy with media interviews that on the Tuesday, I forgot that Fatima Yazbek and Yahya Alhadid from the Gulf Institute for Democracy and Human Rights (GIHDR) were coming to the office with Hakeem's wife, Nani.

My colleague Nicole came to my office door. 'They're here,' she said. 'And by the way, Craig Foster is here with them.'

Craig Foster? My jaw hit the floor. Reaching out to Craig was on my 'to do' list but then the Rahaf crisis had taken over. I hadn't realised he was working in tandem with the Gulf Institute and Hakeem's wife.

I came out to meet them. Nani, looked incredibly distraught and sad. She had returned to Melbourne just before Christmas when Hakeem was transferred to prison. Craig explained his personal interest in the case as a fellow soccer player, and we quickly started to brainstorm about what to do next for Hakeem. Their small group had already visited Amnesty International.

We agreed he needed regular visits at prison – Nani said that Hakeem's last visitor was someone from the Australian embassy on 28 December, two weeks earlier. I explained our staff in Bangkok were unfortunately blocked from prison visits. At that point, Craig offered to go to Bangkok. I was surprised that he was so moved by Hakeem's story that he would travel there. I offered him support from our team in Thailand to help set up advocacy meetings.

Soon after, Evan Jones, an Australian living in Bangkok and working with the Asia Pacific Refugee Rights Network (APRRN), would take on the role of regularly visiting Hakeem in prison, taking him food, updating him on the campaign and generally keeping his spirits up.

Craig's involvement in Hakeem's case was a gamechanger. He led the efforts of organisations in Australia and around the world. He could pull a much bigger crowd of journalists than a bunch of human rights organisations. Hastily assembled, Craig organised a press conference by the steps of the Sydney Opera House, to get Hakeem's case covered more widely in the Australian press.

Australia's Foreign Minister Marise Payne travelled to Thailand to meet with her counterparts in mid-January. I published an op-ed in the *Bangkok Post* about the Thai government's track record of sending people back to authoritarian regimes.[17] While Payne's trip didn't yield any tangible results, a visit from the Foreign Minister certainly made it clear to the Thai government that Hakeem's case mattered to Australians.

We kept asking ourselves why the Thai government was so deferential to Bahrain. Australia spent decades building goodwill with Thailand through trade, aid and security ties. Australia was a closer neighbour geographically, a more strategic regional partner. Perhaps they didn't think that the Australian government cared about the fate of one refugee, given how Australia treated most people seeking asylum – sending them to offshore detention camps. But it was bizarre that the Thai government was willing to put this bilateral relationship on the line for a tiny kingdom in the Persian Gulf. The only plausible explanation was perhaps there was some informal agreement from one kingdom to another?

Craig flew to Bangkok the following week bringing the polish and skill of a professional broadcaster, speaking with eloquence and charisma. He worked closely with Phil to brief diplomats, journalists and UN staff, and they held a joint a press conference on Hakeem's case. Craig also visited Hakeem in prison. He spoke about the experience outside, welling up in tears during an emotional piece to camera for *The Project*, a popular prime time news show on Australia's Channel Ten network. Strictly speaking, Hakeem's case was still a matter of extradition to be judged by Thai courts. But we knew well the power of the Thai senior officials to intervene and call it off.

After Bangkok, Craig flew to Zurich to meet with senior FIFA officials. He lobbied the professional football players union in Amsterdam, Fédération Internationale des Associations de Footballeurs Professionnels (FIFPRO) to seek their support for

Hakeem. The hard work and Craig's personal connections paid off, with FIFA taking a much closer interest in the case.

Having Craig now driving Hakeem's campaign forward was a big relief and meant we at Human Rights Watch could step back. Craig had a singular focus and boundless energy for Hakeem, working nonstop. We supported him in any way we could.

Amnesty International was also playing a greater role in coordinating action on Hakeem's case from Australia. They have a much bigger staff, and I was happy to have them step up. The advocacy network was getting broader. It now included the Professional Footballers Association (PFA), the Australian Council of Trade Unions (ACTU), GIDHR, and a mix of politicians.

Just like in Rahaf's case, the social media campaign continued to build. Amnesty International garnered a petition with tens of thousands of signatures and the hashtag #SaveHakeem started trending on social media. Craig's sporting connections started to pay off, bringing Hakeem's case to broader attention not only in Australia, but internationally.

On 1 February, the #SaveHakeem campaign held a second press conference on the Opera House steps. Craig arrived from the airport after his European advocacy tour. This time, it wasn't just Craig and a few human rights groups, he was amassing broad support across the Australian community. The press pack was larger. And the pressure was building on the Australian government through mainstream media.

Hakeem's extradition hearing was on 4 February. Craig flew back to Thailand for it and went with Phil – shouting words of support and encouragement to Hakeem. They were not alone. FIFA's head of sustainability, Federico Addiechi, was in the courtroom. Australia's ambassador was there, and diplomats from the

US, Canada, Britain, Switzerland, Germany, France, Norway, Sweden, Finland, New Zealand, the Netherlands, Belgium and the European Union.[18]

The hearing was largely a formality. Hakeem's lawyer Nadthasiri (Nat) Bergman noted that her client would contest the extradition to Bahrain and the next court date was set for 23 April.

The image of Hakeem getting off the prison bus to walk to the court room, his legs shackled and barefoot in the Thai prison uniform of a shirt and shorts, surrounded by uniformed guards, shocked the world. Shackling anyone is barbaric. But putting shackles on a professional footballer, whose livelihood depended on his feet, really added insult to injury. Those images quickly went viral and sent the global campaign for Hakeem's freedom into overdrive.

Within twenty-four hours, the #SaveHakeem hashtag reached over 500,000 tweets. UK Premier League footballers with millions of followers, players like Didier Drogba, Robbie Fowler, and Gary Lineker were soon tweeting to #SaveHakeem.

Another influential act was a letter sent on 9 February to the Thai prime minister urging Hakeem's release from the two Aussie cave divers who helped rescue the Wild Boars football team of twelve boys and their coach in Northern Thailand in July 2018.

Things moved quickly over the weekend of 9–10 February. The Thai government dispatched their foreign minister to Bahrain. On the evening of Monday, 11 February, Sunai emailed with good news – it was over. Bahrain had dropped the extradition request!

I felt a wave of relief. Public pressure by a virtual army of human rights activists and concerned individuals from around the world, led by a former Socceroo, had worked. We had managed to raise the stakes and stop Hakeem from being sent back to Bahrain.

On Tuesday morning 12 February, Hakeem arrived at Melbourne Airport to a welcoming crowd of hundreds. A few weeks later, I had dinner with Hakeem and Nani in Melbourne. Hakeem obviously didn't know everything that had occurred on his behalf, but he knew Sunai and Phil had worked very hard to free him. Nani looked like a different person, radiant and relaxed, so happy to have him back.

It took nearly three months and a lot of work for Hakeem to safely return to Australia. Many individuals and organisations worked tirelessly for his release. But the real credit must go to Craig, who truly went above and beyond to save a young man's life. Hakeem's case was not just about one person, it opened people's eyes to the acute levels of repression in Bahrain and how sport was politicised.

Rahaf's case also wasn't just about one brave young woman armed with a smartphone and a Twitter account. Her Bangkok Airport drama set off a chain of events that eventually led the Saudi government to ease some restrictions on women.

Nine months after Rahaf's ordeal, in August 2019, Saudi Arabia's Council of Ministers approved a royal decree that relaxed some of the male guardianship provisions including the one that required permission from a male relative for a woman aged twenty-one or over to travel. Various factors led to that decision, not least the fact that Saudi was hosting the G20 Summit in 2020 and was facing a serious legitimacy crisis after Saudi agents murdered Jamal Khashoggi and the government's detention of prominent women's rights activists. But I am certain that Rahaf's brave voice calling attention to these abuses played a role in it too.

After the publicity around Rahaf and Hakeem, people started contacting Human Rights Watch anytime someone was detained at an airport. Unfortunately, we aren't always able to look into the circumstances of each case and help everyone.

With people travelling more and authoritarian regimes able to carry out digital surveillance across borders, the risks of arbitrary detention and 'hostage diplomacy' seem to be increasing.

And while the Australian government ultimately did the right thing in standing up for Hakeem, this case should serve as a precedent for the government to speak up publicly and consistently for those who are arbitrarily detained. Failing to engage robustly on human rights sends the wrong message to abusive governments in the region, like Thailand, Cambodia, Myanmar and China. It becomes easier to brush Australia off as not committed to rights, or only raising concerns when it suits a political agenda. And that emboldens abusive governments in our region when there is no cost associated with their actions.

When Hakeem and Rahaf's cases emerged, some asked, why did the media and the public get so caught up in the case of just one life? Why did Australians seem to care about the refugee Hakeem, and yet, so many Australians remained unmoved by the hundreds of refugees trapped for years in limbo in Papua New Guinea and Nauru?

It was a good question. Sometimes the plight of one individual is easier for people to connect to and for people to feel like their voice or their action matters. Many Australians can relate to taking a flight to Bangkok, so they can imagine the terror of being unexpectedly detained in a way that they cannot imagine the terror of being detained on a remote Pacific Island. But it was a reminder to apply those lessons learned for others whose plights remained invisible and did not capture the world's attention.

Hakeem was targeted by the Bahraini government as soon as he left Australian soil, but I would also encounter other former refugees and migrants in Australia who had escaped the authoritarian regimes who persecuted them, only to find those same regimes would go to extraordinary lengths to silence their criticism in Australia.

CHAPTER 9

COLLECTIVE PUNISHMENT: SAFE IN AUSTRALIA, DETAINED IN ETHIOPIA

In the cases of Hakeem and Rahaf, we saw how the governments of Bahrain and Saudi Arabia flexed their authoritarian rule beyond their borders. They tried to convince weaker governments to do their bidding and compel the return of 'errant citizens' to punish them for actions that supposedly brought 'shame' to their governments. Yet transnational repression extends all the way to Australia too.

Refugees resettled in Australia might feel safe. They might finally be comfortable enough to join protests or speak publicly about abuses by their home government. But some authoritarian regimes excel at collective punishment – detaining or harassing family members who remain, to silence criticism from abroad.

The situation gets worse, when abusive officials from authoritarian governments travel overseas and feel confident enough to take action against diaspora communities who criticise their rule. That's why governments concerned about human rights need to carefully consider the records of foreign officials from authoritarian governments when approving their visas. The story of collective punishment meted out against relatives of Ethiopian Somali protesters in Australia shows what can happen when there is a failure to vet foreign government officials for their role in human rights violations.

*

It all started with an email to Human Rights Watch's Australia account from a Hotmail address in late June 2016. The subject line read 'Innocent Civilians Have Been Detained in Ogaden Region in Ethiopia.' Unsure about the email's significance or its relevance to Australia, my colleague forwarded it to me.

The email explained that security forces had recently arrested dozens of people in Ethiopia's Somali Regional State (historically referred to as the Ogaden after a Somali clan by that same name), located in the eastern part of Ethiopia, bordering Somalia, Somaliland, and Djibouti. Those arrested were relatives of people protesting in Australia against a visiting Ethiopian government delegation. The email was from the chairman of the Ogaden Association in Western Australia. I had never come across him or the association before, but I had heard of the Ogaden because Human Rights Watch had previously reported on atrocities there.

As I read it, sitting at my desk in the Sydney office, part of the message sent a chill down my spine:

My relatives including two of my brothers and two of my uncles are among those detained and some have [been] tortured; their properties have [been] confiscated and their children were kicked out from their homes. So I would like to have a meeting with you in order to explain the extent of this issue and provide more evidence, documents and reports.

We regularly get emails from people requesting assistance, but as a tiny office, unfortunately, we cannot help everyone. And it can be difficult to know which claims are legitimate. But this one stood out. I wanted to know why people in Ethiopia were being detained because of a protest in Australia.

With my curiosity piqued, I agreed to a meeting and asked the chairman to send through relevant documents. He wrote back straight away and said since he was in Perth, he would send one of his contacts in Sydney to meet me instead.

Responding to that email set off a chain of events.

Like Hakeem, refugees from Ethiopia's Somali Regional State felt safe in their new country to speak up about abuses at home. But their home state at the time was ruled with an iron fist by its regional president, Abdi Mohamoud Omar who did not tolerate dissent, even – it appeared – when that took place halfway around the world in Australia. He still had a way of punishing his opponents – through their relatives at home.

As a global organisation, Human Rights Watch was well-placed to investigate these disturbing allegations. For the victims of these abuses, speaking out publicly entails serious risks of reprisals, so researchers must develop creative methodologies to conduct research and corroborate facts. In this instance, ultimately the sustained documentation of serious human rights abuses helped lead to the arrest and likely prosecution of a state leader.

Before meeting the Ogaden Association representative, I did some reading about Ethiopia's Somali Regional State. Most of the five million residents of the state are ethnic Somali, and also Muslim. Ogadenis are a Somali clan and speak Somali language. About a third of Ethiopia's population is Muslim, making it the second largest religious group after Ethiopian Orthodox Christians. Ethnic Somalis are spread across country borders in the Horn of Africa: when putting lines on maps, colonial powers didn't give much thought to how that would affect people living there.

I had visited Ethiopia once in 2003, almost fifteen years earlier, so I vaguely knew of Somali Regional State. Backpacking through East Africa with my boyfriend and another friend, we'd entered Ethiopia from Kenya through the southern border town of Moyale, about 200 kilometres to the west of Somali Regional State, spending the night in a basic guesthouse.

We had to hitch through northern Kenya and southern Ethiopia – there were no public buses due to the risk of what locals described as 'bandits.' That was the only time I heard mention of the Ogaden. I remember sitting in the back of a truck filled with Ethiopian men and women and us three foreigners.

Bouncing along the road in the dust was as close as I got to the Somali Region. We didn't venture further east. It was known to be a dangerous area – off-limits to tourists.

The Somali Region is one of eleven ethnic regional states in Ethiopia, in addition to two city-states, nine of which gained autonomy in 1992, with their own parliament and president.[1] It is one of Ethiopia's poorest and most underdeveloped regions.[2] Much of the state is arid, and people living in rural areas are traditionally livestock herders. The region has very low levels of literacy, poor infrastructure, and weak governance, due to years of neglect from the central government.

The region has also been wracked by conflict. In the 1970s, there was a full-blown war between Ethiopia and Somalia and ever since there have been more complicated local insurgencies with a confusing kaleidoscope of groups, backed by Somalia or Ethiopia, or Eritrea to the north.

The main insurgent group since the mid-1990s was the Ogaden National Liberation Front (ONLF). In 1992, the ONLF was a peaceful political movement that won the majority of seats in the regional parliament. But after agitating for independence, they fell out with the central government and eventually took up arms against Ethiopia.

The human rights situation in Somali region was summed up in a story published in *The Economist* which stated:

Before August 2018, the Somali region was the most ill-treated place in all of Ethiopia, tyrannized by its then state president, Abdi Mohamoud Omar, who had waged a scorched-earth campaign against secessionist rebels for more than a decade. Backed by the central government, Abdi, and his heavily armed special police force, the Liyu, murdered and raped civilians, imprisoned and tortured tens of thousands of alleged rebels, and, according to Human Rights Watch, committed crimes against humanity.[3]

This is the back story to how, on a Thursday afternoon in mid-July 2016, Shukri Shafe, an Australian Ethiopian Somali man from the Somali Regional State, came to the Human Rights Watch office in Sydney.

In Ethiopia, Shukri had been a junior judge in the regional court system. Here in Australia, he drove for Uber. Shukri's black curly hair was short, with a distinctive shock of white in the front. He looked in his late thirties, but it was hard to tell his exact age. He gently placed a plastic bag filled with documents on the table in the conference room where we met. I asked one of our interns Matthew Abbey to sit in the meeting with me and take notes.

Shukri spoke excellent English, but his voice was soft, so one had to lean forward to catch everything he said. Abdi Mohamoud Omar (also known as Abdi Illey), the President who 'tyrannised' the Somali Regional State, had recently visited Australia, and Shukri wanted us to understand exactly who he was.

In 2006, in his capacity as judge, Shukri ordered the release of three men who prosecutors accused of being ONLF members without sufficient evidence.

In Somali Regional State, the judicial system was prone to political capture. Security forces regularly detained civilians – especially Ogadenis – without any judicial process at all, accusing them of being ONLF members or supporters. A young judge, perhaps Shukri did not realise that ordering the release of suspected militants would attract the attention of authorities and in turn, make himself a target.

Shukri explained he was arrested on September 8, 2006, while on holiday in a neighbouring city of Dire Dawa, about 150 kilometres from the Somali Regional State capital of Jijiga. He said paramilitaries took him to an unofficial jail.

I was detained without charge for one night. Abdi Illey and the military intelligence were there. Abdi Illey was then in charge of the Somali Regional State's Bureau of Security. He beat me with the back of his hand, he hit me so hard that my teeth came through my lip. Two of his bodyguards held my upper body and two others held my legs, and they threw me like an object into the back of a ute. They began to stomp on me. I thought I may have sustained a rib injury.

Shukri described how the next day he and several others were transferred to a military camp and placed in cells underground for several days. He said Abdi Illey was at the camp when they arrived, and there were seven or eight men standing around in military uniforms.

> There was a woman amongst the five of us detainees. Abdi said to the woman, 'If you don't confess to being ONLF then all these men will be in a queue to rape you.' We were all given a paper that said we were against the government, a part of the resistance, but I refused [to sign it]. We were only ever let out [of the cell] for interrogation and torture. We remained in this situation for six days.

After that, Shukri said he was transferred to a military camp inside Jijiga Prison where he was held for a further sixteen months and tortured regularly. He pulled out a document from the plastic bag on the table and gave it to me. It was a letter from the International Committee of the Red Cross confirming his detention in the camp.

I was horrified by what I was hearing, but I wanted to know more. Shukri's careful composed demeanour and the way in which he spread the documents on the table, made him seem very credible. The lawyer in him was carefully presenting the evidence.

Shukri went on:

During this time, I was tortured every week. We were hand-cuffed with our arms over our legs, with the legs pulled up. They would put a rod under our legs and hang us up, so our head falls back, and we hang upside down. I would be hung upside down for periods of fifteen minutes and they would hit my buttocks and feet. It was very painful. They would keep us like this for fifteen to twenty minutes.

Shukri tried to illustrate the torture by acting it out on the floor to show us. Our meeting room has big ceiling-to-floor glass windows that served as one of the walls, like a fishbowl. He had his back to the glass wall, but I could tell my colleagues on the other side were wondering what on earth was going on. Matthew was scrambling to take notes. I could see from his wide-eyed expression, he was shocked by what we were hearing. Shukri continued:

One man became unconscious during the torture. Another man confessed to an explosion that he didn't commit – it occurred in the city while he was in prison. Abdi Illey was present for some of these interrogations when we were hanging upside down and hitting us with the stick. The stick was like a rubber hose with an iron bar inside. Once, Abdi Illey thought the officer was not hitting hard enough [so] he took the stick himself to hit.

At this point, as he told his story, Shukri broke down in tears. It was clear that talking about it made him relive the torture. I told him to take his time and got him some water. He continued:

It was the Federal Court that ordered my release. I was able to get a letter out through a relative, and I asked him to take it to the mobile Federal Court. They ordered my release on 25 December 2007. I was scared they [the paramilitaries] were looking for me again so I hid in Jijiga for five days, before fleeing to Somalia and later Kenya.

He explained how he lived in Kenya as an urban refugee rather than in a camp. After marrying his wife (who was an Australian citizen) in 2009, he was granted a family reunion visa and came to Australia in November 2010. Shukri showed us his UNHCR document from Kenya which verified his status as a refugee.

Then he reached into the plastic bag and pulled out a very battered copy of an old Human Rights Watch report – dated 2008. It documented abuses in the conflict between the Ethiopian government and ONLF. I remembered it: when it came out, I'd just joined Human Rights Watch in New York, but I was busy with our various crises in Asia – the war in Sri Lanka, the aftermath of the cyclone in Burma – and I hadn't paid close attention. It documented the Ethiopian military's brutal counter-insurgency campaign, in which civilians were deliberately and repeatedly attacked, as well as being detained at facilities including military bases like the one where Shukri was tortured. The report was titled *Collective Punishment: War Crimes and Crimes against Humanity in the Ogaden area of Ethiopia's Somali Region* – Ethiopian soldiers singled out the relatives of ONLF suspects for retribution.[4] People were at risk simply by virtue of their perceived affiliation with the ONLF. It reminded me of the Tamils in the Sri Lankan civil war. Ethiopian troops carried out killings, rape, and torture in the Somali Regional State. They displaced entire communities, ordering villagers to leave their homes before burning them down. Human Rights Watch researchers found that these abuses amounted to crimes against humanity and war crimes, among the most serious violations of international law.

Shukri put the palm of his hand on the cover of the report: 'This report has saved a lot of lives. It was a scorched earth campaign. After the report, the killings were not so open. There were still cases of torture and rape. But they stopped burning villages after this report.'

It made me feel quite emotional to know someone had carried one of our reports halfway across the world and held onto it for years because it documented the crimes that they had experienced. I photographed Shukri holding the report – I wanted to share it with our Africa team and let them know the impact of their work. Sometimes, our work seems futile – it was hard to know if it made a difference. And then, other times, like this, I knew it mattered to some people more than we ever knew.

As regional head of security in the Somali Regional State, Abdi Illey had established a regional police force known as 'the Liyu police' (Liyu means special in Amharic, Ethiopia's main language). The Liyu police were made up of ethnic Somalis, including Ogadenis, so they came from the same communities that they were deployed to infiltrate and intimidate. With Abdi Illey as state president, their powers were broadened even further, and they 'eventually took control of almost all security functions once held by the regular police, the custodial police, and the federal military' including running detention facilities and prisons.[5] Allegations of serious human rights abuses in the region continued including killings, rape, arbitrary detention, and forced displacement.

The month before I met Shukri, in June 2016, Abdi Illey visited Australia as a part of a delegation with two other regional state presidents from Ethiopia. I later learned the Australian government facilitated the visit for Ethiopian state leaders to understand how Australia's federal system works. They met with federal and state officials in Canberra, Victoria and Tasmania. Like Australia, Ethiopia's federal system gives considerable autonomy to its states. But to me, the trip sounded suspiciously like a junket, given the challenges of governing Ethiopia were starkly different to Australia. Such trips can be common to build rapport between friendly countries.

Shukri got out his phone and showed me how members of the delegation had proudly posted photographs to Facebook from their meetings with Australian diplomats. I wondered why Abdi Illey's participation in a high-profile governmental tour had raised no alarm bells for anyone at the Department of Foreign Affairs and Trade (DFAT). Shukri said it was Abdi Illey's second visit to Australia.

Besides official meetings, Abdi Illey also met with members of the diaspora – there was a large Ethiopian Somali community in Melbourne. According to Shukri, this was to drum up support for himself and root out those who challenged the government or supported the ONLF. These are communities far from their homeland but still bitterly divided. Shukri said Abdi Illey's meetings with the diaspora were announced on social media and that he 'wanted to find out who his supporters are by their attendance at his events, and also to see who resists his power'.

Members of Shukri's community protested against Abdi Illey's visit. Shukri said he first drove to Canberra, where they interrupted a community event where Abdi Illey was speaking. He showed me shaky images on his smartphone with people shouting angrily in Somali language. As I flicked through the images, Shukri described how he felt seeing Abdi Illey again:

When I saw Abdi, it brought back the pictures in my mind the day he put me in an underground cell . . . it was dark, cold, I was handcuffed and hanging from the roof. I was tortured. In Canberra, I felt like I was being victimised again in a country of freedom, a civilised country where people's human rights are guaranteed.

265

From Canberra, Shukri and others drove to Melbourne to join a larger protest. Shukri told me his version of events, and the rest I pieced together from interviewing other protesters and viewing photos and videos. The TV network Channel Seven also reported on the protest in their evening news bulletin.

Sunday, 12 June 2016, was a sunny winter's day in Melbourne. The demonstration took place on a street outside a conference venue in an industrial part of Epping, a suburb about 20 kilometres north of Melbourne's city centre. There were protesters, as well as Abdi Illey's supporters, and Victorian police present to keep the peace between the two groups.

Abdi Illey's supporters had hired the Epping site for a community meeting with him. It looked like a place to hold wedding receptions, a 1980s-style rectangular building with mirrored tinted windows, set back behind a car park, surrounded by shrubbery. A pair of steel gates provided access in and out of the car park.

About a hundred of so protesters from the Ethiopian Australian diaspora stood on the street outside the venue. Some of them had fled Ethiopia's authoritarian regime, and they objected to the visit of the Ethiopian government delegation. They carried flags and banners saying things like 'No to Abdi Illey' and 'Australia Stop Aiding Dictatorial Regime in Ethiopia'. The mainly male protesters shouted and jostled and filmed one another using their smartphones.

Meanwhile Abdi Illey and several of his supporters stood in the car park inside the gated property of the conference venue. Some of this group were actively filming and photographing the protesters using their smartphones. Later, a protester I interviewed told me he recognised the person filming them as someone from the Ogadeni community in Perth.

A dozen or so police officers formed a line between the protesters and those trying to enter the venue through the gate. Several scuffles broke out, but police largely kept the two groups separate.

Shukri said he recognised one of the men accompanying Abdi Illey as someone he went to school with. He said the man recognised him too and came closer to speak to him. Shukri said: 'He threatened me at the protest saying, "Give me fifteen minutes and I will show you that I will punish you. You will come back to me begging." I told him, "Hey, this is Australia. You can't punish me; this is not Ethiopia." He replied, "I will punish you another way. Give me fifteen minutes and you will see."'

It was a chilling threat. After the protest, Shukri and several others went to a local restaurant. Several hours later, his relatives messaged him from home, his mother (in her seventies), his sister and three brothers were all arrested.

I asked Shukri if there was any other possible reason why his family could have been targeted. Was he sure that it was in relation to the Melbourne protest?

'A neighbour of my mother said the Liyu police asked Mum, "Are you the mother of Shukri? Your son created trouble for the president!" before taking her away. The neighbour said they beat her as they took her out of the house.'

He also said it had happened to others. He confirmed that his sister's ten-year-old child who witnessed the arrest of his sister said the Liyu police asked his sister the same thing, 'Is Shukri your brother?'

Within hours, other protesters started receiving frantic calls and texts on instant messaging apps from friends and family members back home in Ethiopia asking them, 'What did you do?!' It was horrifying to think that halfway around the world people were rounded up and detained because of the actions of their relatives in Australia. It was the textbook definition of 'collective punishment' – the title of our 2008 report.

Shukri said Abdi Illey's supporters had set up an informant network in Australia. I'd heard of informant networks in other diaspora communities. Over the years, members from the Cambodian, Uyghur and Rwandan communities had approached Human Rights Watch concerned about others in their community effectively spying on their human rights activities back to the embassy. Sometimes, it was a blurred line as to whether behaviour that felt intimidating and threatening was actually unlawful.

Cambodians complained about going to protests or community events where unknown people took their photograph without permission. Taking a photograph isn't a crime and linking the photographs to later reprisals was difficult. Still, it had a chilling effect – some were too afraid to go to public events. They tried to keep their heads down and avoid politics. Living in Australia, they found themselves forced to pick a political position on their home government, and if they didn't take a position – that too could be considered proof of a lack of loyalty.

In this case, amongst the Ethiopian Somali community in Australia, there was no doubt about the purpose of pro-government supporters taking photographs of the demonstrators. Protesters were identified and on that basis their family members were picked up.

Australians may wonder how this can happen. How relatives in another country can be rounded up so quickly without any legal process at all? But Ethiopia in 2016 was the textbook example of a police state. The government strictly controlled the internet and mobile technologies to monitor and surveil communications. Across rural Ethiopia, even in the absence of digital records, the government maintained control over its citizens through extensive networks of informants and a grassroots system of surveillance.[6] The authorities kept lists of 'anti-government families', noting who was connected to who, and noting who in the diaspora criticised the government.

Shukri claimed the only way to free your relatives was to record a video statement with pro-government supporters pledging allegiance to the Somali State government, and specifically mentioning Abdi Illey's name. Shukri and others showed me examples of these videos which I couldn't understand, but they reminded me of forced confessions. The videos were posted on Somali State television and social media as propaganda. Shukri explained that this was not just happening in Australia, but also in the diaspora in the US and Europe.

'The [Ethiopian Somali] community in Australia is divided in their views. We feel fear, we feel intimidated. Bringing Abdi Illey here is facilitating him to commit further crimes. Bringing him here is victimising people back home and here. Controversial persons like this should not be invited to Australia. That is why we wanted to inform you about this.'

Shukri showed me letters that his community sent to the then-Justice Minister Michael Keenan and Immigration Minister Peter Dutton complaining about Abdi Illey's visit. They hadn't had any response. They turned to Human Rights Watch, because they did not know who else could help them.

I asked if he had reported the matter to Australian police, but he hadn't – because the crimes were in Ethiopia he didn't think they'd be able to do anything. I urged him and others to make complaints to the Australian Federal Police as soon as possible.

I had expected the meeting to take about thirty minutes, but it had been more than two hours. I told Shukri I'd need to discuss the allegations with my colleagues in the Africa Division, but if we could corroborate his story, it sounded like something we would be able to investigate further. The next day I sent Matthew's detailed account of the interview to Felix Horne, our researcher covering Ethiopia, and to Leslie Lefkow, who had actually interviewed Shukri as part of the 2008 report and was now a Deputy Director in the Africa Division.

Meanwhile we found social media posts and photographs on Australian government accounts and websites, confirming that they had hosted a delegation including Abdi Mohamoud Omar in Canberra. I recognised one of the senior DFAT diplomats. We copied all the web pages: I didn't want them disappearing once we started asking questions.

Felix, based in Canada, wrote back overnight saying he'd received similar emails from diaspora groups in Australia. He knew exactly who Abdi Illey was and said Ethiopian Somalis in Europe and North America had experienced similar problems.

We agreed to do further interviews with the community in Australia and raise the matter with the Australian government. A Human Rights Watch statement documenting the abuse would serve as a powerful public record to explain why governments should not issue visas to those implicated in serious human rights violations. I hoped the publicity might lead to pressure for family members in Ethiopia to be released, but Felix was not optimistic – he thought it could just as easily lead to further retaliation, and the community had to understand those risks if they wanted to proceed and go public. I said I would explain this to everyone we interviewed.

Despite being our Ethiopia researcher, Felix had only been to the country once since starting with us in 2010. That year, Ethiopia passed a law effectively outlawing groups like ours –

it made illegal any work carried out by a foreign NGO that touched on human rights or governance issues. The Ethiopian government had deported a previous Human Rights Watch researcher and blocked another from entry at the airport. The overall climate of repression made it impossible to travel and carry out human rights interviews in-country.

So Felix had had to be creative, like other researchers who work on closed countries, like North Korea, China, or Iran. He'd built contacts with diplomats, journalists, diaspora communities, and people who had recently fled the country. He used satellite imagery and digital verification techniques and conducted interviews remotely using encrypted apps to keep in-country sources safe. Despite these challenges, he'd built an impressive profile of reports on issues ranging from digital surveillance, and the lack of media freedom, to killings and arbitrary detention of ethnic minorities in various parts in the country. On this subject, however, we'd have to do without sources in Ethiopia. Even an encrypted app would be far too risky and place our sources in danger.

Over the next two months, I interviewed ten people from the Ogadeni community in Sydney and Melbourne. Most people spoke to me on the condition of anonymity. I checked and cross-checked facts by asking people what they saw and heard at the protest, and to confirm the situation of their family members back home. All of it supported Shukri's account. Two people overheard Shukri being threatened and identified the same person who threatened him. The interviewees described how not only their relatives were detained, in some cases, livestock was confiscated, and properties were seized too. There was no legal process.

One of the Ethiopian Somali Australians in Melbourne told me:

After the protest finished, [our] relatives were arrested back home for no reason. Their camels, their houses were taken. These people know nothing of Australia. The reason we were protesting was because we were trying to show solidarity to our people back home. We wanted to be the voice for them, since they have no voice, since they cannot speak against the government because they're scared they'll be killed.

He expressed his frustration and fear: 'But now, I don't feel safe here. I thought I was safe. I came here as a refugee. I thought now I will be in a free country.'

He stopped for a minute looking down at his hands and thinking about what to say next.

Even now people here in our community are scared to come and talk to you. I asked them, come, and speak to this lady. Tell her what happened. But they are too afraid. Can you imagine, in 2016, people living in Australia who escaped from Ethiopia, who are still scared of Ethiopia. They can't even express their opinions; they can't say anything.

His voice quivered and he put his hands in his pockets. It was a cold day, and he was wearing a dark coat. I didn't know what to say. I agreed with him. I found it sickening that the repressive authoritarian state followed people all the way to the land where they should be free and safe.

As I conducted the interviews, some interviewees acknowledged they supported the ONLF. Others did not but fleeing the Ethiopian government's abuses was why many of them were in Australia. I learned that some family members initially rounded up were later released, particularly the sick and elderly, sometimes

on condition their Australian relatives make a video apologis-
ing to Abdi Illey for their 'anti-government' behaviour. Shukri's
mother and sister were freed after about five weeks in detention.

We decided to put together a video of our own to accompany
our statement. For security reasons, we obscured the identities
of the protesters we interviewed – we filmed their hands, and
backlit their bodies – but Shukri wanted to show his face. He
said Abdi Illey already knew of his involvement in the protests
in Australia.

Camerawoman Mayeta Clark and I flew to Melbourne to
record the video. We visited the street in Epping where the
protest occurred so I could do a short 'piece-to-camera'. It was a
quiet suburban street lined with trees, with a mix of commercial
and industrial buildings – I found it hard to imagine it full of
police and protesters. I recognised the metal gates to the parking
lot and the building labelled 'Golden Star' that I had seen in so
many cellphone videos.

We'd just started filming on the street when a middle-aged
man emerged from the Golden Star building and started yelling
at us to put the camera away. Coming out onto the street, he
tried to stop us from filming, waving his hands in front of the
camera. Calmly, we told him it was a public place and we had
the right to film. I warned him that if he didn't back off, I would
call the police. But he grew increasingly agitated, blocking our
camera, and shouting close to my face.

So I made the call and within five minutes a police car arrived
with two cops, a man, and a woman. We described what we were
trying to do, and the male cop relayed to the man exactly what
we had said – that yes, we had the right to film on the street,
it's a public space. Funny how when it's said by an armed man
in a blue uniform instead of by two young women, the effect is

immediate. The man backed off and disappeared back inside the building. We continued filming without any further incident.

As we completed our video interviews, we sent the footage to our multimedia team in New York who put the package together. Felix worked on the press release.

Our introduction to Australia's Ethiopian Somali community came at a hectic time for our Sydney office. We were juggling multiple projects, including supporting a colleague visiting Nauru to interview refugees and asylum seekers. We worked on the Ethiopia project when we could.

As we prepared our documentation, I began to register our concerns with various Australian officials about Abdi Illey's visit both orally and in writing. I informed them about the repercussions for relatives of protesters who were Australian citizens. We wrote to DFAT formally with a list of questions prior to releasing our public statement, so that we could incorporate their views. They responded by letter saying that they intended to raise recent events of concern with the Ethiopian government. In response to our question as to why Abdi Illey was issued an Australian visa given his problematic human rights record, DFAT wrote:

> All non-citizens wishing to enter Australia are assessed against relevant public interest criteria, including foreign policy interest, national security and character requirements in accordance with relevant legislation. This includes foreign officials with potential character concerns or subject to allegations of human rights abuses.[7]

It was a deliberately general and unhelpful response.

In the letter, DFAT confirmed what Shukri had told us, that Abdi Illey had visited Australia twice – in 2012 and 2016.

The letter noted 'both visits were funded and instigated by the Ethiopian government'.

DFAT's response did not explain why the Australian government allowed Abdi Illey to visit, despite his troubling human rights record. I found a parliamentary speech made by Justice Minister Michael Keenan from 2014 mentioning human rights violations in the Ogaden and that he had met with members of the diaspora who had raised concerns about 'allegations of rape, torture, genocide and kidnapping'.[8] He said that 'Australia has raised the issue of human rights within the Ogaden region directly with the government of Ethiopia, including through representations made by Australia's ambassador there as recently as 15 January this year.' So surely, Australia was aware of Abdi Illey's problematic human rights record.

Cynically I wondered if Australia turned a blind eye for economic and political reasons. Australian companies in mining, energy, and agriculture were exploring trade opportunities there. We discovered that in July 2016 an Australian trade delegation had visited the country.

A strong public statement from Human Rights Watch would mean that in future there could be no actual or feigned ignorance about Abdi Illey's rights record – by Australia or any other democratic government. We would set out the facts so that any immigration officer making visa 'character assessments' would have publicly accessible information about exactly what can go wrong if a known human rights abuser is invited to a country and then uses that visit to intimidate and threaten people from that county in their new home.

As we prepared our report and video, I talked to the ABC then-evening news program, *Lateline*, proposing that they consider a deep dive into this story. I had had positive experiences working with them on other topics. *Lateline* were keen and worked on their own investigative piece, and we agreed to put out our releases simultaneously. Initially it was meant to be released in late October, but their interview schedule pushed it back to Monday, 7 November.

My heart sank when they suggested the date change. It wasn't ideal – that was the same week as the 2016 US Presidential election. The election would likely drown out other news, so I agreed with reluctance.

'It better be worth it!' Felix wrote to me.

In late October, a few days before the release, I spoke to Shukri to check if he had any final updates on family members or if anything had changed.

Shukri said his three brothers remained in detention. But then he told me about a UN official, Mustafa Omer, from Ethiopia's Somali Regional State, who worked in Nairobi. Mustafa had publicly criticised Abdi Illey and the Somali regional government. In a social media post, Mustafa said that Liyu police rounded up his father and younger brother back home and that his brother was executed in front of his father.

Shukri shared Mustafa's heartbreaking Facebook post with me. It was horrifying to read. Just like with the protesters in Australia, apparently Mustafa was given an ultimatum to retract his criticism of the regime or else his family would pay the price. The Facebook post said:

> The Somali Regional State President Abdi Mohamud Omer today executed my younger brother Faysal Muhumed Omer ... My brother is not killed because I oppose the government (which by the way is my constitutional right) and in any case my opposition should not lead my family

members to death. This death is ordered to prove a point: Abdi Mohamud Omer is the most powerful person in Ethiopia and nobody can save anyone he doesn't like. As I promised I will not rest one day before I get justice for my family but more importantly for the thousands of people suffering like me but lack the strength to say no to injustice.

It was a brave statement. And it wouldn't be the last we would hear from Mustafa Omer.[9]

I asked Shukri if he still wanted to go ahead, given security concerns for his family members. I told him we could postpone it or cut him out of the film if he was not comfortable. *Lateline* would understand. But Shukri stayed firm, telling me the information needed to be made public. He felt that he needed to take a public stand against Abdi Illey, otherwise those back home and in Australia would continue to live their lives in fear.

Monday, 7 November, came, and we were hastily preparing to release the report and video.[10] I was excited to watch the *Lateline* story that evening. But things didn't go to plan. Lateline pulled it at the last minute due to an internal problem. I was upset. We couldn't hold back our release – it was already with several outlets embargoed and so we pushed ahead. But it was frustrating, because we had counted on the *Lateline* story to build the initial coverage.

The *Lateline* piece aired the next evening, Tuesday, alongside segments anticipating the US election outcome.[11] It was powerful, compelling and at eleven minutes an unusually long package for an evening news program. It delved deeper into the issues around the video-taped 'pledges of allegiance' to Abdi Illey in exchange for the release of family members. The journalist even confronted some members of the pro-government community here in Australia.

I thought it was excellent. I was just gutted about the timing. The big media splash that we had hoped for did not exactly go to plan. But at least the story of Shukri and other Ethiopian Somali Australians was in the public domain, and it would still have a lasting impact. To their credit, *Lateline* did another follow-up story in early December.

In the days after our report and video came out, our office was flooded with email messages of thanks from Ogadenis in Australia and around the world. They did not care about the US election; they were just happy that someone was paying attention to what was happening in Somali Regional State.

A few weeks later, Shukri called with both good and bad news. When I answered the phone, I was sitting at my desk eating lunch. Shukri spoke in his usual calm measured voice. The good was that his three brothers and several other family members of the protesters had been released. They were skinny and malnourished after nearly six months in detention. Shukri said his brothers were still wearing the same clothes they wore when they were arrested, but at least they were alive. I felt so relieved!

'That's great, Shukri, I'm so happy for you!' I said.

But then the bad. Shukri's tone turned solemn, his sister and her husband were picked up by the authorities. It was like a revolving door of detention.

By this stage, Shukri's family were too scared to talk to him directly, so he was speaking to them via intermediaries in a third country. But the arrests seemed to be a direct result of him speaking out. He was obviously worried sick about the fate of his sister. She was forty-seven years old with ten children.

I suddenly lost my appetite. We had discussed the risk of reprisals, but that doesn't make it any easier when it happens. It's always a tough decision to know whether or not to go public.

For months afterwards, I would second-guess that decision. Should we have done things differently? Perhaps we should have been more adamant that Shukri not share his identity. Would it have made any difference? The publicity did have a positive impact in getting Shukri's brothers and several others released. But the new detentions were hard to accept.

Lateline's follow-up story included the reprisals against Shukri's sister and brother-in-law. The Ethiopian embassy denied they were in government custody, but we knew that the central government did not run Somali Regional State, they left everything to the state government, run by Abdi Illey. We kept DFAT informed and urged Australian officials to press for the release of Shukri's relatives. Months went by. Other relatives of Australian protesters were freed. The husband of Shukri's sister was released.

One small positive thing was at least we knew where Shukri's sister was being held, in a police station rather than a prison or military camp. Family members could take her food, and occasionally see and talk to her. But months turned into a year. Finally, in early 2018, I got a message from Shukri that his sister was free. She was ok, he said, and back with her children. But that was all he knew.

About a year after our report came out, one of the protesters we interviewed got back in touch to say his brother, Ali (pseudonym), who had been detained in Somali Regional State had fled to Kenya. He left because he faced ongoing harassment by the Liyu police about his brother's activities in Australia. I asked if my Human Rights Watch colleague in Nairobi could interview Ali to learn more about his experience.

In Nairobi, our assistant researcher on Somalia interviewed Ali and provided many details of the violence and reprisals faced by relatives of protesters in detention. Their treatment was even worse than I had feared.

Ali confirmed that Liyu police came for him on 12 June 2016 – the same day as the Melbourne protest. They took him and five others in a vehicle and drove them to the top of a small mountain near the town of Qabri Dahare.

'At the mountain, we met eight people who were arrested from different towns and villages the same day including my mum. I was really surprised to see my mum there. We were all asked to sit there. We were not told why we were arrested.'

He said a lorry arrived and they were taken in the vehicle with about fifty others to a police camp, where more people arrived, including Ali's sister. About seventy people total were at the camp, men detained separately from the women. Liyu police transferred half the people to another camp, but Ali was in the group that remained. Officers then started to interrogate them about the activities of their relatives in Australia, and with the interrogations came beatings.

'He [the Liyu police officer] asked us whether we knew why we were arrested? We said no. He said, "You are relatives of bad people who demonstrated against our president in Australia." He said, "The government is everywhere, it is in Australia, it is in every house in Ethiopia, and it is everywhere in the world. We now want to see what your relatives can do for you".'

Ali explained that the beatings continued every time the Liyu police officers interrogated him. Some of the older and sick people in their group were released after about a week, including his mum.

After several months, the officers moved them to a different hut and Ali said he was detained with three men who said they were the brothers of Shukri Shafe in Australia.

'We were sleeping on the ground; we were given a small dry bread every twenty-four hours. The Liyu police came and beat us every night. I was taken outside the hut at night and was beaten with sticks and the back of the gun. I would become unconscious. They kept asking me for my brother's number which I did not know.'

In November, one of the men became ill. Ali was transferred to a police station and the beatings stopped. This timing was soon after the release of our report and the *Lateline* story. Ali was released in late November 2016. He was not brought before a court the entire time and a family member had to act as a guarantor for his release. Ali had no home to return to because their property was confiscated so he joined his wife and children who were living with their in-laws. Still, intelligence officers kept turning up to question him, so after several months he left for Kenya, leaving the rest of his family behind.

I felt very sad reading the transcript of the interview. It confirmed everything we had been told by the Ethiopian Somali community in Australia. It filled in many gaps in how the Liyu police treated the relatives after they were picked up.

Following our report, in late 2016, Australian officials confirmed that Abdi Illey would not receive a visa to travel to Australia again. Felix said our work would be significant for Europe and North America too. I took comfort in the fact that these horrible events hopefully would not occur again and that Abdi Illey's world at least had gotten a little smaller.

My work on Ethiopia's Somali Regional State largely ended there, although I kept in touch with Shukri occasionally. But Human Rights Watch wasn't done with Abdi Illey. Under his abusive rule, it was hardly surprising that a broader pattern of arbitrary arrest, detention and torture in the state began to emerge.

From 2016 to 2018, separately from our Australia report, Felix was interviewing Ethiopian Somalis in refugee communities in Kenya and other countries. He started researching a notorious prison in Jijiga, known as 'Jail Ogaden' because so many Ogadenis were detained there. Most of those inside Jail Ogaden were accused of affiliation with ONLF, only a handful ever saw a court.

Felix and other colleagues interviewed seventy former prisoners, as well as government officials and security forces including Liyu police. The interviews uncovered a pattern of horrific torture and mistreatment of detainees at the prison, and disgusting detention conditions. Detainees described electric shocks to their genitals, rape, being publicly humiliated and forced to carry out sexual acts in front of others, prisoners tortured to death and their rotting corpses remaining in the cells for days.

We also had twenty-five hours of leaked video testimony from prison guards at Jail Ogaden. In 2011, officials carried out an evaluation of prison guard performance and filmed it at the request of Abdi Illey. Years later, one of his advisers left Ethiopia and shared the footage with Human Rights Watch. In the video, the guards confirmed what prisoners were telling Felix in interviews. They described in chilling detail torturing, raping, and extorting money from prisoners, at the direction of various senior officials at Jail Ogaden.[12]

The prison staff were managed by the Liyu police, who reported to Abdi Illey. And Abdi Illey himself appeared regularly to personally harangue the detainees.[13] As Felix got closer to finalising the report on Jail Ogaden for release in mid-2018, the political situation was changing rapidly in Ethiopia.

In April 2018, after months of unrest leading to the resignation of Ethiopia's former Prime Minister Hailemariam Desalegn, the Parliament appointed a new Prime Minister, Dr Abiy Ahmed. In his first few weeks in office, Abiy quickly announced sweeping reforms.

He released political prisoners and reached out to Ethiopians in the diaspora and banned opposition parties like ONLF. After years of repressive rule in Ethiopia, Abiy suddenly seemed like a ray of hope. He officially ended two decades of hostilities with Eritrea – for which he won the Nobel Peace Prize in 2019. But by late 2019, the rights environment had begun to deteriorate in the country, with increased reports of security force abuses, communal violence and mass displacement.

Fast-forward to 2020 and Abiy Ahmed's reputation as a peaceful reformer was in tatters. In November 2020, the Ethiopian government and its allies, including Eritrean forces, began military operations in the northern Tigray region against the region's ruling party, the Tigray People's Liberation Front (TPLF). Human Rights Watch has documented horrific massacres and sexual violence by all warring parties. It has also documented a brutal ethnic cleansing campaign against Tigrayans by Amhara forces and officials in Western Tigray. Many of these abuses constitute war crimes and crimes against humanity.[14]

But back in mid-2018, the Tigray conflict had not yet started and Abiy was still considered a reformer, getting international recognition and praise for his efforts to bring peace to Ethiopia. Somali Regional State, however, was not high on his list of priorities.

That changed after our Jail Ogaden report came out on 5 July 2018. The report attracted widespread attention in international, Ethiopian and Somali media, especially because of the leaked material from prison guards. It became a source of shame for the Ethiopian central government who distanced themselves from the abuses and demanded answers from Abdi Illey and regional officials.

Under pressure from the central government, in the days that followed, Abdi Illey suddenly announced that all prisoners would be released from Jail Ogaden. He stated the prison would be closed and converted into a mosque. Many prisoners were released that day. Several days later, the Prime Minister's office asked Abdi Illey to resign, apparently at least in part due to Human Rights Watch's report.

Publicly, Abdi Illey now began throwing his support behind Abiy and his reform agenda, asking for forgiveness. Meanwhile he blamed the former head of Ethiopian intelligence, Getachew Assefa, for directing the abuses by Liyu police in Somali Regional State. But in Jijiga, there were bouts of sectarian unrest in early August 2018. Groups loyal to Abdi Illey including Liyu police and a youth militant group attacked non-Somali people and offices, burning homes and property, as a message to the central government. The Ethiopian Orthodox church said eight of its churches were burned, and more than fifteen people, including seven priests, killed. Hundreds lost their homes.

On 6 August 2018, after ignoring calls to step down for several weeks, Abdi Illey finally resigned as president of Somali Regional State. On 27 August, federal police came to his compound and arrested him on suspicion of human rights violations primarily related to the deadly violence earlier that month. He was flown to Addis Ababa, where he remains in prison.

It was a stunning development for the man who seemed untouchable for a decade. He travelled the world spreading fear amongst diaspora communities while ordering the detention of families of his enemies. Now, finally it seemed he would face justice for his crimes.

Felix finally visited Somali Regional State and Jail Ogaden for the first time in 2019.

'Abdi Illey's arrest meant everything to the victims of these abuses. People had completely given up hope. It was the first step towards healing and recovery for a society that had been destroyed for many years. This was an important step towards justice and accountability,' Felix said, reflecting on his trip there.

In a final twist of fate, the person Abiy appointed to replace Abdi Illey was Mustafa Omer. Mustafa was the UN official who blamed Abdi Illey for the killing of his brother in that heartfelt Facebook post.

As state president, Mustafa shut down Jail Ogaden permanently, and announced plans to turn it into a museum. He established an auditor general to investigate the state government finances. Attempts were made to re-train the much-feared Liyu police, though abuses continue to be reported, and a truth and reconciliation process has been initiated.

At the time of writing, Abdi Illey is still in custody awaiting his trial. Human Rights Watch first named Abdi Illey in our July 2008 report, *Collective Punishment*. Ten years later, in 2018 we named him again in the *Jail Ogaden* report. Two months later, he was detained. I still remember that day when Shukri came to the office and pulled out that battered Human Rights Watch report that he had carried with him across the world. In 2020 he returned to Ethiopia for the first time since he fled in 2007.

We write our reports to expose the truth about human rights violations. We always hope the perpetrators of those abuses will be held to account for their crimes. But getting justice can take a very long time. It takes patience and persistence.

And I was about to discover that even in countries like Australia where the rule of law is protected, with functioning civil society, independent media and judiciary, some of the most egregious human rights abuses against certain minorities persist. They continue because the people experiencing those abuses have been largely invisible and excluded from the political conversation. And because it's not just about exposing the abuse, but about fundamentally changing the system.

PART IV

AUSTRALIA

CHAPTER 10

A MENTAL HEALTH CRISIS IN AUSTRALIA'S PRISONS

Aboriginal and Torres Strait Islander readers should be aware that this chapter contains images and names of people who have passed away. In many Indigenous Australia communities, it is common practice that when a member of the community dies, the person's name is changed in accordance with cultural beliefs. Names here are shared with the consent of the families.

On the morning of 16 December 2015, a thirty-six-year-old Aboriginal man, Mr Jackamarra, left home for what he thought would be a routine court appearance in Broome, Western Australia. His mother, Georgette, recalls that he called out as he left the house, 'Mum, put the chicken out, I'll come back and cook you supper.'

But Mr Jackamarra, whose first name is withheld for cultural reasons, never came back. Hours later he was found dead, hanging from the partition of a shower block in Broome Regional Prison. More than three years later, the coroner ruled it a suicide.

In 2019, a few months after the coroner released her report into his death, I visited Broome and met with Mr Jackamarra's family – Georgette, his younger brother Shaquille, and two of his aunties. We ate breakfast together at a café, sitting outside on the verandah. I was there as part of a Human Rights Watch investigation into deaths in prisons related to inadequate mental health support.

Despite the fact that forty per cent of all prisoners in Australia have a mental health condition, prisons are not designed with mental wellbeing in mind. Detention exacerbates psychological problems – I saw that already on Manus Island. At worst this manifests with self-harm and suicide. A significant proportion – one fifth – of Indigenous deaths in custody are people with mental health conditions who end their lives.

Experts have been repeating and reiterating the same recommendations to reduce Indigenous deaths in custody for decades. Back in the 1980s, the problem of systemic failures resulting in Indigenous people dying in custody was so acute that in 1987 the federal government announced a Royal Commission inquiry into the issue, the highest level of public inquiry in Australia. Over four years, the Royal Commission examined ninety-nine deaths over a period of ten years and issued a damning final report in 1991 with more than 330 recommendations.[1] In the thirty years since then, there have been more than 512 Indigenous deaths in custody, at least 320 of which have taken place in prisons.[2] Deaths continue because many of the Commission's recommendations were never implemented, especially those that focused on preventing First Nations people from going to prison in the first place.

Today, Indigenous people are still imprisoned at disproportionate rates. In Western Australia, for example, Aboriginal people make up four per cent of the population, and yet they are thirty-nine per cent of the adult prison population.[3] As I saw in our research, simply changing the physical infrastructure of prisons to remove tools for self-harm is not enough: governments need to address the overincarceration of Indigenous people, provide alternatives to incarceration, and ensure those who wind up in prison get culturally appropriate and adequate mental health support.

Despite growing up in Perth, I had never visited Broome before. It always felt such a long way away – more than 2000 kilometres into the Kimberley, that vast and sparsely populated region in the remote northwest, a twenty-four-hour drive or a two-and-a half-hour flight from Perth. In fact, both Darwin in the Northern Territory, and Dili, the capital of Timor-Leste, are geographically closer to Broome than Perth. When I got there the intense colours of the landscape took my breath away. The vibrant red earth was a stark contrast to the turquoise water and the bright blue sky. A fine red dust settled over every surface, on my skin, and in my eyes. It's a stunningly beautiful place.

The town is on the traditional lands of the Yawuru people who have lived in the area for over thirty thousand years. Broome (or Rubibi as the Yawuru people call it) became a pearling town in the 1880s. In the early days, pearlers shamefully rounded up Aboriginal people and forced them to dive for mother-of-pearl shell, to make buttons for shirts. After a few years, changes to regulations and diving technology ended the forced labour and attracted low-paid divers from Japan and Southeast Asia. This made Broome an unusually diverse town for that time, although the neighbourhoods were largely segregated between whites and non-whites. Today, the town population of 16,000 is still a melting pot of Aboriginal, Asian and white

Australians – twenty-eight per cent are Aboriginal.[4] Mr Jackamarra himself was of mixed Aboriginal and Indonesian heritage.

Broome is also famous for Cable Beach, twenty-two kilometres of squeaky white sand, with crystal clear water, camel rides at sunset, and the occasional crocodile. While tourists mainly stay in resorts watching the sun set over Cable Beach on the west side, the town centre or Old Broome is a few kilometres away on the eastern side of the peninsula. Wide streets are lined with modest buildings, many made from corrugated iron. The prison is in the middle of the town, across the road from the courthouse, marked by a small sign beside an enormous boab tree. The towering tree is a momentary distraction from the imposing steel fences, razor wire, and exterior prison walls.

The prison itself is a mix of dilapidated and decrepit old buildings. The coroner's report into Mr Jackamarra's death described the prison as 'a structure both confronting and depressing'.[5] Part of the prison dates back to 1894, while most of its cell blocks were built in 1945, making it the oldest working prison in Western Australia. Hot and dry through the Australian winters, Broome is uncomfortably sticky and monsoonal through the summers.

The Western Australian government has an independent Inspector of Custodial Services who conducts routine inspections of each prison every three years, writing up reports for the parliament. The reports are public and are a valuable insight into what occurs behind those prison walls and how prisoners are treated. Sifting through the reports, I could see government officials had debated whether to shut the Broome prison down for years. As discussions dragged on, it remained open, with only small renovations to improve the very worst bits. The Inspector described it as 'unfit for purpose' in both his 2017 and 2020 inspection reports.[6]

When I visited in 2019 with my colleague from Sydney, Nicole Tooby, it was hot, still, and quiet. Unlike other prisons I have been to, there was a lack of work, recreation, or other activities for prisoners. In the middle of the day, prisoners sat around smoking or sleeping in the cells.

When we visited, all the staff appeared to be white, and most of the prisoners were Black. This, amidst the rundown buildings and fences, made me feel like I was walking into some archaic system of apartheid. Later, officials from Corrective Services told us in a letter that Broome prison has the highest proportion of Aboriginal staff in the state, at thirteen per cent.[7] Perhaps we happened to be there on a day when there were no visibly Aboriginal staff working, or more were subsequently recruited. The Inspector of Custodial Services described Broome as an Aboriginal prison – since eighty per cent of detainees are Indigenous.[8]

The prison has one remaining building from the 1890s period – the bull pen – a large caged-in enclosure with a roof used to house Aboriginal prisoners at the turn of the twentieth century. A horrific relic of Australia's brutal colonial past, it is heritage listed. When we visited, it was a recreational area for prisoners, with a pool table inside. When the prison was desperately overcrowded, authorities had debated whether to use the bullpen as a temporary dormitory, but thankfully decided that given its painful history, it would be culturally inappropriate.[9] But I struggled to understand why the bullpen has been given a heritage listing yet remains in active use in a jail that houses mainly Aboriginal prisoners. It felt to me to be deeply insulting to Indigenous people and a daily reminder of what their ancestors had to bear.

In comparison, just over 200 kilometres away in Derby, the West Kimberley prison had been built in 2012 specifically with the cultural needs of Indigenous prisoners in mind. But while West Kimberley was a better option for Aboriginal prisoners in the region, the courts were still in Broome, and so its aging prison is still in use, especially for prisoners who are on remand (not yet sentenced) or in transit.

Being 'on Country' or remaining on the region of land to which they and their ancestors belong, is very important to Aboriginal people, who have a spiritual connection to the land. Sending Indigenous people to prisons far away or 'out of Country' also makes it more difficult for them to cope and for relatives to visit.

Mr Jackamarra, who lived in Broome most of his life, was all too familiar with its prison. His family said he had been there more than twenty times. He was well known to the prison staff. He had a personality disorder and experienced paranoia and severe anxiety.

That morning in December he went to court around 9 am for a bailable arson offence. Mr Jackamarra was expecting his uncle to sign the bail surety and thought he would be home by dinner time. But he had forgotten to tell his uncle about the court date, and when he tried to call him that morning, he learned that his uncle was working in an Aboriginal community located several hours drive away. At the court, Mr Jackamarra was placed in the court's holding cells until someone could be located to sign the surety.

As he waited in the cell, Mr Jackamarra became more and more distressed. He asked for his mental health medication. He began banging his head against the wall. He said he wanted to go 'across the road' which officers assumed meant to Broome prison. I know all this from the detailed coroner's report into his death.[10]

A private company was responsible for security at the courthouse. Their officers observed Mr Jackamarra, and around

11.40 am, they transferred him across the road to the prison in the back of the truck once it became clear that the bailpapers were unlikely to be signed that day.

One of the staff involved in the transfer coincidentally was an uncle of Mr Jackamarra. The uncle told the coroner he seemed 'lively and pretty happy' and he did not think he was at risk of self-harm.[11] Staff noted in their records that he had been banging his head against the wall, but somehow that fact was not shared with prison authorities.

Officers took Mr Jackamarra to the prison's maximum-security unit, where it's standard procedure for remand prisoners to be held. The prisoners and officers call it 'maxi'. Some prisoners called it 'the cage'. Maxi is a bleak and cramped unit at the back of the prison made up of seven cells with twenty-eight beds. Besides the cells, there was a communal sitting area caged in on all sides, making it very claustrophobic, in direct line of sight to prison officers. One cannot see the sky.

The Inspector's 2017 report on Broome prison referred to conditions there as 'inhumane and degrading'. He noted, 'Cells were crowded, with some prisoners sleeping on cell floors. There was no space for physical activity or recreation, and most prisoners spent their days lying around watching television, or sitting out on the dark, caged-in patio.'[12]

Shortly after arriving at prison, Mr Jackamarra spoke to a female Aboriginal prison support officer. She was a familiar face; she had known him since he was a child. In that conversation she recalls him crying and calling her Aunty. When she asked him, 'Are you going to do anything silly?' he replied no, he wouldn't be there for long. She understandably thought that meant he would be released soon on bail. Based on that conversation, the officer did not assess him to be at imminent risk of self-harm.

But less than three hours after he arrived at the prison, he took his own life by hanging himself with his shirt in the shower block. Another prisoner discovered his body shortly after 2 pm. Mr Jackamarra's death is one of hundreds of Indigenous deaths in Australian prisons that have occurred since the Royal Commission issued its report in 1991.

Pat Dodson was the only Aboriginal Commissioner on the Royal Commission into Aboriginal Deaths in Custody. He is a Yawuru man from Broome, now a Labor senator. Prior to entering parliament in 2016, Dodson had a long track record as a prominent activist. He also is a former Roman Catholic priest.

Reflecting on the lack of progress since 1991, he puts it down to a lack of political will, accountability and institutionalised racism. 'When I was at the Royal Commission, my job was to look at underlying issues – health, housing, education, employment, services for people with mental health issues. Underlying issues weren't being addressed, and they still aren't really. We keep doing justice on the cheap. There got to be an accountability board of some type, the accountability structures are all internal, they are not delivering the outcomes that we expect.' He continued, 'People in institutional structures – police, courts, custodial officers, medical people slip back into the modus operandi and allow stereotypical views to dominate their responses to people of colour. Making reforms to institutional structures has to happen.'

Mr Jackamarra's death in 2015 showed a litany of failures. His mental health history was well known to prison authorities. The coroner's report showed that he had a history of self-harm attempts during other prison stays and in admissions to Broome hospital. She recommended changes in how information is shared between prisons and medical services and urged that mental health staff should assess prisoners with mental health needs or past self-harm attempts on arrival. But she also noted that 'there was no therapeutic alternative to keep an inmate safe, in the circumstances of Mr Jackamarra.'

This is the bleak reality of Australia's prison system. Locking any person up in a confined space for an extended period of time increases the risk of self-harm, but this is especially acute for Indigenous people with mental health conditions who have tried to hurt themselves before. Dodson told me, 'It's about Western culture and an authoritarian system butting up against people from a very different culture and societal background. The frustration, anxiety and the total diminishment of someone in custody leads them to take their lives, because they feel like the only power they have left. Custodial people normally are not attuned to that.'

Mr Jackamarra's story was all too familiar. He first entered a juvenile detention centre at age eleven for breaking and entering. His mother, Georgette, is slim with sad eyes, and softly spoken. Sitting at the café, looking at old family photographs on a smartphone, Georgette described how when police detained him as a child, she would ask to be locked up in the cell with him to play cards until he calmed down. 'His anxiety went through the roof in detention,' she said.

Mr Jackamarra had repeated stints in and out of juvenile detention and adult jails from age eighteen. He struggled with substance and alcohol abuse. As he got older, the offences became more violent. 'Off the drugs, he was a happy, caring person,' his godmother said. 'He loved life, he loved his family, and he loved his mum.'

His mother and brother said he was trying to turn his life around for his two children. He was taking a hospitality course at a technical college. His passions were cooking and music. Returning to prison that day was likely triggering for him. His mood swings could be volatile, he had been prescribed mood stabilisers, the medication that he was asking for when he was detained.

The week before his death, Mr Jackamarra presented to Broome Hospital's emergency department having paranoid delusions. The hospital referred him to the Kimberley Mental Health and Drug Service (KMHDS) in Broome for a possible placement in a rehabilitation facility. But no further action was taken. I was troubled that despite the warning signs, the system had failed him.

My colleagues scrutinised more than a hundred coronial inquest reports as part of our investigation into deaths in custody related to disability in Western Australia.[13] We found that in the decade from 2010 to 2020, of 102 people who died in WA prisons, sixty-one had a disability, including mental health conditions. Of those with a disability, fifty-eight per cent died because of a lack of support provided by the prison, suicide, or violence. Half of those deaths were Indigenous people.

Many of these deaths were preventable. They occurred because of the severely inadequate mental health support in prisons. This was a problem that I'd already seen firsthand. More than two years before that visit to Broome, I accompanied my colleague, Kriti Sharma, an expert in disability rights, to visit six male and female prisons in Western Australia and Queensland to examine the treatment of prisoners with disabilities.

We interviewed prison staff – including officers, medical staff and counsellors, prisoners as well as their families, lawyers, and those providing services in prison. When people think of a 'disability', they often think of people who are blind, deaf, or have a physical impairment. But disabilities include cognitive impairments or affecting thinking, perhaps from an acquired brain injury caused by a head trauma – a car accident or a bashing – or cognitive impairments from alcoholism, substance abuse, or foetal alcohol syndrome. By far the most common disabilities in prison are mental health conditions – including autism, schizophrenia, paranoia, bipolar disorder, depression and severe anxiety.

While eighteen per cent of Australia's population has a disability, this goes up to nearly fifty per cent when it comes to the Australian prison population.[14] But Australian prisons are not built with people with disabilities in mind. They are designed for punishment.

People with acute mental health needs can end up in jail for myriad reasons. Sometimes their mental health condition hasn't been properly supported in the community and they act in ways that put themselves or others at risk. Some of the people we interviewed committed crimes to obtain money or drugs. Others as a cry for help. Sometimes people did not understand they were breaking the law. As a result, prisons have become a vast repository for people with mental health conditions. Overrepresented among them are Indigenous people with mental health needs, who face a criminal justice system that is discriminatory, racist, and far more likely to send them to prison than other Australians.

My colleague Kriti is from India and travelled to Australia to do this research. Kriti is in her early thirties and has a warm, caring and bubbly personality. She is wise beyond her years and has led investigations on abuses against people with disabilities all over the world. Immediately before she came to Australia for this project, she had just completed a harrowing report examining how people with mental health conditions in Indonesia are shackled or chained up in the absence of proper psychological support.

Kriti coached me on how to interview people with disabilities. She helped me to learn what to look out for, what kinds of questions to ask, how to obtain consent, and importantly, when to stop a line of questioning.

Even the process of entering a prison environment as an approved visitor is stressful. You can't take anything with you – no bag, no wallet, no phone, no recording equipment. Just a notebook and a pen. You pass these items through an X-ray machine and walk through a metal detector. Your photo ID is taken from you upon entry.

I wore trousers instead of a skirt or dress for comfort and security. Prisons officials tell you to avoid wearing the same colour as the prisoners' uniforms (which might be green or maroon – it varies from prison to prison). You'll be issued a panic alarm and are shown how to use it in case of an emergency. Some of the panic alarms are automatically set to go off if they move into a certain position. Every time I went to the loo, I was worried I was going to accidentally set it off and have prison officers bursting into the bathrooms!

Once you've passed through the security checkpoint where you register and get your alarm, you enter the prison compound – a seemingly endless sequence of doors locking and unlocking, walking past fences or walls compartmentalising the different areas of the prison. As a visitor, I immediately felt dependent on the staff who were required to escort me from place to place.

Kriti and I toured different prisons to get a better sense of the physical surroundings and the layout of individual units. We interviewed the staff, trying to understand their perspectives on problems. Then we would turn our attention to the detainees.

Prisoner interviews present numerous challenges and involve navigating a range of ethical dilemmas. It is even more challenging when you add cognitive disabilities or mental health conditions into the mix. These were some of the most difficult interviews I have done in my career. We cannot protect people in prison. At the end of the day, we go home. The inmates and the officers remain.

The first issue is how to conduct interviews safely but privately. At times, the officers were reluctant to leave me alone with an interviewee, particularly some male prisoners with mental health conditions who might be volatile or pose security risks. I would negotiate with the officer accordingly, and we'd try to find a suitable space balancing privacy with safety. It was never appropriate to interview someone in the presence of an officer. If that was the only alternative, I would just decline to do the interview altogether.

One prisoner I interviewed in Western Australia had an obsessive compulsive disorder. He proudly showed me his spotlessly clean cell, everything neatly in place. I asked him if he had a cellmate. He said no, he stabbed the last one, so now he was alone. I asked him if he'd faced any bullying in prison, and he admitted being bashed up a while back, but then he threw boiling water on the person who attacked him, so they didn't do it again. That interview took place outdoors in a courtyard. We were under camera surveillance, but officers couldn't hear our conversation. Other prisoners sat in the courtyard at other tables, smoking and drinking cups of tea.

Other interviews took place in rooms with large windows or common spaces with good visibility. If the security risk was lower, especially in women's prisons, we'd use private meeting rooms. We didn't interview anyone inside their cell.

Building rapport with prisoners is difficult. Time is limited. They were sometimes hauled out of their cells to talk to us, in which case we were immediately associated with the officers. We always clarified to interviewees that we are independent of the government, and we write reports that will be made public and that is how their testimony (which is anonymised) will be used. We also explained that we can't help to get them out of prison.

Sometimes prisoners did not want to talk to us – we were strangers and not Indigenous, they didn't know whether to trust us, and sometimes they just didn't care. Other times, the officers said, 'This one won't talk to you,' but sometimes they would when we approached them directly. Those with severe cognitive impairments or conditions like schizophrenia sometimes find it difficult to communicate. So that means we need to be extra careful getting consent, asking for it several times throughout the interview, and clearly explaining how we will use the information. It's always important to avoid re-traumatising people, especially people with mental health conditions who are in a closed environment. Our 'do no harm' policy at Human Rights Watch means that both the process of interviewing and exposure of abuses through reporting should consider any additional risks or negative effects for the interviewee. If it is not possible to mitigate these risks, then we should cease the work – either stop the interview or not use the information.

And then there is the matter of corroboration. Usually, we won't rely on just one person's allegation of an abuse. In prison, verification can be challenging. We attempted to carefully cross-check claims of abuses with other prisoners or staff without breaking confidentiality. So that means asking people open-ended questions and hoping they'll substantiate what you've been told.

302

For instance, if someone tells you they were raped by their cellmate and that they reported it, we need to confirm that a sexual assault was reported in that unit and see what action was taken, to see if basic facts of the story match up. So, we ask the staff, 'Have any sexual assaults occurred? In which units? When? What action was taken?' rather than asking about any specific case.

As part of obtaining consent to conduct an interview, we explain that information from the interviews will be made publicly available in a report that will be on the internet. We are careful to maintain confidentiality, and when disclosing abuses, we rarely revealed the prison where the abuse took place to avoid the possibility of retaliation. Everyone we spoke to was anonymised in our reports, unless they had passed away and we had consent from the family. We only shared specific information with prison authorities in a very limited set of circumstances, to protect someone's safety and where they gave explicit consent. I always gave my email address to those I interviewed so they had a means of getting in touch.

And then there's the lingo. When I started doing these interviews, Kriti, who had already travelled to several prisons around the state, kindly prepared a 'cheat sheet' for me of the terms she had picked up, so I would be able to understand. Her savvy skills and nous meant she'd already picked up some good Aussie slang.

A *screw* is a guard. *Cellie* is a cellmate. *Down the back* is being sent to a punishment unit. *Spends* are your canteen points or entitlements, that a prisoner earns through work or good behaviour. A *dog* is an informer. To *neck up* is to self-harm (attempt suicide). Then *Hakea. Acacia. Boronia. Melaleuca.* These words weren't slang. In Western Australia, someone named the prisons after native plants, perhaps thinking it brought beauty to ugly places.

Now when I see an Acacia tree or a Hakea flower I always think of the prison.

Visiting prisons is suffocating, I always felt slightly on edge inside. The hierarchies are immediately and clearly defined between those with power and those without. As a visitor, you are someone with power, with the freedom to come and go from those gates. And it's an artificially constructed world where random people of the same sex are confined together in a system built deliberately to discipline and punish.

At the end of the day, when we left a prison, Kriti and I would decompress. Since most of the interviews we conducted were one-on-one, we talked about interviews that went well, what didn't, and discussed strategies for interviewing more effectively the next day.

I'd try and do something nice at the end of each day to unwind. I'd go out for a run, a walk, or head to the beach for a swim. Being outdoors in nature and looking up at the big blue cloudless sky was calming. But it was hard to shake off the knowledge that you had left behind vulnerable people who were now locked in their cells for the night for the next twelve or thirteen hours. I couldn't get my mind off it.

Some of the prisons we visited were in and around Perth, the city where I grew up. It was a week before Christmas in 2016 and a scorcher of a summer already – extremely unpleasant if you are detained in a tiny cell without air conditioning and sometimes without even a fan. One was Bandyup Women's Prison. To get there, you have to drive through the Swan Valley, an area dotted with wineries – popular with day trippers from Perth. But Bandyup, like Broome prison, is publicly run and well past its prime. It was built in 1969. I had been there once before – when I was a law school student studying criminology in the 1990s. On that visit, I remembered meeting one detainee, a seemingly sweet old lady working in the prison library. I later learned that she was Catherine Burnie, one half of a notorious couple that terrorised Perth's southern suburbs in the 1980s engaging in a spree of abduction, rape, and the murder of several young women.

When I returned to Bandyup in that summer of 2016, it did not look like much had changed, but now it was desperately overcrowded. There were 360 prisoners living in a space that was designed for 209. The state government had recently converted part of a men's prison, Hakea, into a new separate facility for women, Melaleuca, named after a species of myrtle or tea tree, but no one had been transferred there yet.

At Bandyup, women were doubled up in tiny cells designed for one – which often meant someone sleeping on a mattress on the floor, next to an open toilet. It was disgusting, and oppressively hot – with temperatures in the low forties Celsius. Only one unit out of seven had air conditioning. That unit, of newer demountable buildings, housed prisoners who were pregnant, vulnerable, or unwell.

Everywhere else, prisoners had to make do with portable desk fans which they had to buy from the canteen. Locking people up in small rooms for fifteen hours per day in such heat without proper air flow felt inhumane. At Bandyup, one of the prisoners, Kate (pseudonym), explained the daily routine, 'At 7.15 am they open the doors [to the cells]. We are locked in again from 11.45 to 1.30 over lunch. Then dinner is at 5 pm. At 6 pm they lock the doors again. It's a long night. I'd prefer to be alone. There's a lot of cattiness between inmates.'

Kate was in her sixties. She had depression. She told me she had tried to burn down her house with herself and her family in

305

it. She shared her cell with two others. She had no fan, but one of her *cellies* did, so she was fortunate. She had arrived in Bandyup two weeks ago and had no money and no chance yet to earn her *spends* to purchase a fan.

When we visited Bandyup, forty-eight per cent of the prison population was Aboriginal. Many were 'out of Country' meaning they were not from Perth. Leanne (pseudonym) was from a town in the far north – near the Northern Territory border. She said she was on a brief visit to Perth when she was arrested and jailed for disorderly conduct. She'd previously been in prison up north, but this time, being out of Country it was more difficult. Leanne heard voices. She had a cognitive impairment, which she said was the result of a particularly brutal beating by her former partner.

Sally (pseudonym) was a Noongar woman in her twenties – vivacious and talkative. She said in a detached tone, 'I'm paranoid schizophrenic, like my mum.' Sally told me how as a teenager, a close relative died of a drug overdose in her arms. After that, she wasn't the same. She told me, 'I couldn't speak. At one point, I had a nervous breakdown. I wandered the streets. That was when I ended up in Boronia [another prison]. I lost my mind over there.'

Sally described her battles with drug addiction. 'I was homeless when I got out last time. No support. I got back on the drugs. I need to learn from my mistakes. Adopt protective strategies. I want to get on a methadone program. I need it for my mental health. I have no limits, that's my problem.'

Particularly among the Indigenous women with disabilities who we interviewed, there were recurrent stories of domestic violence, substance abuse, committing crimes with or for their partners, and ending up going to prison.

June Oscar is the Aboriginal and Torres Strait Islander Social Justice Commissioner at the Australian Human Rights Commission in Sydney. She's a proud Bunuba woman from Fitzroy Crossing in the Kimberley region – a four-hour-drive inland from Broome. At a speech in 2018 delivered at the University of Western Australia, she expressed her concern about the dramatic rise in incarceration of Indigenous women:

> We're locking up Indigenous women faster and more often than any other state. Incarceration should always be a last resort, so what is wrong, why is incarceration becoming one of the first responses to social issues in Australia?
>
> In the moments when these women have needed care and compassion and a system willing to respond to their needs, both in the immediate and long-term, they have been left with only authoritative judgement. Their prison cells, quite literally the physical manifestation of their complete isolation from all forms of support.[15]

June's words encapsulated the experiences of women I met inside Bandyup. Prison should be the last resort, yet so many Indigenous women were in a cycle of imprisonment and neglect. Mental health needs of women inside Bandyup were not being met. A damning 2017 report about Bandyup prison by the Inspector of Custodial Services noted: 'Mental health care at Bandyup remained crisis driven. It was not delivered in a holistic manner, and women suffering from depression or other psychological problems were missing out on support services.'

We heard a repeated refrain in male and female prisons at opposite ends of the country, from Western Australia to Queensland. Requests to see psychologists went unanswered for days, weeks, sometimes even months. Minor mental health conditions deteriorated. People started 'acting out' to get attention, harming others or self-harming – cutting themselves, swallowing things – whatever they could get their hands on. One man told me how he swallowed the batteries from a remote control so that he would be removed from the punishment unit. The sad reality is that the only way to get medical attention was to make your situation worse than others'.

In the very worst cases, like Mr Jackamarra's and dozens of other deaths in custody, people commit suicide.

Since the 1991 Royal Commission governments have taken some steps to change the physical infrastructure of prisons to try to reduce suicide. Prisons have identified and removed 'ligature points' (where things can be tied to) from most cells so that people cannot hang themselves. Things like razor blades, belts or shoelaces are forbidden, or their use is strictly controlled. But fixing the physical surroundings and removing tools for self-harm can only do so much if cultural and mental health support is lacking.

Solutions to address these problems are well known and include measures to reduce the numbers of Indigenous people who are incarcerated, through adopting measures to divert people from police custody, repealing punitive bail practices, and mandatory sentencing laws. Pat Dodson reiterated the main recommendation from the Royal Commission was about alternatives to incarceration, 'There still aren't other options for magistrates or police to send people to. For instance, we know what the behaviours of people are like when under the misuse of alcohol or drugs. There should be a place that is provided within a medical set up for when police officers are beyond their wits. They should, as a first response, take someone who is displaying signs of ill-health to that clinic where they can be held, supervised, and treated, rather than holding them in custody as a first response.'

Larger prisons may have crisis or safety units with inbuilt CCTV cameras to provide twenty-four-hour observation care for prisoners who are at acute risk of self-harm. These crisis units might be keeping people alive, but they are far from therapeutic. Improving mental health also comes through ensuring prisoners have adequate time outside their cells and meaningful human contact including with staff specialised in caring for people with mental health conditions. Peer-to-peer support (from other prisoners especially amongst Indigenous prisoners) can help and Aboriginal and Torres Strait Islander staff and more culturally appropriate mental health services delivered by First Nations organisations is required.

We visited several safety units at different prisons. The spaces were clinical, austere, and cold. 'This is not a place to get better. It's a place to keep them alive,' a prison psychologist told me.

Some crisis units were located as part of the medical wing of the prison, meaning access to trained medical professionals is close at hand. Some cells had padded walls to protect people from themselves. But putting anyone alone, wearing only a rip-proof smock in a small, padded cell, with the lights on 24/7 is enough to give anyone anxiety or depression. Not surprisingly, it tends to exacerbate rather than alleviate mental health conditions.

I saw this myself in the prisons we visited. In a safety unit in a prison in Queensland, I met shaggy-haired Brian (pseudonym) who had bipolar disorder and post-traumatic stress disorder (PTSD). I noticed abrasions on his forehead. He seemed sad and anxious. He confided, 'I was headbutting the walls. I'm agitated in here. I can't access anything to self-harm. I just want to die.'

Later, when I spoke to a prison psychologist, he told me: 'People like Brian should not be in prison at all, he should be in a proper mental health facility but there isn't space. The beds tend to go to people in the community, because the feeling is prisoners are being cared for in prison. Yesterday a bed almost came up for Brian, but then it is gone already to someone else.'

In another prison in Queensland, I met Tom in his twenties who had bipolar disorder and Attention Deficit Hyperactivity Disorder (ADHD). He told me, 'My son died a month and a half ago, he was twelve days old. They sent me to the safety unit for two weeks. I didn't self-harm before going to the safety unit, though I have in the past. The safety unit isn't good. The lights in there, they are on all the time. It drives you crazy those lights. You can't sleep. They make you stew on your problems. I would say anything to get out of there.'

Because people in the crisis unit are at risk of self-harm, the lights remain on, to ensure they remain under 24-hour camera surveillance. It's supposed to be for the prisoner's wellbeing, but it often feels to the prisoner like a form of sleep deprivation.

Prison is not just for punishment, it is meant to be a place for reform and rehabilitation. When I visited the prison in Broome, it didn't have a crisis unit, psychologist or a mental health nurse. It only had one very overwhelmed counsellor. Three and a half years after the death of Mr Jackamarra, the Inspector visited Broome prison again. The mental health services were abysmal. He reported that the only psychology services for prisoners were fortnightly telehealth consultations – a phone or video call with a psychologist based at a prison near Perth.[16] He noted that demand for the fulltime counsellor's services was so strong that they could only handle individuals in crisis or at risk of harm.[17] The Inspector wrote in his report, 'mental health care was largely reactionary. Staff expressed fear that too many vulnerable prisoners were escaping attention, and not receiving any service.' A staff survey conducted as part of the prison inspection found a quarter of the staff respondents felt mental health services were unacceptable, and more than half did not feel adequately trained in suicide prevention.[18] Clearly, there had been a failure to learn lessons and implement changes after the death of Mr Jackamarra.[19]

Our prisons research in Queensland and Western Australia in 2016 and 2017 formed the basis of a Human Rights Watch report, released in February 2018, *'I Needed Help, Instead I was Punished': Abuse and Neglect of Prisoners with Disabilities in Australia.*

The 2019 interviews with the families of prisoners who died in custody, led to a follow-up report in September 2020, *'He's Never Coming Back': People with Disabilities Dying in Western Australia's Prisons.*[20] That report focused on deaths in custody related to inadequate mental health care. Kriti researched and wrote both reports. I helped with interviews, providing the Australian context, particularly on recommendations and the advocacy strategy. It was a good match of our respective skills.

Both reports received extensive media coverage at the time of release, and support from some staff working inside prisons and Corrective Services. The Ministers of Corrective Services in both Western Australia and Queensland were predictably defensive and pushed back on calls to end solitary confinement of people with disabilities. But the reports had some impact. In 2018 and 2019, the Queensland government allocated an extra $2.9 million in annual funding to improve services to prisoners with a disability or mental illness.[21] Queensland also developed new tools to screen prisoners for intellectual disability upon entry into prison.

In Western Australia, Bandyup now has a new thirty-two-bed special unit to provide greater support to prisoners with mental health needs. And Western Australia's Inspector of Custodial Services now specifically includes disability and mental health in his inspection standards.

We submitted information to a new Royal Commission established in 2019 to examine the abuse and neglect of people with disabilities. It wasn't clear whether this Royal Commission would include prisons, so we urged the Commissioners to do so, and especially the situation of Indigenous people with disabilities who are incarcerated. It felt demoralising that another Royal Commission was looking at these issues, thirty years after a previous one had failed.

It all comes down to a dire lack of political will to improve prisoner welfare. Politicians think short term in terms of their election cycles and it's popular to be 'tough on crime', but that attitude ends up costing all of us. Politicians should address the social and financial consequences of using prisons to house large numbers of people who are mentally unwell. Because if we are serious about reducing recidivism then prisons need to be places that are better equipped to help people with mental health needs and intellectual disabilities. If not, then when they are released, they are even less likely to be resilient and able to cope with adjusting back to life outside.

Prison authorities in Western Australia and Queensland gave Human Rights Watch access to prisons to document these problems, because some individuals at the top recognised the problems and wanted solutions. Better mental health support makes for a healthier prison environment for both staff and prisoners. Being transparent and sharing the facts about what occurs inside prisons and how prisoners are treated in the first step towards genuine reform.

Back in Broome, I think of the red dust settling on the surfaces inside the prison, a reminder to prisoners of life outside. In May 2019, the Western Australian government committed to building a new facility near Broome with a cultural and rehabilitative focus for Indigenous prisoners. But things are moving at a glacial pace. A site was only confirmed in February 2022. Construction is expected in 2027–8.[22] Meanwhile, Broome Regional Prison is still in use. The inspector releases his periodic reports about its decay, and people held there continue to suffer largely in silence.

In June 2020, people all over the world marched to protest the death of George Floyd who was murdered by police in Minneapolis in the United States. His death touched a nerve for Black people around the world about racist policing. Tens of thousands took to the streets of cities and towns all around Australia in solidarity with the global Black Lives Matter movement. Protesters drew attention to the lack of accountability for Indigenous deaths in custody. It was a wake-up call for many non-Indigenous Australians that this country has its own reckoning with racist policies and deaths in custody.

Senator Dodson made a fiery speech in Australia's parliament where he lamented the lack of progress over the last thirty years, 'For too long there have been nice words and good intentions, but the lack of action and commitment has not seen a reduction in deaths in custody; it's seen an escalation in the social indicators that diminish First Nations people and diminish us as a nation.'

Human Rights Commissioner June Oscar also pondered what the Black Lives Matter movement means for Australia, where inequality and discrimination faced by Indigenous people for centuries continues in the cycle of incarceration. When asked by

The Guardian to reflect on her vision for the decade after 2020, she wrote poignantly:

> It is time we stopped pretending that meaningful change can happen in a system that is grounded in denial. So, in 2020, as a nation, we need to turn away from denial as usual and towards truth. Truth is difficult for many of us to confront, particularly the truths about the foundations of this nation and the ongoing impact of inequality on our people ... Change is possible when you tell the truth, or when you listen deeply and enable truth to be brought to the surface. The more truth is told, the more support for truth grows in this nation.[23]

The truth-telling has only just begun.

CHAPTER 11

ACADEMIC FREEDOM, CHINA AND AUSTRALIAN UNIVERSITIES

When I was at uni in Perth in the 1990s, if the Dalai Lama came to speak on campus, it would have been the height of cool. The Dalai Lama won the Nobel Peace Prize in 1989. By the 1990s, the spiritual leader of Tibet had achieved global celebrity status. Back then, no one would think twice about joining campus protests calling for a Free Tibet or hosting meetings on the rights of Tibetans.

Nearly two decades later, in 2015, the Dalai Lama did visit a university in Perth, the University of Western Australia (UWA). By all accounts the visit was a success, he spoke on the rather anodyne topic of 'The Importance of Education'.

But three years after that visit, the university's official student representative body, the student guild, passed a peculiar motion. It noted how a visit from the Dalai Lama could 'offend' some students and said the guild 'does not support the decision to host the Dalai Lama or his representatives at UWA.' It urged the university to liaise with the guild to ensure guests do not 'unnecessarily offend or upset groups within the student community.'

It was a strange position to take, and it seemed obvious that nationalistic Chinese students on the guild must have been behind it.

Students from China are entitled to voice their views on the Dalai Lama of course. But I was stunned to see how a revered icon of peace could be shunned as a divisive and 'offensive' figure.

The Dalai Lama motion spoke volumes about how dependence on income from international students from mainland China was changing the fabric of Australia's universities. Institutions that proudly championed free speech were becoming places where some sensitive subjects were best avoided.

Higher education is big business. In 2021, the sector was Australia's fourth largest export, right behind iron ore, coal and gas.[1] And students from China make up forty per cent of all students coming to Australia.[2] While the majority of Chinese students studying in Australia don't dare take the risk of getting involved in politics, a curious minority are keen to learn about democracy and human rights, and excited to use their studies in Australia to expand their world view. There is also another vocal minority who do not tolerate any criticism of the motherland. This nationalistic fervour has increased during the last decade under President Xi Jinping. Overseas students have become a target of the Chinese Communist Party (CCP)'s propaganda efforts to influence citizens abroad.

International students make vital contributions to life and diversity on campus. But the lucrative revenue from international education has meant some university administrators have become quick to shy away from topics that might offend pro-Chinese government students, like human rights in China, Tibet, Xinjiang, Taiwan or Hong Kong. Pro-Chinese government supporters have harassed and intimidated other students and staff on campus who express views critical of the Chinese government.

In 2020, I got a practical lesson in how this plays out when I myself became the target of a ferocious campaign by pro-Chinese government supporters over some comments I made on Hong Kong to a university publication. Being at the centre of a controversy is uncomfortable and stressful, but it can also be an opportunity to stand up and advocate for change.

This experience was also a reminder that institutions as well as governments are responsible for protecting rights. Universities need to be proactive in safeguarding academic freedom. And I saw how Human Rights Watch's detailed investigative reporting and sustained advocacy combined with political pressure made a difference.

1 August, 2020 was a sunny Saturday morning in the middle of the Sydney winter. I woke up with a hangover, hurriedly throwing some clothes in a bag for a weekend away with my girl-friends. It had been a busy week at work. I had done several media interviews about the protests in Hong Kong, including one with the communications team at the University of New South Wales (UNSW), where I was an adjunct lecturer in the law school. The university had contacted me seeking comments for a story they were publishing on their website and I gave them some quotes. With Sydney only recently out of lockdown, I headed to the pub after work on Friday evening, where I promptly consumed a few too many wines.

As my husband dropped me off at a friend's house in the morning, all I could think about was crawling back to bed. Instead, we were heading off for a weekend in the Blue Mountains, about ninety minutes from Sydney. Climbing into the car, my phone beeped with a text message. It was Sophie McNeill, the former ABC reporter at the forefront of helping Rahaf Mohammed in

Bangkok, and now my Human Rights Watch colleague, our brand-new Australia researcher.

'Did you see this?' She linked to a tweet by Badiucao, a Chinese-Australian artist and human rights activist.

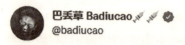
巴丢草 Badiucao ⚡⚡ ✓
@badiucao

An unacceptable disgrace.
@UNSW deletes tweet of an article about #HongKong human rights abuse by @PearsonElaine , AUS director of @hrw, over pressure from Chinese nationalists who r mobilized by Chinese app #Wechat (Weixin) and email Chinese consolate for "help" from Australia

9:08 AM · Aug 1, 2020 · Twitter for iPhone

402 Retweets   55 Quote Tweets   697 Likes

I hadn't seen it. That morning, it had taken all my energy just to pack and get my hiking gear on. I examined the screenshots attached to Badiucao's tweet trying to make sense of them. I could see he was upset, but I was struggling to put the pieces together. Some of it was in Chinese. One was a screenshot of a deleted tweet from @UNSW's account which included one of my quotes about Hong Kong. It said:

'Now is a pivotal moment to bring attention to the rapidly deteriorating situation in Hong Kong.' @UNSWLaw's Elaine Pearson says 'now is the time' for the international community to put pressure on China to wind back infringements on human rights.

It linked to the UNSW article. Nothing surprising there, I thought – that was indeed what I told the UNSW media team.

Then there was a screenshot of a letter from a Chinese law student calling the article 'totally unacceptable' and claiming it represented the view of the university because it was posted on the university's official news site. The student demanded an apology from UNSW and the withdrawal of the article. Another screenshot said that law students had complained to the Chinese embassy.

My drowsy eyes widened in shock. Besides my day job at Human Rights Watch, I taught the occasional human rights class as an adjunct lecturer in UNSW's law school and sat on the advisory committee to the Australian Human Rights Institute, which was part of the law school.

That past year, Hong Kong was rocked by enormous street protests. More than a million people, young and old, marched repeatedly against Beijing's encroachment on democratic freedoms. The Chinese government had promised Hong Kongers they would retain their democratic and autonomous form of government after handover from the British in 1997, for at least fifty years under the 'One country, two systems' principle. But protests erupted over a proposed law that would allow Beijing to transfer criminal suspects from Hong Kong to mainland China.

After months of demonstrations – at times violent – the government withdrew the extradition bill. But any victory by protesters was short-lived.

In response, the Chinese government rushed through an incredibly repressive national security law to quash freedom of assembly and free expression. In typical Chinese Communist Party fashion, the exact content of the bill was a closely guarded secret until it became law. On June 30, 2020, it passed.

After the law passed, we discovered it was even worse than analysts expected. It provided a checklist of the usual tools of tyranny: banning participation in protests, sweeping new powers to the police, creating new specialised secret security agencies, denying people rights to a fair trial in national security cases, imposing restrictions on civil society and the media, and weakening judicial oversight.

The law criminalised conducting advocacy about Hong Kong's human rights issues with foreign governments anywhere in the world. This was unprecedented. My colleagues in Human Rights Watch's China team published a detailed analysis of how the law would provide the legal pretext to stamp out demonstrations and support for democracy in Hong Kong.

When UNSW's media representative called me for an interview, I told them that the national security law was very problematic. It made all sorts of things that were ordinary and unremarkable in a democracy suddenly illegal. I suggested foreign governments should call on UN Secretary-General António Guterres to appoint a special envoy on Hong Kong, in line with a recommendation that parliamentarians from the UK, Canada, Australia and New Zealand had recently proposed. I didn't think twice about the interview. We called for UN mandates on crisis situations all the time.

The university published the article on its website on Friday 31 July, posting a tweet with one of my quotes, and a link to the article from the @UNSW Twitter account. I remember thinking at the time that it was a waste to publish it on a Friday afternoon, when it would get little attention. But clearly I was wrong. That morning, the university's media team had already referred a couple of journalists seeking follow-up interviews.

So, as I rode in the car, I was initially puzzled by Badiucao's tweets. I clicked on the link to the story in the tweet. The link worked. I saw that Badiucao had also sent a direct message on Twitter to alert me to the news:

Speechless, he wrote.

Badiucao (or Badi as I call him) is an artist, born in China but living in Melbourne, now an Australian citizen. He looks like a typical thirty-something Melbourne hipster, with stylish glasses and a bushy beard. His satirical cartoons largely mock the Chinese Communist Party. Initially, Badi kept his identity a secret for security reasons – 'the Chinese Banksy' some people called him. A filmmaker had even made a documentary about him and he would go on to win the Victor Havel Human Rights Prize for creative dissent, a prominent international award for free expression.

After authorities interrogated his family members back in China, Badi realised there was no use in keeping his identity secret anymore. Pressure from Chinese authorities had forced him to cancel an art show in Hong Kong in 2018. I had met Badi the previous year, when we connected over human rights concerns in China and Hong Kong. We were friends.

I replied to him:

Badi, as far as I know UNSW is standing by the article. The article is still accessible?

He wrote back immediately:

It was down a short period of time
And a tweet of it has been deleted

He forwarded me more tweets which claimed that the UNSW tweet and article had been deleted following pressure from the Chinese consulate and nationalistic students.

I responded to Badi:

Not sure what happened but they been asking me to do media on it, so I don't think they took it down due to pressure – it might just have been a glitch

He replied:

I think there is a chaotic decision on it
ask them why the tweet is deleted
I don't think it's a glitch

He forwarded me some more links from Chinese academics saying the article had been deleted. When I tried to access the story again, just a few minutes later, the link was broken.

I was confused. I called the UNSW media representative who had interviewed me for the piece – but as it was Saturday and she didn't monitor the university's social media accounts, she wasn't sure what was happening. She said she would get back to me.

Taking this all in from the car was making me feel queasy. My hangover intensified. I put the phone down and tried to concentrate on catching up with my friends. We hadn't seen each other in months. After arriving in the mountains, we went hiking for several hours.

I tried not to worry about it. But whenever we stopped and I opened my phone, there was a slew of new messages on Twitter. Random people were tagging me in posts about the article being censored.

As I pieced things together, it appeared that soon after UNSW posted the article and tweeted about it, Chinese social media users, some claiming to be students, had flooded UNSW's social media accounts with angry messages.

Initially, the university responded by tweeting again from its institutional account saying, 'The opinions expressed by our academics do not always represent the views of UNSW. We have a long and valued relationship with Greater China going back 60 years.'

But by Saturday morning, both tweets and the article were deleted. Within hours, the article appeared back online again, but on the law school page, not on the main media page where it had been previously.

My hangover was now long gone and I wanted to put my phone away for the weekend and relax. But the messages kept coming, and I was waiting to hear an explanation from someone at the university before jumping into the Twitter fray.

By 6.30 pm on Saturday evening I heard from Badiucao again:

巴丢草 Badiucao ✒️ ✒️ ☑️
@badiucao

⋯

now even the infamous Chinese nationalist tabloid GT
is joinning the scandal!
@UNSW make a stand!

> 🅖🆃 **Global Times** ☑️ @globaltimesnews · Aug 1, 2020
> 🏮 China state-affiliated media
> . @UNSW is under attack from outraged Chinese students after it published an
> article denouncing the "human rights issue" in Hong Kong. Although the article
> was soon deleted, students are still furious and demand an apology.
> bit.ly/39NjNMQ

7:16 PM · Aug 1, 2020 · Twitter for iPhone

22 Retweets   2 Quote Tweets   56 Likes

I had been resting in the hotel room, but sat bolt upright.
I had never been quoted in the *Global Times* before! It was the
Chinese government's primary English language tabloid, and
their story was entitled 'Australian university under attack for

article "interfering" in HK affairs'.[3] The article referred to me as 'Professor Pearson', and the inaccurate promotion made me smile, though the rest of the article did not.

It described how Chinese students had successfully pressured an Australian university over a 'controversial' article denouncing the 'human rights issue' in Hong Kong. Outraged students claimed to be 'ashamed to be a UNSWer' and denounced the article as 'blatant interference in China's internal affairs and support for "Hong Kong independence".' The article stated that as a result of student pressure, the university deleted the article.

I was stunned.

There was no reporting in Australian media, but coverage by a Chinese-government outlet gave the issue some international prominence. My Human Rights Watch colleagues in Europe and the US were now waking up on their Saturday mornings, seeing the same tweets and asking me what was happening. I told them I was still seeking clarification from the university and not to tweet.

We went out for dinner and returned to the hotel for a drink. While my girlfriends were messing around on their dating apps, I read out the *Global Times* story to them and tried to explain what was happening. We laughed at the absurdity of the situation, but deep down I felt worried. I wanted to get back to Sydney where I could focus on the situation properly.

When I woke up Sunday morning, there was a text from my husband, who closely follows Australian news and politics: 'I saw this thing on twitter about UNSW & China yesterday, but I didn't realise that it was about YOU!!' he wrote.

Now, I felt even more uneasy. The story clearly was no longer confined to a small group of China-watchers on the internet.

In some ways, there was an irony to me being targeted by pro-Chinese government supporters. Not because I am part-Chinese, but because I was more aware than most Australians of how pro-Chinese government supporters tried to silence or harass academics and students for their views on China.

Since 2015, Human Rights Watch had been tracking Chinese government threats to academic freedom in Australia and other countries.[4] Led by our China Director Sophie Richardson in Washington DC, I had helped by conducting some interviews with academics and students in Australia.

As more students from China studied abroad, reports began surfacing about problems faced by some students and academics who were critical of the Chinese government. It was like the Dalai Lama incident at UWA but happening everywhere. We started documenting incidents of censorship, surveillance and harassment of students and academics not just in Australia, but in Canada, France, the UK, and the US. Activities that many students take for granted – attending public talks, discussing politics in class became risky activities if they touched on certain topics, especially if you were a student from China.

These students may have hoped they could express themselves freely when studying in the West, but the long arm of the Chinese state effectively followed them wherever they went. Pro-democracy students described how the presence of other mainland students on campus made them feel under surveillance. They described receiving threats for comments they posted online or events they participated in. In some cases, authorities questioned their family members back home about their student activities abroad to send a clear message of intimidation. Chinese authorities were effectively saying, 'You might be out of the country, but we've got our eyes on you, and we know who your family is.'

It reminded me of the surveillance and harassment that Ethiopian Somalis living in Australia endured. And how they felt that despite being in Australia, they were still not free and scared of the Ethiopian state.

In 2018 and 2019, protests broke out on Australian university campuses in solidarity with the people of Hong Kong as well as ethnic Uyghurs who were facing mass detention in political re-education camps in China's Xinjiang region. Pro-democracy students from China who participated in the protests or who wrote on 'Lennon walls' – a mass of impromptu sticky notes of solidarity messages – said they felt threatened or monitored by other students from the mainland.

In 2019, Human Rights Watch held a screening in a Sydney cinema of a documentary film about Badiucao, *China's Artful Dissident*. Before the event, we received phone calls from anxious mainland and Hong Kong pro-democracy students who wished to attend. They wanted to know what security measures were in place to keep pro-nationalists out. Some asked if they should wear masks to obscure their identity. We hired security guards for the screening, but also cautioned that we were unable to vet everyone who attended the film. The event thankfully took place without incident, but it was a reminder of the concerns students faced in even deciding to attend a film screening.

For academics in Australia, teaching anything related to China also became a minefield. Classroom discussions that touched on sensitive topics like Tiananmen Square, Xinjiang, Tibet or Taiwan resulted in complaints from some nationalistic Chinese students, even in non-political classes. In 2017 in Newcastle, a Chinese student secretly recorded an exchange with a lecturer who referred to Taiwan as a country. The student said this was offensive and leaked the recording to Chinese-language media.[5]

327

I spoke to a lecturer who was a specialist in Chinese studies and taught students from the mainland in the social sciences. He said there was no point offering alternate views.

'The first year, I did teach Chinese students and I thought I would try giving them human rights materials. But it's not worth it. They just shut down and won't engage. They presume that it's part of some grand anti-China conspiracy.'

Self-censoring in teaching topics related to China seemed like it was becoming routine.

In April 2019, drawing on our research findings around the world, Human Rights Watch released a 12-point code of conduct, calling on colleges and universities to take steps to prevent the harassment of (mainly) Chinese students.[6] We urged universities to speak up for academic freedom, monitor and report any harassment and surveillance of students, and be transparent around research partnerships with Chinese government entities and institutions. It was intended to provide a starting point for discussions with both university administrators and governments. Here in Australia, I wrote letters to vice-chancellors, sought meetings, and responded to queries from journalists.

So I wasn't entirely surprised when my comments on Hong Kong sparked an outcry online from pro-Chinese government students. I had seen it happen to others, it just feels strange when it happens to you.

Social media users called for me to recant my views, to apologise to Chinese students, some urged the university to sack me. Some of them called me a terrorist. It was hard to know if the accounts were actual university students or pro-Chinese government trolls, but it was probably some combination of both. Some urged a boycott of the university. They felt that because they paid fees to UNSW, they could demand the silencing of views they did not like. Thankfully, most of the messages targeted the university rather than me directly.

One Twitter user started a list of hyperbolic demands in English and Chinese:

'Liberate the Campus, The Revolution of Our time'

1. Refund all fees of Chinese students and victims of anti-China propaganda immediately.
2. Issue an official apology to Chinese students.
3. Fire all UNSW employees involved in drafting, posting and quibbling for the terrorism supporting posts.
4. Principal [Vice-Chancellor] Ian Jacobs must step down for encouraging and allowing anti-China propaganda on the campus.
5. Expel all riot supporters and separatism sympathisers from the university.

By Sunday evening, despite the slew of angry Twitter messages and *Global Times* article, I still had not heard from anyone in the university's media team so I emailed the university's Communications director asking what had happened.

I woke up Monday morning to what felt like a barrage of media requests from Australian and foreign journalists. Sydney's main tabloid, the *Daily Telegraph*, ran a story about the fiasco with a large photo of me and the headline 'Academic cut off after criticising Chinese abuses in Hong Kong'. It wrongly claimed that I was the author of the article. That error was consistently repeated in much of the Australian press coverage.

Australian media focused on how a leading academic institution had effectively caved to the demands of pro-Chinese government students and censored an article about human rights in Hong Kong. As the incident gathered steam, and in the absence of any communication from the university, I felt I should clarify what occurred. I decided to do a Twitter thread instead to set the record straight:

@PearsonElaine
THREAD: I'm belatedly weighing in on a recent @UNSW article on Hong Kong which quotes me. I am an adjunct lecturer in law @UNSW as well as the Australia Director @hrw
https://law.unsw.edu.au/news/china-needs-international-pressure-to-end-hong-kong-wrongs . . .

Replying to
@PearsonElaine
Firstly, UNSW's media team approached me for the story and asked for my views on the human rights impacts of Hong Kong's national security law. I gave my views. The story was published by UNSW. I did not write it.

I understand there was a backlash from some pro-Chinese Communist Party supporters complaining about the article and asking UNSW to remove it.

A tweet from UNSW quoting me and promoting the Hong Kong story was suddenly deleted, and twice the story was removed briefly from the UNSW website, but then later reappeared.

It is back online – but it is not being promoted anymore on UNSW's main newsroom page. You can read it here: https://law.unsw.edu.au/news/china-needs-international-pressure-to-end-hong-kong-wrongs . . .

China's pro-CCP mouthpiece the Global Times also weighed in attacking the university for publishing the article:

Australian university under attack for article 'interfering' HK affairs[7]

I am seeking clarification from UNSW on what occurred. I hope UNSW will reaffirm its protection of academic freedom and make it clear that academic freedom does not mean caving to censorship demands by some people over views they disagree with.

Safeguarding the human rights of Hong Kong people is not something that should be controversial.
@hrw has long documented concerns about Chinese government threats to academic freedom at universities around the world, including Australia. All Australian universities should be taking this seriously.
[I linked to Human Rights Watch's Code of Conduct for Universities and Colleges to Counter Chinese Government Threats][8]

I posted the thread and tried to get on with other work.

Around lunchtime, the head of UNSW's Communications unit called me back and explained that the online campaign against the Hong Kong article had come as a total shock to them. He said they were concerned about the volume and tone of online comments flooding the university's social media accounts, something they had never experienced before. At that time, they made a snap decision, admittedly the wrong one, to remove the post. In putting the article back online, the university were standing firm by free speech for their academics. He justified deleting the tweets by saying there was ambiguity about whether my views in the article represented the university's position – which was how some Chinese social media users interpreted it.

While I empathised with the university media team struggling to take control of a fluid situation over a weekend, I felt their response was weak. I wasn't advocating for anything particularly controversial – I had merely called out human rights violations in Hong Kong. I felt frustrated and abandoned by the university's pitiful response, especially given the interview was something they had initiated.

All day, my phone kept ringing and pinging with text messages. Conservative radio and television chat shows that were never usually interested in human rights stories were suddenly inviting me on as a guest. I declined as I was concerned that some commentators would manipulate the incident into a xenophobic anti-Chinese rant. On Twitter, I noticed 'UNSW' was trending and seeing that gave me a sick, anxious feeling. I was used to engaging with the media regularly, but not usually about myself.

That week, my colleagues at Human Rights Watch – in particular the two Sophies – our Australia researcher Sophie McNeill and China director Sophie Richardson were incredibly supportive and gave me good advice in how to respond. Sophie McNeill had only started working for us the week before – I was thrilled she had made the jump from journalism to activism. She was not only a hardworking, smart and savvy media operator, but she was also kind and compassionate – a winning combination for Human Rights Watch. My husband gave me the best communications advice that Monday – 'Stop looking at your phone. Either turn it off or give it to me.'

An editor at the *Sydney Morning Herald* saw my Twitter thread and asked if I would like to write an op-ed about what occurred. I agreed, explaining why this incident was a critical test not just for UNSW, but other universities on academic freedom.

I thought it was important to respond. If I was quiet, the pro-Chinese government voices would think they had won their battle in silencing critical voices speaking up on Hong Kong. And the university certainly wasn't speaking up on my behalf.

Also, I wanted to make the point that not all students from China were pro-Chinese government nationalists. There were others on campus from China and Hong Kong who were also feeling silenced and intimidated– that's how we found out about the campaign to get the article removed in the first place. We interviewed one UNSW law student from China. He told us:

> I wanted to study abroad to have a way of life so I'm not afraid to share my opinion. In our law department there are a lot of students who share the same opinion as me, but they are too afraid to speak out, they are afraid of retaliation . . . If you protest against the CCP abroad, they will find people you love and hurt them to make you pay.

Those words really broke my heart. These students were closely watching how the university responded to this case, and yet they felt invisible. I quoted the student in my op-ed.

On Monday night, I chatted with Sophie Richardson in Washington DC. Her China team had been analysing some of the online trolling in Chinese and English. Some of the social media users had picked up that I was half-Chinese and questioned why I would be taking such a stance 'against the motherland'. She had a warning for me, 'I don't want to alarm you, but please just be aware of your surroundings and who is around you the next few days. I know it seems crazy but just remember, what happened in New Zealand to Anne-Marie Brady.'

Anne-Marie Brady is an academic who writes on Chinese government interference. Her home and office in Christchurch were broken into twice. Her car had been tampered with, and she had received threats. Then in my growing paranoia I remembered that, in July, two Chinese activists living in New Zealand who were on their way to testify before a parliamentary committee about China died in a car crash. I had heard the whispers from some Chinese human rights activists who did not think the crash was an accident, even though there was no proof that was the case.

I went to bed late Monday night with all these thoughts swirling through my overactive imagination. I had nightmares about Jamal Khashoggi-type scenarios – the Saudi dissident who went into a consulate and never came out, because agents allegedly chopped him into pieces.

I got up at 5.30 am and groggily went downstairs to the kitchen to grab a glass of water. As I turned to go back upstairs, I stopped short in my tracks. Our blinds were open, and I could see straight into an apartment window across the road. We had lived in the street for several years and I had never seen anyone in that window. Their curtains were always drawn closed, the lights occasionally did go on and off, so I knew someone lived there but I didn't know who.

Now, in the pre-dawn hours, the lights were on, the curtains were open, and there were two young men of East Asian appearance, possibly Chinese, standing and making weird hand gestures directly, it seemed, at me.

I stared back at them, stunned and confused. Snapping into a panic, I raced upstairs to grab my phone. I came back downstairs slowly, without turning on the light, and filmed them silently for several minutes. My mind churned. First off, I was furious, how dare they try and intimidate me. I was rattled. But the hand gestures were . . . odd.

They clearly weren't spies – or weren't very good ones, because they had left their lights on. *Weird. Did they want me to notice them? Was this a stunt to intimidate me?* I rubbed my eyes; thinking I am clearly devoid of sleep, I needed a second opinion.

I woke up my husband. He came down the stairs, looked at them for a few moments and snapped our blinds shut. 'Elaine, they are nerds. They are students playing computer games. Go back to sleep,' he said as he turned and lumbered back up the stairs to bed.

Now I felt like an idiot. I peeked back through the blinds. Sure enough I could see the top of a computer monitor and the hand gestures that I had initially interpreted as threatening were in fact directed at the computer screen. They were playing a Wii or some other computer game.

Days later, I laughed about it, embarrassed. But I also worried that in my stressed-out state I had made snap judgements about two young men on the basis of race. Me, a forty-something Asian-Australian woman who monitors human rights abuses for a living.

My paranoia aside, for the rest of the week it felt like I was in the middle of a mini-media storm as journalists chased various angles. Senators and diplomats contacted me with notes of concern and to check the facts of what had occurred. Politicians from both major parties spoke up condemning the university's actions in censoring one of its staff. There was increasing pressure on the university to respond and publicly explain its actions. My op-ed went online Tuesday and in the print edition of the *Sydney Morning Herald* on Wednesday.[9]

On Wednesday at 5 pm, five days after the initial posting of the article, the Vice-Chancellor of UNSW, Ian Jacobs, emailed a letter to all staff.[10] He apologised for the mistake of removing the tweet and reiterated the university's commitment to freedom of expression and academic freedom. He said:

We will not restrict the right of staff, students or others to express their views however challenging or controversial, as long as they remain within the legal constraints of Australia. Our University is rightly a place where many different views and opinions are expressed and vigorously debated. We expect those engaged in these debates to treat others with respect and we will not limit freedom of expression within the law simply because some find it offensive or challenging.

The email also said: 'This is an example of the challenges universities face in navigating issues of freedom of speech in a complex world. At UNSW we will continue to acknowledge and learn from our mistakes, while holding firm to our policy and principles.'

I was both happy and relieved to see the Vice-Chancellor apologise and articulate strong support for the principle of free speech. It felt like a small but important victory, especially after several days of the university saying little except to distance themselves from my views.

But I was disappointed the letter went only to staff, not students. Nor was it translated into Chinese. I immediately asked university colleagues why they didn't put it on the website. Eventually, five days later, they did.

The other thing that irked me about the response was the glaring omission of the words Hong Kong or China. The university seemed to be carefully tiptoeing around the substance to avoid any further confrontations by pro-Chinese government students. For anyone who had not been following the news, it would be hard to figure out exactly what had occurred and who was responsible.

UNSW wasn't alone in being afraid to call out China. I saw this happen repeatedly when I met with other university leaders urging them to adopt the code of conduct. I mentioned it when I later gave parliamentary testimony on this topic: no one ever wanted to say 'the C-word': China. That was the biggest hurdle we faced in advocating with universities and governments on our code of conduct. None would call out China directly.

'If you target just one country, it's counter-productive. It could lead to racism or xenophobia against Chinese students,' one university administrator told us.

'Aren't other authoritarian governments acting like this on campuses?' a government minister asked me.

I pointed out, in all those meetings, the fact that our research had found that only one government was acting in this coordinated, targeted way – the Chinese government, and forty per cent of all international students came from China. I said that it was fine if measures taken also protected students from other authoritarian countries too. But the failure to acknowledge that the Chinese government was actively encouraging the harassment and censorship of other views was a mistake. The responses would be vague and not targeted enough to have the desired impact.

Following the Vice-Chancellor's apology, I responded in a private letter, acknowledging his statement but also making several recommendations for follow-up. It felt strange to be 'making recommendations' on behalf of Human Rights Watch, something I had been doing for more than a decade, but now on a matter of my own personal experience.

I urged the university to convene a public meeting on the topic for students and staff to identify what went wrong, and reinforce procedures to report acts of intimidation, harassment and censorship. I asked for a thorough investigation of the online campaign targeting the university. I had seen screenshots of social media chats on the Chinese app, WeChat and in one of the chats, a social media user threatened to report a UNSW student to the Chinese consulate because they spoke against the campaign targeting the university for the article on Hong Kong. That deeply worried me.

I thought the Vice-Chancellor's statement of apology would set the matter to rest. But China's *Global Times* published another story the next day: 'UNSW apologises to Chinese students after controversial Hong Kong article'.[11] It divulged details of a very different statement in Chinese that UNSW's Pro-Vice Chancellor (International), Laurie Pearcey, had emailed to 'Chinese partners' including students. It emerged this letter was sent first thing Monday morning – two days before the Vice-Chancellor's letter in English to university staff.[12]

I couldn't believe it. While Vice-Chancellor Jacobs apologised for deleting the tweet and made a strong commitment to free expression and academic freedom, Pearcey referred to the content of the tweet as 'misleading' and said 'we are deeply disturbed by the trouble the incident has caused to everyone' – making no mention of free speech whatsoever. It was clear the university's first response was to placate its Chinese partners rather than protect the academic freedom of staff or students, which only came belatedly following intense Australian media scrutiny.

The two letters set off another round of media articles, and by Friday, even Australia's Prime Minister Scott Morrison, a UNSW alum, was asked to weigh in on that matter on talkback radio, saying, 'I find in managing the relationship with China, you've just got to be consistent.'[13]

A month later, Sophie Richardson and I had a thirty-minute Zoom meeting with the UNSW leadership to discuss the matter. It was one of those slightly awkward Zoom calls with too many people giving lengthy introductions and that doesn't leave enough time to discuss the substance. It was clear that the university felt the matter had been put to rest; that a mistake had been made, they had accepted responsibility, and did not think there was any need to act on the recommendations made in my letter. Vice-Chancellor Jacobs felt further public discussion of the issue could stoke racial tensions between students and he felt existing policies and standards on academic freedom were more than adequate. No one seemed willing or able to investigate the online harassment campaign or hold social media users accountable for making threats. At one point in the call, a visibly-irritated Jacobs told me that 'This university is a bastion of free speech' and that 'You should be celebrating the fact that UNSW has one of the best free speech policies in the country, if not the world.'

'Celebrating?' I queried in a flat tone.

There was an awkward pause. Clearly Jacobs had no idea what the past few weeks had meant, not just to me, but for academics working on China and students from China and Hong Kong who supported human rights. Policies to defend academic freedom might exist on paper, but it was up to universities to make students and staff aware of them and hold people accountable when they did not.

The experience with UNSW provided us with the impetus to conduct further research on this issue. My colleagues working on China felt that the views of students from China who supported democracy and human rights were the voices missing in the debate. The unfortunate fallout from the incident was that these students felt even more isolated and ignored than ever, and that they lacked protection from Australian institutions.

We knew that we needed to pull together more examples to show that this incident was not a one-off. Sophie McNeill, our Australia researcher, took on the project with vigour. Publishing testimonies of students from China studying at Australian universities would not only help universities understand the issues and how to protect these students, but also reaffirm to the students that they were not alone.

What started as a small project quickly turned into something bigger due to Sophie's extraordinary research skills. In addition to students from China, she found many academics had relevant experiences to share. After several months, Sophie interviewed forty-eight students and academics from seventeen Australian universities across six states and territories. She quickly turned those interviews into a report.

Getting people to talk was not easy. Some students were terrified to disclose their experiences to Human Rights Watch, and yet they spoke up because they wanted things to change. Interviews took place via encrypted messaging apps and over secure networks for security reasons.

Around the time Sophie completed the research, in February 2021, we were invited to testify before the Parliamentary Joint Committee on Intelligence and Security who were conducting an inquiry examining foreign interference threats to higher education. Their inquiry was prompted by a series of events at universities, including the incident at UNSW. Sophie and I testified, immediately after the head of Australia's Security and Intelligence Organisation (ASIO). The Committee also heard evidence from university vice-chancellors. The parliamentary hearing was effectively putting universities on notice that if they did not take steps to address threats to academic freedom, the government would step in and make them.

In June 2021, we published our findings in a report entitled 'They Don't Understand the Fear We Have': How China's Long Arm of Repression Undermines Academic Freedom at Australia's Universities.[14] The report was a catalyst for change within the university sector. Before and after the release, we met with senior officials, politicians, and university leaders to discuss our recommendations. The Department of Home Affairs had already convened a University Foreign Interference Taskforce (UFIT), involving leadership from across the university sector. We were invited to brief them. Initially, the taskforce was narrowly focused on problematic research partnerships and cyber-security issues. Our report contributed to a revision of their guidelines on foreign interference for the university sector. The new guidelines addressed issues of censorship, self-censorship and harassment of students. They also encouraged universities to educate students about state-backed harassment and to report such concerns at their universities.

We also had direct follow-up to our recommendations from the parliament. In March 2022, the Parliamentary Joint Committee on Intelligence and Security released its report on national security risks in the higher education sector, the inquiry to which Sophie and I gave evidence. The Committee's report adopted several of Human Rights Watch's recommendations urging the universities to monitor and report on state-backed harassment and intimidation and adopt practical steps to deter students who report on activities of fellow students to foreign governments.[15] Getting our recommendations endorsed by a parliamentary committee and a foreign interference task force was a critical step forward, the next step was making sure universities implemented them.

I was encouraged that following the release of our report, UNSW welcomed it and announced a new awareness-raising campaign for students and staff about state-backed harassment. Another university, the University of Technology, Sydney (UTS) also initiated new orientation materials for foreign students letting them know that if they face threats, doxing or surveillance for their opinions, how they can report it.

By mid 2021, the attitudes of both the government and university administrators had changed dramatically from 2019 when we first launched Human Rights Watch's global code of conduct for academic freedom. Back then, we were met with denials that there was any problem of foreign interference. The change in attitude also reflected the growing awareness about China's atrocious record of repression both at home and abroad. My colleagues at Human Rights Watch had documented both the mass detention of more than a million Uyghurs in so-called 'political re-education' camps as well as the ways in which the Chinese government intimidated and harassed members of the Uyghur diaspora to try and silence their advocacy for detained relatives.

And in Hong Kong, the very subject of the article that caused such a controversy, the downward spiral of human rights continued. Young student activists who led the Hong Kong protest movement, like Joshua Wong, Agnes Chow and Ivan Lam, had only recently graduated from university themselves, but they were now behind bars. The national security law was having its desired effect in discouraging criticism and protests against the Hong Kong and Chinese governments both in and outside China.

China is a very different country to the one from which my grandmother fled to avoid starvation a century ago. Now it's an economic powerhouse, forging closer trade and security ties with many countries around the world. And Chinese parents send their children to study in the West for greater opportunities. But deeply ingrained views of nationalism born out of decades of propaganda, censorship and surveillance is not something that can be unlearned overnight. And it also does not help that some Chinese students face racism and exclusion which only reinforces their views about the West as anti-Chinese.

University is an opportunity to educate and encourage an exchange of ideas. It should be an opening to counter intolerance, ignorance and fear, based on facts and reasoning. Certainly for me, it was the start of my journey of political and social awakening two decades ago that sparked in me a desire to embark on this career in human rights. I hope that some day all students have the same opportunities to test their curiosity and their preconceptions. To question, not to accept. And to feel comfortable enough to stand out, not to blend in.

EPILOGUE

As I write this final chapter, in June 2022, authoritarianism and human rights violations are surging in many of the countries that I have covered during the course of my career. Democracy is under attack in places where it has long been taken for granted. Some abusive leaders have taken power by force, determined to eliminate even the pretence of elections altogether. Others exploit existing democratic processes that have been weakened by disinformation, corruption, and ineffectual institutions that should be providing a check on power, and even going through the charade of holding elections that are neither free nor fair – Ken Roth calls them 'zombie democracies'.[1]

I was last in Kyiv in 2002 to document the trafficking of women from Ukraine to Western Europe for Anti-Slavery International. Now, in the space of three months, more than six million Ukrainians have fled their homes and their country following Russia's invasion in February 2022. Just as we verified a litany of war crimes in Sri Lanka's conflict, Human Rights Watch has sent a team of researchers into Ukraine to monitor and report on violations of the laws of war by both sides. They have primarily found summary executions, torture and indiscriminate attacks on civilians by Russian forces.

Across much of Asia, there is a terrible sense of déjà vu as abusive leaders from the past or their descendants are making a comeback. The Taliban is back in power after seizing Kabul in August 2021. Military leaders overthrew an elected civilian government in Myanmar in February that same year.

In Sri Lanka, former Defence Secretary Gotabaya Rajapaksa was elected President in 2019, appointing his brother Mahinda as Prime Minister. As of July 2022, an economic crisis and popular protests have forced the two brothers to resign and Gotabaya to flee the country.

Rodrigo Duterte is no longer in charge of the Philippines, as each president can only serve a single six-year term, but the new president is Ferdinand 'Bongbong' Marcos Jr, the son of the late dictator, Ferdinand Marcos, who was ousted by the People Power Revolution in 1986. Bongbong's vice-president is Duterte's daughter, Sara.

In China, there are no elections and President Xi Jinping looks set to begin an unprecedented third five-year term as leader after abolishing term limits. China's economic rise has not been accompanied by greater freedoms as many in the West had blindly hoped – instead the government has doubled down on repression. Hong Kong's liberal democracy has been systematically dismantled and pro-democracy supporters are fleeing the city-state in droves while the remaining leaders of the protest movement are imprisoned.

Meanwhile, in China's northwest region of Xinjiang, Uyghurs and other Turkic Muslims face the slow but methodical and ruthless erasure of their culture, language and religion. Human Rights Watch has said these abuses amount to crimes against humanity. More than a million people have been locked up without any due process in political re-education centres for alleged extremism. The list of so-called 'suspicious' acts includes things such as travelling to Muslim countries such as Turkey or Malaysia on holiday, giving up alcohol, men growing beards, women wearing headscarves, or saying 'Salam' instead of 'Ni hao' as a greeting. Even for those outside the camps, their daily lives are so heavily surveilled by the Chinese state that Uyghurs modify their everyday behaviour and their speech to try and avoid attention from the authorities. It is chilling.

It would be easy to feel despondent or fatalistic about the state of the world. But I'm not.

Because on all these issues, my colleagues and human rights defenders are meticulously documenting the injustices and raising the alarm, holding abusive governments to account. Our work can be painstaking and draining, and change can take a long time. I stay motivated by celebrating the small but meaningful wins – the freedom of Hakeem or Rahaf, or others who we have advocated on behalf of.

And I remind myself that things could be worse if we didn't do what we do. Exposing human rights violations raises the cost of committing those violations. In that sense, we hold the line, we stop the roof from falling in.

We don't always get the result we want. We don't always end the senseless killings, free those who should never have been detained, or find out what happened to relatives who disappear. We don't always get to see the perpetrators investigated, prosecuted and convicted for their crimes. But when human rights abusers know that someone is watching, recording, and exposing these violations, it raises the stakes, putting the threat of accountability into the calculus of their decisions.

Even when we cannot end an abuse, the detailed fact-finding reports by Human Rights Watch, other NGOs or by UN investigators, that place the testimony of victims and witnesses on the record is a vital source of truth. I have seen how these written documents, as well as speaking truth to power before a parliamentary committee, the UN or an official hearing, provide solace and comfort to individuals and families whose stories have not been told, or who have been censored or ignored. As Australian Aboriginal activist June Oscar said, 'change is possible when you tell the truth'.[2]

The UN is imperfect and often slow to respond, but it is still an important moderating force. I was fortunate in my career to see early on how NGOs can influence different mechanisms of the UN and its member states. Whatever governments claim, UN reports are meaningful because they are an objective account of facts. Abusive governments will pull out all the stops to avoid investigation and possible censure by the UN. I think of the families of the disappeared in Sri Lanka, and how one of the mothers told me the only progress achieved in-country was because of the work done to raise Sri Lanka's war crimes in Geneva, when their own domestic mechanisms failed. In the Philippines, the UN report on 'drug war' killings was an acknowledgement that these events had occurred and that the state was responsible. But mobilising governments to make these reports happen took years.

Yet the UN institution itself is under threat as the Chinese government tries to reshape the international system to make it one that is less focused on accountability and more on 'technical cooperation'. To counter these trends, democratic countries that care about human rights need to do more to work together and push back against authoritarianism. This means using the UN system consistently to pressure any government that commits serious human rights violations and making sure powerful nations like the US or China do not evade accountability.

As we have seen in the examples of Saudi Arabia, Bahrain, China and Ethiopia, authoritarian regimes no longer confine repression to within their borders. As people move around the world, abusive governments get savvier at trying to repress and control people in other countries, sometimes using family members as hostages. Such threats to silence diaspora communities must be taken seriously, and democratic governments and institutions need to recognise and address it.

Sometimes, with that heady mix of patience, timing and opportunity we do achieve some of the enduring change that we always hope for. We may get a treaty, or a law passed that protects the rights of victims or funding to do the same, or see a human rights abuser charged for their crimes. And one strength of Human Rights Watch is how the staff strategically seize opportunities to make change.

For the change to hold, it requires vigilance, and truly listening and working alongside those whose rights we seek to protect. As human rights defenders, we have a duty to amplify the voices of others who are marginalised.

Listening to affected groups whether they are migrants, sex workers or prisoners is something practical I learned early in my career. I have often recalled my experiences in Nigeria and Nepal, when well-meaning or paternalistic organisations and institutions failed to listen and give agency to the individuals they sought to protect. It is a lesson that has stayed with me.

Courageous individuals give me hope. This book has enabled me to share some of the untold stories of just a few of the incredible people I have met throughout my career. Their tireless and brave work defending rights gives me the inspiration and energy to keep pushing for change. I think of people like Leila de Lima in the Philippines who continues her work from detention. I think of those who proactively use their power and influence to help others like Craig Foster or who bravely challenge their governments and take risks for us all to have a better brighter future.

Across Asia, the rise in authoritarianism and the frontal assault on genuine political representation is provoking new movements led by young people, often university students. This solidarity across borders in support of democracy in Asia is known loosely as the Milk Tea Alliance, in a nod to the popular beverage.[3]

When governments make it impossible for them to run for office or disqualify their preferred candidates, they are taking to the streets and going online to agitate for change, despite the huge risks to their freedom and safety. People like Hong Kong's former legislator twenty-nine-year-old Nathan Law, now living in exile, twenty-three-year-old Thai student leader Panusaya 'Rung' Sithijirawattanakul who bravely called for reform of the monarchy in Thailand, or thirty-year-old Thinzar Shunlei Yi, an activist in hiding from Myanmar who grew up in a miliary family, but now works to raise awareness about the junta's abuses, and to convince serving members of the military to defect.

Milk Tea activists are using social media as a tool for building solidarity among others, both in and between countries, and to explore and share innovative ways of organising. Some of the movements are leaderless, with flat non-hierarchical structures, applying transparent and democratic techniques to their own organising. They often involve artists and musicians to help change the mindset of ordinary citizens.

I wrote this book to give a more intimate account of what human rights work involves. And to step back and look at the broader trends over recent years, because some stories don't fit neatly into the fact-finding reports released by NGOs.

As human rights defenders, we report the facts objectively without emotion. We evaluate the violations against international law, adopting a legalistic tone. We don't discuss how our backgrounds shape our empathy and experiences in documenting abuses. Nor do we speak about the toll that working on human rights violations, day after day, year after year, can take.

I wanted to bring the reader with me as I travelled, giving them a window into how we do our work, the professionalism required, the boundaries needed, the considerations we weigh up, the steps we take to try and protect people's safety, and how we make change and how change happens – two very different things. One of my objectives was to remind readers that human rights violations are not just something that occur far away to 'other' people, but that they affect all of us, and we can all take small actions every day to improve human rights.

A few weeks after the 2022 Australian election I asked Aboriginal Senator Pat Dodson if he had any advice for young activists today. He said, 'Don't let the sense of disempowerment crush you. Look towards the enormous achievements that are being made by our contemporary leaders. Young people have got a serious role to play to make and shape this future to be a better place. Without you, we won't get there. They are vital to the future, and to be the leaders to help this nation heal itself. Look towards the future you want. Be the change.'

Change comes when people push back against oppression, but sometimes they need our solidarity.

There are many more stories of marginalised and oppressed people, and of the human rights defenders who remain resilient and defiant, persevering with grit and determination.

They push back. And so should we.

ACKNOWLEDGEMENTS

This book would not have been possible without the generous support and encouragement of my family, friends and colleagues. As all writers quickly realise, there are far too many people who have helped out in ways great and small to try and thank everyone over a few pages – my apologies to anyone I may have overlooked!

I would like to start by thanking my smart, fierce and passionate colleagues at Human Rights Watch. Some of you pestered me to write these stories, reviewed chapters, helped me navigate tricky issues and graciously let me write about these events – thank you. A special shout out to Carlos Conde, Andreas Harsono, Sophie McNeill, Sunai Phasuk, Sophie Richardson, Phil Robertson, Jim Ross, Joseph Saunders, Ken Roth, Minky Worden, Maya Wang, Yaqiu Wang, Felix Horne, Laetitia Bader, Anietie Ewang, Mausi Segun, Aya Mazjoub. Beyond these individuals, thank you to everyone at Human Rights Watch especially the Asia Division and Australia teams (Georgie Bright, Nicole Tooby, Pippa Brown, Tayla Hall, Gill McGregor, Kate Rosenberg, Sophia Katsinas, Tamanna Abdi) for your solidarity, commitment and generous spirit.

To the wonderful mentors who have guided me along the way – Mike Dottridge, Thetis Mangahas, Brad Adams, Jan Boontinand and Bandana Pattanaik, thank you for being the bosses that have mastered that most delicate of arts: giving staff autonomy and space but also helping us grow and become better researchers, advocates and managers. To Fernand de Varennes and Simon Gipson, thank you for being so encouraging to an idealistic young student.

To all the activists, lawyers and collaborators who have taught me so much and stirred me on to keep fighting the good fight, including Sayed Ahmed Alwadaei, Hakeem al-Araibi, Ruth Barson, Behrouz Boochani, Badiucao, Lin Chew, Agnes Chow, Leila de Lima, Hugh de Kretser, Melissa Ditmore, Pat Dodson, Craig Foster, Damian Griffis, Emily Howie, Shaquille Jackamarra, Surang Janyam, Ann Jordan, Michael Kirby, Nathan Law, Mark Lock, Imran Mohammad, Rahaf Mohammed, Abdul 'Aziz' Muhamat, Bruno Moens, George Newhouse, Bisi Olateru-Olagbegi, Meena Poudel, Geoffrey Robertson, Jen Robinson, Thanush Selverasa, Shukri Shafe, Mala Singh, Thinzar Shunlei Yi, Panusaya 'Rung' Sithijirawattanakul, Marjan Wijers, Daniel Webb, Joshua Wong, Vicky Xu, Cathy Zimmerman and so many others who, for various reasons, can't be named here.

To the kind folks who offered me the chance to escape my living room to more creative (and quiet) writing spaces – thank you to the Allisons, Corahs, McGarrys, and Morrisons.

To Elissa Baillie and Marcus Fazio for first workshopping the idea of a book with me, and then so patiently encouraging me to write it – I am so very grateful. To members of the Australia Committee at Human Rights Watch for your wide-ranging and most generous support. To Maria Farmer for always being there to impart your practical and precise PR wisdom. And to the wonderful team at Simon & Schuster for seeing something in my vision for this book, and helping me make it a reality.

To all my dear friends in Sydney and around the world who have supported me in this process, feeding me, stealing me away for drinks, sharing ideas, and putting up with me, especially over the last two years as I have tried to focus – thank you.

To my family, especially Mum, Nigel, Cheryl, Ian, Chris, my Aunty Rosemarie, Uncle Patrick and Jill, for letting me share these stories with the world, and to Chean Wai and Uncle Henry for painstakingly translating the audio files from the Singaporean archives.

And finally, to my husband Cameron, who has shared so much of this journey. My first reader and editor, sounding board and critic. Without your love and support this book would never have started, and would probably never have finished. Thank you and I love you.

NOTES

Prologue

1   John Pilger, *A Secret Country*, Knopf, 1991.
2   Pauline Hanson, 1996 Maiden Speech to Parliament (full transcript) as reprinted in the *Sydney Morning Herald*, September 15, 2016. https://www. smh.com.au/politics/federal/pauline-hansons-1996-maiden-speech-to-parliament-full-transcript-20160915-grgjv3.html
3   Transcript of the Prime Minister the Hon. John Howard MP Press Conference, Parliament House, May 7, 1997. https://pmtranscripts.pmc. gov.au/release/transcript-10331

Chapter 1

1   Foundation Against Trafficking in Women, International Human Rights Law Group, Global Alliance Against Traffic in Women, *Human Rights Standards for the Treatment of Trafficked Persons*, 1999. https://www.gaatw.org/books_ pdf/hrs_eng1.pdf
2   'Giving the customer what he wants', *The Economist*, Feb 12, 1998. https:// www.economist.com/special/1998/02/12/giving-the-customer-what-he-wants
3   Marjan Wijers and Lin Lap-Chew, 'Trafficking in Women: Forced Labour and Slavery-Like Practices in Marriage, Domestic Labour and Prostitution', Women Ink, 1997.
4   NGO Consultation, 'Trafficking and the Global Sex Industry: Need for Human Rights Framework', 1999. https://imadr.org/wordpress/wp-content/ uploads/2013/01/T2-1.-NGO-consultation-1999.06.pdf
5   Ibid.

6 Ibid.

7 Jo Bindman and Jo Doezema, *Redefining Prostitution as Sex Work on the International Agenda*, Anti-Slavery International, 1997.

8 Melissa Ditmore, *Encyclopedia of Prostitution and Sex Work*, Greenwood Press, 2006. https://melissaditmore.com/books/encyclopedia-of-prostitution-and-sex-work/

9 Elaine Pearson, 'Human Rights and Trafficking in Persons: A Handbook', GAATW, 2000. https://www.gaatw.org/books_pdf/Human%20Rights%20and%20Trafficking%20in%20Person.pdf

10 Article 3 of UN Protocol to Prevent, Suppress and Punish Trafficking in Persons Especially Women and Children, supplementing the United Nations Convention against Transnational Organized Crime (2000):

For the purposes of this Protocol:

(a) "Trafficking in persons" shall mean the recruitment, transportation, transfer, harbouring or receipt of persons, by means of the threat or use of force or other forms of coercion, of abduction, of fraud, of deception, of the abuse of power or of a position of vulnerability or of the giving or receiving of payments or benefits to achieve the consent of a person having control over another person, for the purpose of exploitation. Exploitation shall include, at a minimum, the exploitation of the prostitution of others or other forms of sexual exploitation, forced labour or services, slavery or practices similar to slavery, servitude or the removal of organs;

(b) The consent of a victim of trafficking in persons to the intended exploitation set forth in subparagraph (a) of this article shall be irrelevant where any of the means set forth in subparagraph (a) have been used;

(c) The recruitment, transportation, transfer, harbouring or receipt of a child for the purpose of exploitation shall be considered "trafficking in persons" even if this does not involve any of the means set forth in subparagraph (a) of this article;

(d) "Child" shall mean any person under eighteen years of age.

11 Elaine Pearson, 'Human Rights and Trafficking in Persons: A Handbook', GAATW, 2000. https://www.gaatw.org/books_pdf/Human%20Rights%20and%20Trafficking%20in%20Person.pdf

Chapter 2

1 Stephen Kastoryano, et al, 'Street Prostitution Zones and Crime', *Cato Institute Research Briefs*, April 2017. https://www.cato.org/sites/cato.org/files/pubs/pdf/research-brief-74-updated.pdf

2   Human Rights Watch, '"Everyone's in on the Game": Corruption and Human Rights Abuses by the Nigeria Police Force', August 2010. https://www.hrw.org/report/2010/08/17/everyones-game/corruption-and-human-rights-abuses-nigeria-police-force#

3   Adaobi Tricia Nwaubani, 'A Voodoo Curse on Human Traffickers', *New York Times*, March 24, 2018. https://www.nytimes.com/2018/03/24/opinion/sunday/voodoo-curse-human-traffickers.html

4   Pearson, Elaine. *Human Traffic, Human Rights: Redefining Victim Protection*, Anti-Slavery International, 2002. http://www.antislavery.org/wp-content/uploads/2017/01/hum_traff_hum_rights_redef_vic_protec_final_full.pdf

5   Human Rights Watch, 'You Pray for Death: Trafficking of Women and Girls in Nigeria', August 27, 2019. https://www.hrw.org/report/2019/08/27/you-pray-death/trafficking-women-and-girls-nigeria

Chapter 3

1   Human Rights Watch, 'Between a Rock and a Hard Place: Civilians Struggle to Survive in Nepal's Civil War', October 6, 2004. https://www.hrw.org/report/2004/10/06/between-rock-and-hard-place/civilians-struggle-survive-nepals-civil-war

2   For the years 2003 and 2004. Human Rights Watch, 'Nepal: Security Forces "Disappear" Hundreds of Civilians', March 1, 2005. https://www.hrw.org/news/2005/03/01/nepal-security-forces-disappear-hundreds-civilians

3   Human Rights Watch, 'Between a Rock and a Hard Place: Civilians Struggle to Survive in Nepal's Civil War', October 6, 2004. https://www.hrw.org/report/2004/10/06/between-rock-and-hard-place/civilians-struggle-survive-nepals-civil-war

Chapter 4

1   Human Rights Watch, 'Recurring Nightmare: State Responsibility for "Disappearances" and Abductions in Sri Lanka', March 2008. https://www.hrw.org/reports/srilanka0308.pdf

2   Human Rights Watch, 'Sri Lanka: "Disappearances" by Security Forces a National Crisis', March 6, 2008. https://www.hrw.org/news/2008/03/06/sri-lanka-disappearances-security-forces-national-crisis

3   United nations, 'Report of the Working Group on Enforced or Involuntary Disappearances', August 2021, A/HRC/48/57. https://undocs.org/A/HRC/48/57

4   See United Nations, 'Report of the Secretary-General's Panel of Experts on Accountability in Sri Lanka', March 31, 2011. https://www.securitycouncilreport.org/atf/cf/%7B65BFCF9B-6D27-4E9C-8CD3-CF6E4FF96FF9%7D/POC%20Rep%20on%20Account%20in%20Sri%20Lanka.pdf

5 United Nations, 'Report of the Human Rights Council on its Eleventh special session: Assistance to Sri Lanka in the promotion and protection of human rights,' May 19, 2009. https://ap.ohchr.org/documents/dpage_e. aspx?si=A/HRC/S-11/2

6 United Nations, 'Report of the Secretary-General's Panel of Experts on Accountability in Sri Lanka', March 31, 2011. https://www.security councilreport.org/atf/cf/%7B65BFCF9B-6D27-4E9C-8CD3-CF6E 4FF96FF9%7D/POC%20Rep%20on%20Account%20in%20Sri%20 Lanka.pdf

7 Niro Kandasamy, 'The Sri Lankan state is using violence to unleash fury on its citizens, as its political and economic crisis deepens', *The Conversation*, May 12, 2022. https://theconversation.com/the-sri-lankan-state-is-using-violence-to-unleash-fury-on-its-citizens-as-its-political-and-economic-crisis-deepens-182937

Chapter 5

1 Oliver Holmes, 'Rodrigo Duterte vows to kill 3 million drug addicts and likens himself to Hitler', *The Guardian*, October 1, 2016. https://www. theguardian.com/world/2016/sep/30/rodrigo-duterte-vows-to-kill-3-million-drug-addicts-and-likens-himself-to-hitler

2 Stephanie Nebehay, 'U.N. to step up rights work in Philippines after drug war killings', October 8, 2020, Reuters. https://www.reuters.com/article/ us-philippines-rights-idUSKBN26S24K

3 Oliver Holmes, 'Duterte says children killed in Philippines drug war are "collateral damage",' *The Guardian*, October 17, 2016. https://www. theguardian.com/world/2016/oct/17/duterte-says-children-killed-in-philippines-drug-war-are-collateral-damage

4 William Branigin, 'Davao Known as Philippines' "Murder Capital",' *The Washington Post*, August 8, 1985. https://www.washingtonpost.com/archive/ politics/1985/08/08/davao-known-as-philippines-murder-capital/ ce938055-0f5d-451c-9420-c2da95277dad/

5 Human Rights Watch, '"You Can Die Any Time": Death Squad Killings in Mindanao', April 2009. https://www.hrw.org/reports/philippines0409 web_0.pdf

6 Human Rights Watch, 'Scared Silent: Impunity for Extrajudicial Killings in the Philippines', June 2007. https://www.hrw.org/reports/2007/philip pines0607/philippines0607web.pdf

7 Jeffrey M. Tupas, 'Where crime suspects live dangerously', *Philippine Daily Inquirer*, February 15, 2009.

8   United Nations, 'Report of the Special Rapporteur on Extrajudicial, Summary or Arbitrary Executions, Philip Alston, on his mission to Philippines (12–21 February 2007), A/HRC/8/3/Add.2, April 16, 2008. https://digitallibrary.un.org/record/626743?ln=en

9   A *barangay* is the smallest administrative unit of government in the Philippines.

10 Cheryll D. Fiel, 'Last son alive', *Davao Today*, December 5, 2006. http://davaotoday.com/main/politics/crime-public-safety/last-son-alive/

11 Human Rights Watch, 'You Can Die Any Time': Death Squad Killings in Mindanao', April 2009. https://www.hrw.org/sites/default/files/reports/philippines0409webwcover_0.pdf

12 Alan Sipress, 'Vigilante killings alarm Philippines citizens', *The Washington Post*, November 30, 2003.

13 Jeffrey M. Tupas, 'Where crime suspects live dangerously', *Philippine Daily Inquirer*, February 15, 2009.

14 Human Rights Watch, 'You Can Die Any Time': Death Squad Killings in Mindanao', April 2009. https://www.hrw.org/reports/philippines0409web_0.pdf

15 Human Rights Watch, 'Scared Silent: Impunity for Extrajudicial Killings in the Philippines', June 2007. https://www.hrw.org/reports/2007/philippines0607/philippines0607web.pdf

16 At the national level in late April 2009, the Office of the Ombudsman, an independent government agency that investigates and prosecutes criminal acts by government officials, told reporters that it also would initiate investigations into the killings.

17 Human Rights Watch, 'License to Kill: Philippine Police Killings in Duterte's "War on Drugs"', March 2017. https://www.hrw.org/report/2017/03/02/license-kill/philippine-police-killings-dutertes-war-drugs

18 Yuji Vincent Gonzales, 'Allegations of "DDS" member in Senate hearing', *Philippine Daily Inquirer*, September 15, 2016. https://newsinfo.inquirer.net/815550/summary-allegations-of-confessed-dds-member-in-senate-hearing#ixzz6xqnWPcD4

19 Human Rights Council, Situation of human rights in the Philippines: Report of the United Nations High Commissioner for Human Rights, A/HRC/44/22, June 29, 2020. https://www.ohchr.org/Documents/Countries/PH/Philippines-HRC44-AEV.pdf

20 Fatou Bensouda, 'Statement of the Prosecutor of the International Criminal Court, Fatou Bensouda concerning the situation in the Republic of the Philippines', International Criminal Court, October 13, 2016. https://www.

icc-cpi.int/news/statement-prosecutor-international-criminal-court-fatou-bensouda-concerning-situation-republic

21   Ibid.

Chapter 6

1   Andreas Harsono, *Race, Islam and Power: Ethnic and Religious Violence in Post-Suharto Indonesia*, Monash University Press, 2019.

2   The Ministry of Religious Affairs extends official recognition to six religions Islam, Catholicism, Protestantism, Buddhism, Hinduism, and Confucianism.

3   Human Rights Watch, '"I Wanted to Run Away" Abusive Dress Codes for Women and Girls in Indonesia', March 18, 2021. https://www.hrw.org/report/2021/03/18/i-wanted-run-away/abusive-dress-codes-women-and-girls-indonesia

4   Ibid.

5   Thi Thu Huong Dang, *The role of Islam in the democratization process of Indonesia in the post-Soeharto period*, Grin Verlag, 2009.

6   'Q&A: What you need to know about sharia in Aceh,' *Jakarta Post*, March 4, 2018. https://www.thejakartapost.com/news/2018/03/04/qa-what-you-need-to-know-about-acehs-Sharia-law.html

7   Human Rights Watch, '"I Wanted to Run Away": Abusive Dress Codes for Women and Girls in Indonesia', March 18, 2021. https://www.hrw.org/report/2021/03/18/i-wanted-run-away/abusive-dress-codes-women-and-girls-indonesia

8   Human Rights Watch, 'France: Headscarf Ban Violates Religious Freedom', February 27, 2004. https://www.hrw.org/news/2004/02/26/france-headscarf-ban-violates-religious-freedom

9   Ibid.

10   Human Rights Watch, 'Indonesia: New Aceh Law Imposes Torture', October 11, 2009. https://www.hrw.org/news/2009/10/11/indonesia-new-aceh-law-imposes-torture

11   Human Rights Watch, 'Policing Morality Abuses in the Application of Sharia in Aceh, Indonesia', November 30, 2010. https://www.hrw.org/sites/default/files/reports/indonesia1210WebVersionToPost.pdf

12   Human Rights Watch, 'Indonesia: Aceh's New Islamic Laws Violate Rights', October 2, 2014. https://www.hrw.org/news/2014/10/02/indonesia-acehs-new-islamic-laws-violate-rights

13   Human Rights Watch, '"I Wanted to Run Away": Abusive Dress Codes for Women and Girls in Indonesia', March 18, 2021. https://www.hrw.org/report/2021/03/18/i-wanted-run-away/abusive-dress-codes-women-and-girls-indonesia

14   A regency is an administrative division in Indonesia, a level below a province.

15   Human Rights Watch, '"I Wanted to Run Away": Abusive Dress Codes for Women and Girls in Indonesia', March 18, 2021. https://www.hrw.org/ sites/default/files/media_2021/03/indonesia0321_web_0.pdf

16   Human Rights Watch, 'India: Prohibit Degrading "Test" for Rape', September 26, 2010. https://www.hrw.org/news/2010/09/06/india-prohibit-degrading-test-rape

17   Human Rights Watch, Indonesia, '"Virginity Tests" for Female Police', November 17, 2014. https://www.hrw.org/news/2014/11/17/indonesia-virginity-tests-female-police

18   Julia Suryakusuma, 'Roe v. Wade and Indonesia's 2024 presidential election', *Jakarta Post*, July 2, 2022. https://www.thejakartapost.com/opinion/2022/ 07/05/roe-v-wade-and-indonesias-2024-presidential-election.html

19   The three ministers that signed the decree were Education Minister Nadiem Makarim, Home Affairs Minister Tito Karnavian and Religious Affairs Minister Yaqut Cholil Qoumas.

20   Human Rights Watch, 'Indonesia: Enforce Dress Code Ban', February 5, 2021. https://www.hrw.org/news/2021/02/05/indonesia-enforce-dress-code-ban

21   The organisation that filed the petition was the Minangkabau Customary Institution (LKAAM).

22   Tamalia Alisjahbana, 'West Sumatra Ombudsman warns school and Regional Education Board that mandatory hijab in public schools is illegal', *Independent Observer*, June 17, 2021. https://observerid.com/west-sumatra-ombudsman-warns-school-and-regional-education-board-that-mandatory-hijab-in-public-schools-is-illegal/

Chapter 7

1   UNSW Kaldor Centre for International Refugee Law, 'Factsheet: Offshore processing an overview', Updated August 2021. https://www. kaldorcentre.unsw.edu.au/sites/kaldorcentre.unsw.edu.au/files/factsheet_ offshore_processing_overview.pdf

2   Australian Associated Press, 'Trials Conclude at Los Negros', *Sydney Morning Herald*, April 10, 1951. https://trove.nla.gov.au/newspaper/article/ 18207736

3   Amnesty International, 'This is Still Breaking People: Update on Human rights violations at Australia's asylum seeker processing centre on Manus Island, Papua New Guinea', May 2014. https://www.amnesty.org.au/wp-content/uploads/2016/09/This_is_still_breaking_people_update_from_ Manus_Island.pdf

4 Iranian Kurdish Reza Barati was beaten to death by staff working at the detention centre in February 2014. Iranian Hamid Khazaei died from septicaemia after cutting his foot and receiving inadequate medical care. Human Rights Law Centre and Human Rights Watch, 'Australia/Papua New Guinea: The Pacific Non-Solution', July 15, 2015. https://www.hrw.org/news/2015/07/15/australia/papua-new-guinea-pacific-non-solution

5 Behrouz Boochani, *No Friend but the Mountains*. Picador, 2018, 128.

6 Imran Mohammad Fazal Hoque, 'I have never experienced safety since I was born': Life in the Manus 'death centre', *Sydney Morning Herald*, April 21, 2017. https://www.smh.com.au/politics/federal/i-have-never-experienced-safety-since-i-was-born-life-in-the-manus-death-centre-20170417-gvm168.html

7 Human Rights Watch, Australia/PNG: 'Refugees Face Unchecked Violence', October 25, 2017. https://www.hrw.org/news/2017/10/25/australia/png-refugees-face-unchecked-violence

8 Imran Mohammad, 'I was born stateless and persecuted in Myanmar. Here is what it took for me to come to the U.S.', *LA Times*, July 23, 2018. https://www.latimes.com/opinion/op-ed/la-oe-mohammed-stateless-manus-island-20180723-story.html

9 Behrouz Boochani, *No Friend but the Mountains*. Picador, 2018.

Chapter 8

1 Tom Malinowski, 'Prison Island', *Foreign Policy*, May 7, 2012. https://foreignpolicy.com/2012/05/07/prison-island/

2 Tom Malinowski was appointed Assistant Secretary for Democracy, Human Rights, and Labor.

3 Reem Khalifa, 'US diplomat says Bahrain expulsion "not about me"', July 9, 2014, Associated Press. https://apnews.com/article/e0891faa717f433a84c32a4f81b9af81

4 Steve Cannane and Clare Blumer, 'Missed emails, bureaucratic bungles: How Home Affairs and the AFP contributed to Hakeem al-Araibi's time in a Thai jail', ABC News, October 11, 2019. https://www.abc.net.au/news/2019-10-11/bungles-that-led-to-hakeem-al-araibi-being-locked-up-in-thailand/11583270

5 See for instance Human Rights Watch, 'Thailand: Cambodian Refugees Forcibly Returned', November 12, 2021. https://www.hrw.org/news/2021/11/12/thailand-cambodian-refugees-forcibly-returned and Human Rights Watch, 'Thailand: More Uighurs Face Forced Return to China', March 21, 2014. https://www.hrw.org/news/2014/03/21/thailand-more-uighurs-face-forced-return-china

6   Amnesty International, 'Thailand: Between a rock and a hard place', September 28, 2017. https://www.amnesty.org/en/wp-content/uploads/2021/05/ASA3970312017ENGLISH.pdf

7   Ibid.

8   Bahrain Institute for Rights And Democracy, 'Bahraini Refugee Footballer Facing Deportation in Thailand', November 29, 2018. https://birdbh.org/2018/11/bahraini-refugee-footballer-facing-deportation-in-thailand/ and Human Rights Watch, 'Thailand: Don't Send Back Bahraini Dissident', November 30, 2018. https://www.hrw.org/news/2018/11/30/thailand-dont-send-back-bahraini-dissident

9   Steve Cannane and Clare Blumer, 'Missed emails, bureaucratic bungles: How Home Affairs and the AFP contributed to Hakeem al-Araibi's time in a Thai jail', ABC News, October 11, 2019. https://www.abc.net.au/news/2019-10-11/bungles-that-led-to-hakeem-al-araibi-being-locked-up-in-thailand/11583270

10 'Refugee footballer in Thailand denied flight back to Australia', SBS, December 2, 2018. https://www.sbs.com.au/news/article/refugee-footballer-in-thailand-denied-flight-back-to-australia/uyqb97kjq

11 Rebecca R. Ruiz, 'Shadow of Human Rights Abuse Follows Contender in FIFA Vote', *New York Times*, February 24, 2016. https://www.nytimes.com/2016/02/25/sports/soccer/sheikhs-candidacy-opens-new-door-to-criticism-of-fifa-human-rights.html

12 Ibid. *[Hakeem called for FIFA to investigate allegations concerning Sheikh Salman and the arrest and alleged torture of Bahraini athletes who peacefully protested in 2011.]*

13 Human Rights Watch, 'Boxed In Women and Saudi Arabia's Male Guardianship System', July 16, 2016. https://www.hrw.org/sites/default/files/report_pdf/saudiarabia0716web.pdf

14 Human Rights Watch, 'Fleeing Woman Returned to Saudi Arabia Against Her Will', April 14, 2017. https://www.hrw.org/news/2017/04/14/fleeing-woman-returned-saudi-arabia-against-her-will

15 Todd Ruiz, '"We won't send someone to their death," Thai immigration chief says', *KhaoSod English*, January 7, 2019. https://www.khaosodenglish.com/news/2019/01/07/we-wont-send-someone-to-their-death-thai-immigration-chief-says/

16 Helen Chen, 'UN finds Saudi teen in Bangkok is a refugee, Dutton vows "no special treatment"', SBS, January 9, 2019. https://www.sbs.com.au/chinese/english/un-finds-saudi-teen-in-bangkok-is-a-refugee-dutton-vows-no-special-treatment

17 Elaine Pearson, 'Thailand must release al-Araibi', January 11, 2019, *Bangkok Post*. https://www.bangkokpost.com/opinion/opinion/1609214/thailand-must-release-al-araibi

18 James Massola, '"I was crying inside": Melbourne soccer player Hakeem al-Araibi on the bungle that landed him in a Thai jail', *Sydney Morning Herald*, April 13, 2019. https://www.smh.com.au/world/asia/i-was-crying-inside-melbourne-soccer-player-hakeem-al-araibi-on-the-bungle-that-landed-him-in-a-thai-jail-20190409-p51cck.html

Chapter 9

1 Human Rights Watch, 'Collective Punishment War Crimes and Crimes against Humanity in the Ogaden area of Ethiopia's Somali Regional State', June 2008. https://www.hrw.org/reports/2008/ethiopia0608/ethiopia0608web.pdf

2 UNICEF Ethiopia and Central Statistical Agency of Ethiopia, 'Faces of poverty: Studying the overlap between monetary and multidimensional child poverty in Ethiopia', July 2020. https://www.unicef.org/ethiopia/media/3761/file/Faces%20of%20Poverty.pdf

3 'Ethiopia's most repressive state is reforming', *The Economist*, October 3, 2019. https://www.economist.com/middle-east-and-africa/2019/10/03/ethiopias-most-repressive-state-is-reforming

4 Human Rights Watch, 'Collective Punishment War Crimes and Crimes against Humanity in the Ogaden area of Ethiopia's Somali Regional State', June 2008. https://www.hrw.org/report/2008/06/12/collective-punishment/war-crimes-and-crimes-against-humanity-ogaden-area

5 Tobias Hagman, 'Fast politics, slow justice: Ethiopia's Somali region two years after Abdi Illey', London School of Economics Conflict Research Programme briefing paper, September 11, 2020. https://www.lse.ac.uk/ideas/Assets/Documents/Conflict-Research-Programme/crp-memos/Hagmann-Two-years-after-Iley-final.pdf

6 For more information on Ethiopia's surveillance state please see Human Rights Watch, '"They Know Everything We Do" Telecom and Internet Surveillance in Ethiopia', March 25, 2014. https://www.hrw.org/report/2014/03/25/they-know-everything-we-do/telecom-and-internet-surveillance-ethiopia

7 Human Rights Watch, 'Australia: Protests Prompt Ethiopia Reprisals,' November 7, 2016. https://www.hrw.org/sites/default/files/supporting_resources/australia_government_response_to_hrw.pdf

8 Michael Keenan MP, 'Constituency Statements: Ogaden Community Association of Western Australia', Federation Chamber, February 26, 2014.

https://parlinfo.aph.gov.au/parlInfo/search/display/display.w3p;query=
Id%3A%22chamber%2Fhansardr%2F3c6f5db6-8f8b-4848-b3cb-aba0b
158565b%2F0180%22

9   Mustafa M. Omer, 'Death foretold: the killing of my brother', Wardheer
    News, November 25, 2016. https://wardheernews.com/death-foretold-the-
    killing-of-my-brother/

10 Human Rights Watch, 'Australia: Protests Prompt Ethiopia Reprisals',
    November 7, 2016. https://www.hrw.org/news/2016/11/07/australia-protests-
    prompt-ethiopia-reprisals

11 'How a small protest in Australia has had major repercussions in Africa',
    ABC Lateline, November 9, 2016 [*note: the episode aired on Tuesday
    8 November, but the link was posted online on 9 November*]. https://www.
    abc.net.au/lateline/how-a-small-protest-in-australia-has-had-major/
    8010462

12 Human Rights Watch, '"We are Like the Dead" Torture and other Human
    Rights Abuses in Jail Ogaden, Somali Regional State, Ethiopia', July 2018.
    https://www.hrw.org/report/2018/07/04/we-are-dead/torture-and-other-
    human-rights-abuses-jail-ogaden-somali-regional

13 Ibid.

14 Amnesty International and Human Rights Watch, '"We Will Erase You
    From This Land": Crimes Against Humanity and Ethnic Cleansing in
    Ethiopia's Western Tigray Zone', April 6, 2022. https://www.hrw.org/
    report/2022/04/06/we-will-erase-you-land/crimes-against-humanity-and-
    ethnic-cleansing-ethiopias

Chapter 10

1   'Recommendations from the RCIADIC', Common Grace. Accessed July 10,
    2022. https://www.commongrace.org.au/339_recommendations_from_the_
    rciadic

2   Australian Institute of Criminology, 'Deaths in Custody in Australia'.
    Updated: June 7, 2022. https://www.aic.gov.au/statistics/deaths-custody-
    australia

3   Human Rights Watch, '"He's Never Coming Back": People with Disabil-
    ities Dying in Western Australia's Prisons', September 2020. https://www.
    hrw.org/report/2020/09/15/hes-never-coming-back/people-disabilities-
    dying-western-australias-prisons

4   Australian Bureau of Statistics, 2016 census data. Accessed July 10, 2022.
    https://quickstats.censusdata.abs.gov.au/census_services/getproduct/census/
    2016/quickstat/LGA50980

5   Coroner's Court of Western Australia, 'Record of Investigation into the Death of Khamsani Victor Jackamarra', May 9, 2019. https://www.coroners court.wa.gov.au/_files/inquest-2019/Jackamarra%20(Khamsani)%20 finding.pdf

6   Office of the Inspector General of Custodial Services (WA), 'Report 126: 2019 Inspection of Broome Regional Prison,' January 2020. https://www.oics.wa. gov.au/reports/126-inspection-of-broome-regional-prison/key-findings/ and Office of the Inspector General of Custodial Services (WA), 'Report 112: 2017 Inspection of Broome Regional Prison', August 2017. https:// www.oics.wa.gov.au/reports/112-report-of-an-announced-inspection-of-broome-regional-prison/

7   Tony Hassall, WA Commissioner of Corrective Services, Letter to Human Rights Watch, 'Prisoners with Disabilities in Corrective Services Australia', July 14, 2020. https://www.hrw.org/sites/default/files/media_2020/09/ Annex%20I.pdf

8   Office of the Inspector General of Custodial Services (WA), 'Report 126: 2019 Inspection of Broome Regional Prison,' January 2020. https://www.oics. wa.gov.au/reports/126-inspection-of-broome-regional-prison/key-findings/

9   Office of the Inspector General of Custodial Services (WA), 'Report 112: 2017 Inspection of Broome Regional Prison', August 2017. https://www. oics.wa.gov.au/wp-content/uploads/2017/11/Broome-Report-112-web.pdf

10   Coroner's Court of Western Australia, 'Record of Investigation into the Death of Khamsani Victor Jackamarra', May 9, 2019. https://www.coroners court.wa.gov.au/_files/inquest-2019/Jackamarra%20(Khamsani)%20 finding.pdf

11   Ibid.

12   Office of the Inspector General of Custodial Services (WA), 'Report 112: 2017 Inspection of Broome Regional Prison', August 2017. https://www. oics.wa.gov.au/reports/112-report-of-an-announced-inspection-of-broome-regional-prison/

13   Human Rights Watch, '"He's Never Coming Back": People with Disabilities Dying in Western Australia's Prisons', September 2020. https://www. hrw.org/report/2020/09/15/hes-never-coming-back/people-disabilities-dying-western-australias-prisons

14   Human Rights Watch, '"I Needed Help, Instead I Was Punished": Abuse and Neglect of Prisoners with Disabilities in Australia', 2018. https://www. hrw.org/news/2018/02/06/australia-prisoners-disabilities-neglected-abused

15   June Oscar, UWA 2018 Grace Vaughan Lecture, 'The collective power and potential of Aboriginal and Torres Strait Islander women and girls:

Recognising their human rights in achieving equality', May 1, 2018. https://www.ias.uwa.edu.au/__data/assets/pdf_file/0019/3106009/18.05.01-2018-Grace-Vaughan-memorial-Lecture-Speech-by-June-Oscar-AO.pdf

16   Office of the Inspector General of Custodial Services (WA), 'Report 126: 2019 Inspection of Broome Regional Prison', January 2020. https://www.oics.wa.gov.au/wp-content/uploads/2020/03/Broome-Regional-Prison-Report-126.pdf

17   Ibid.

18   Ibid.

19   'All prisoners with mental health issues and/or past self-harm attempts in custody should be assessed by mental health staff at reception.' Coroner's Court of Western Australia, 'Record of Investigation into the Death of Khamsani Victor Jackamarra', May 9, 2019. https://www.coronerscourt.wa.gov.au/_files/inquest-2019/Jackamarra%20(Khamsani)%20finding.pdf

20   Human Rights Watch, '"He's Never Coming Back": People with Disabilities Dying in Western Australia's Prisons', September 2020. https://www.hrw.org/report/2020/09/15/hes-never-coming-back/people-disabilities-dying-western-australias-prisons

21   Queensland Government, 2018–19 Budget Papers, Queensland Corrective Services Service Delivery Statement. https://s3.treasury.qld.gov.au/files/SDS-Queensland-Corrective-Services-2018-19.pdf and Queensland Minister for Corrective Services Mark Ryan, Media Statement, 'Queensland Government invests in regional jobs as a part of criminal justice system reform', June 11, 2019. https://statements.qld.gov.au/statements/87589

22   Bill Johnston, WA Minister for Corrective Services, Media Statement, 'Preferred site identified for new Broome Regional Prison', February 10, 2022. https://www.mediastatements.wa.gov.au/Pages/McGowan/2022/02/Preferred-site-identified-for-new-Broome-Regional-Prison.aspx

23   June Oscar, 'Reaching our potential as a nation begins with truth-telling', *The Guardian*, January 31, 2020. https://www.theguardian.com/australia-news/2020/jan/31/june-oscars-2020s-vision-reaching-our-potential-as-a-nation-begins-with-truth-telling

Chapter 11

1   John Brumby, 'Foreign students are our fourth largest export, even with the pandemic', *Sydney Morning Herald*, February 19, 2021. https://www.smh.com.au/national/foreign-students-are-our-fourth-largest-export-even-with-the-pandemic-20210218-p573pz.html

2   Salvatore Babones, 'The China Student Boom and the Risks It Poses to Australian Universities', Centre for Independent Studies, Sydney, August. https://www.cis.org.au/wp-content/uploads/2019/08/ap5.pdf

3   Zhao Yusha, 'Australian university under attack for article "interfering" [in] HK affairs', August 1, 2020, *Global Times*. https://www.globaltimes.cn/content/1196340.shtml

4   Human Rights Watch, 'China: Government Threats to Academic Freedom Abroad', March 21, 2019. https://www.hrw.org/news/2019/03/21/china-government-threats-academic-freedom-abroad

5   Primrose Riordan, 'Uni lecturer targeted over "separate Taiwan"', *The Australian*, August 24, 2019. https://www.theaustralian.com.au/higher-education/university-lecturer-targeted-over-separate-taiwan-materials/news-story/79febfc3fd91f84604173c79a1f249a3

6   Human Rights Watch, 'China: Government Threats to Academic Freedom Abroad', March 21, 2019. https://www.hrw.org/news/2019/03/21/china-government-threats-academic-freedom-abroad

7   https://www.globaltimes.cn/content/1196340.shtml

8   Human Rights Watch, 'Resisting Chinese Government Efforts to Undermine Academic Freedom Abroad: A Code of Conduct for Colleges, Universities, and Academic Institutions Worldwide', March 2019. https://www.hrw.org/sites/default/files/media_2020/09/190321_china_academic_freedom_coc.pdf

9   Elaine Pearson, 'Critical test of academic freedom for Australian universities', *Sydney Morning Herald*, August 4, 2020. https://www.smh.com.au/national/critical-test-of-academic-freedom-for-australian-universities-20200804-p55iec.html

10 Professor Ian Jacobs, President and Vice-Chancellor of the University of New South Wales (UNSW), Statement on Freedom of Speech, August 10, 2020. https://www.president.unsw.edu.au/news/statement-freedom-speech

11 Zhao Yusha, 'UNSW apologises to Chinese students after controversial Hong Kong article', *Global Times*, August 6, 2020. https://www.globaltimes.cn/content/1196895.shtml

12 Naaman Zhou, 'UNSW criticised for letter in Chinese with no mention of freedom of speech', *The Guardian*, August 6, 2020. https://www.theguardian.com/australia-news/2020/aug/07/unsw-criticised-for-letter-in-chinese-with-no-mention-of-freedom-of-speech

13 Prime Minister Scott Morrison, Interview with Ben Fordham, 2GB, August 7, 2020 [radio broadcast transcript]. https://pmtranscripts.pmc.gov.au/release/transcript-42969

BEN FORDHAM [journalist]: The University of New South Wales has been caught out deleting information that was critical of China and they have now been caught out offering two different apologies. So in Australia, the university apologised for cancelling free speech in China. In China, they've apologised for causing distress with misleading posts. What do you make of what's happened at the University of New South Wales?

PRIME MINISTER: Well, I'm an alumni of the University of New South Wales, and I think people have always got to tell the same story wherever they are. That's certainly my practice when it comes to managing these sensitive issues. And I find in managing the relationship with China, you've just got to be consistent. And I always am. The Government is always and Australia always is. And I think everyone should follow that path.

14 Human Rights Watch, '"They Don't Understand the Fear We Have": How China's Long Arm of Repression Undermines Academic Freedom at Australia's Universities', June 2021. https://www.hrw.org/sites/default/files/media_2021/07/australia0621_web.pdf

15 Parliament of the Commonwealth of Australia, Parliamentary Joint Committee on Intelligence and Security (PJCIS), 'Inquiry into national security risks affecting the Australian higher education and research sector', March 2022. https://parlinfo.aph.gov.au/parlInfo/download/committees/reportjnt/024611/toc_pdf/Inquiryintonationalsecurityrisks affectingtheAustralianhighereducationandresearchsector.pdf;fileType= application%2Fpdf

Epilogue

1 Kenneth Roth, 'The Age of Zombie Democracies: Why Autocrats are abandoning even the pretense of democratic rituals', *Foreign Affairs*, July 28, 2021. https://www.foreignaffairs.com/articles/americas/2021-07-28/age-zombie-democracies

2 June Oscar, 'Reaching our potential as a nation begins with truth-telling', *The Guardian*, January 31, 2020. https://www.theguardian.com/australia-news/2020/jan/31/june-oscars-2020s-vision-reaching-our-potential-as-a-nation-begins-with-truth-telling

3 Laignee Barron, '"We Share the Ideals of Democracy." How the Milk Tea Alliance Is Brewing Solidarity Among Activists in Asia and Beyond', *Time*, October 28, 2020. https://time.com/5904114/milk-tea-alliance/